STEERING THE COURSE

STEERING THE COURSE

A Memoir   SAM HUGHES

McGill-Queen's University Press
Montreal & Kingston · London · Ithaca

© McGill-Queen's University Press 2000
ISBN 0-7735-2042-2

Legal deposit second quarter 2000
Bibliothèque nationale du Québec

Printed in Canada on acid-free paper

McGill-Queen's University Press acknowledges the
financial support of the Government of Canada
through the Book Publishing Industry Development
Program (BPIDP) for its publishing activities. We
also acknowledge the support of the Canada
Council for the Arts for our publishing program.

Canadian Cataloguing in Publication Data

Hughes, S. H. S.
    Steering the Course : A Memoir
    Includes index.
    ISBN 0-7735-2042-2
    1. Hughes, S. H. S. 2. Ontario. Supreme Court –
Biography. 3. Judges – Ontario – Biography. I. Title.
KE416.H83A3 2000   347.713'03534   C99-901443-9

Typeset in New Baskerville 10.5/13

To Helen,

for sixty years

Contents

Acknowledgments

I wish to acknowledge with grateful thanks the help given me in preparing this book by the Joanne Goodman Foundation at the University of Western Ontario and its executants, my friends the Hon. E.A. Goodman, PC, OC, QC, LiD, etc., and Professor Neville Thompson, PhD, through whom I was able to secure secretarial assistance and particularly several versions of the dictated type-script flawlessly produced by Susan Goddard.

To my friend Sir William Doughty I owe resolution of the problem of what to call the book, the title of which reflects his abiding interest in rowing developed from his experience as an oarsman and as captain of the Trinity College Boat Club of Dublin. All the other expressions of opinion in these pages are my own without qualification.

To Helen, my wife, my daughter, Lynn Clappison, her husband, John, and my son, Sam, it is beyond me to express the gratitude they deserve and these arid words must suffice.

S.H.

Folkestone, England, 1915. The author is perched on his namesake grandfather's knee, flanked by proud parents, with his father wearing the ribbon on the DSO won at the Second Battle of Ypres in April of that year.

This was the first of two University of Toronto senior crews of which the author was coxswain, both victorious in the annual two-mile race with McGill. *From left to right:* Professor T.R. Loudon, coach, the author, Messrs Gibson, Willis, Jackson, Skey, Warren, Dowling, Annis, and O'Flynn. Gordon Bradshaw, with the trophy, was spare man.

Helen went from Welland to England as a member of
the Red Cross Overseas Corps in 1943. For two years in
London her service was accompanied by enemy bombs,
V.1's, and V.2's.

Taken by my neighbour, Gerald Campbell, in my library
shortly after my appointment in 1958 as High Court judge
of the Supreme Court of Ontario. (Courtesy Ashley and
Crippen, Toronto)

In a Toronto garden, 1984. *From left to right:* Susie Clappison beside her grandmother, the author, his daughter Lynn Clappison, her husband, John Clappison, and their elder daughter, Sarah. The third grandchild, Geoffrey Hughes, stands with his father, Sam, on the right (Courtesy Ronald Miller Photography, Toronto)

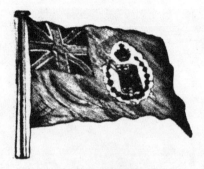

THE OLD FLAG!

THE OLD LEADER!

THE OLD POLICY

AND

Sam Hughes

A photograph of the legend that appears on the silk ribbon of an election favour made to incorporate the names of candidates of the 1891 Liberal-Conservative party. It was found in the family bible of Clerk of the Senate John MacNeill's secretary, who generously gave it to me. Note the flag abandoned by the Laurier government in favour of the Union Jack.

At the 1969 Ontario government press conference, the author holds the first volume of his four volume report on the Atlantic Acceptance Corporation Inquiry. (Courtesy *The Toronto Star*)

STEERING THE COURSE

Origins

I was born in my father's house, as was then the custom, in the pleasant Pacific city of Victoria on October 24, 1913. My father, Garnet Hughes, who had been chief engineer on location with the Canadian Northern Railway, had recently become chief engineer for the Dominion Department of Public Works on Vancouver Island. My grandfather, Sam Hughes, had for two years been minister of militia and defence for Canada and, with an eye for ominous signs of danger in Europe, had converted this often somnolent government department into a hive of activity.

British Columbia had, in the course of some forty years of Confederation, scarcely shed the influence of the Hudson's Bay Company, of which it had once been a fief. My mother, Elizabeth Irene (*née* Newling), English born but raised in Victoria since infancy, used to tell me about local people questioning visitors with the salutation "Are you from the coast or Canada?"

The domestic lives of people in Victoria of even modest means in those days were firmly based upon a large and industrious community of Chinese immigrants (if immigrants they could be called, given their doubtful status), virtually all male because of the prohibitory head tax demanded for females wishing to enter Canada. These men, universally known in the language of the day as "Chinamen," were a tight organization of domestic servants; and when in our household a male child was born, their "tong" recalled our Chinaman without notice to my parents and substituted a man who was senior on the rota. This man appeared on the doorstep of our Chamberlain Street address, taking over from his predecessors the customary duties of cook, houseboy, gardener, and general factotum, and in addition the delicate task of weaning a male child from a mother who had suffered from a difficult delivery and could henceforth bear no children. The newcomer, a young Cantonese of endearing character, speedily became a confidant of my parents. He was known as Hong, and for years after we had parted company and he had returned to Canton, I received tins of Chinese tea sent by him but from no address for acknowledgment and thanks.

The Chinese community in Victoria was dominated by the "importers," men who had become wealthy from lending money to the incoming Chinese who were required to pay the stiff head tax. My father had, on one occasion, come to the assistance of an elderly Chinese woman who had been shoved aside by people boarding a bus. Some time later, he and my mother were invited to dine with an importer of Mandarin stock by the name of Li Mong Kow (which is as near as I can get to rendering a name I have never seen in any form of writing), whose mother was the old lady my father had helped. This entertainment took place in a magnificent mansion concealed in a warehouse in the dock area. My parents' host was a man of parts and learning, and a story that circulated about him illustrates how workaday Anglo-Saxons patronized the Chinese, customarily addressing them in pidgin English and expecting a response in kind. Li Mong Kow, in the course of cashing a cheque at his bank, had been addressed by the teller, "You likee gold, you likee notes?" He had replied, "Young man, if you have any difficulty in speaking the English language, I can oblige you in French, German, and Spanish."

Victoria had traditionally been populated largely by retired English people, but at this time it was beginning to experience a significant number of arrivals from eastern Canada, one of whom was Arthur W. Currie, from Strathroy, Ontario. Currie, a not very prosperous real estate agent in Victoria, had militia experience and he and my father became friends and were instrumental in the embodiment of the 50th Gordon Highlanders of Canada, Currie becoming commanding officer with the rank of lieutenant-colonel and my father his second in command with the rank of major.

In my father's case, some explanation of this rapid promotion should be given. He had been the battalion sergeant-major (the highest cadet rank) at the Royal Military College (RMC) of Canada in Kingston in 1902, and even prior to going to the college, he had risen to the rank of captain in the 45th Regiment in his home town of Lindsay. He had entered the college with the highest marks in the entrance examination obtained across Canada. In due course, he received the gold medal and sword of honour, symbolic of academic achievement and practical military knowledge, and had been offered a commission in the Royal Engineers at Woolwich in England. This opportunity, with splendid promise of early promotion, had been declined because of my grandfather's opposition, engendered by one of his periodic differences of opinion with the British War Office. In the intervening years my father had spent most of his time in the bush on railway business, sometimes living in isolation from white society but in close contact with the aboriginals. It was not until he reached Victoria that his interest in military matters revived. He and Colonel Currie embarked on the Militia Staff Course together, so that when the Gordon Highlanders took form, they were sufficiently qualified to hold their respective ranks.

Alerted by my father to Currie's exceptional qualities, my grandfather looked with favour on the commanding officer of the Gordon Highlanders; and when the war broke out in 1914, he chose him as a brigade commander in the Canadian Expeditionary Force, not only launching Currie on his course to great distinction but saving his credit as a businessman in Victoria. Later in the war, as the star of Sam Hughes declined and that of Sir Arthur Currie rose, there was a falling-out in matters of military organization, but nothing like the quarrel that Currie's biographer and many later historians have tried to foster. When Currie died, my father was one of his pallbearers, and when I was chairman of the Civil Service Commission of Canada in Ottawa in the 1960s, his son, Garner, was a congenial member of my staff and Lady Currie was at all times friendly on the few occasions when we met.

As an independent entity, the Gordon Highlanders of Canada did not survive the extensive reorganization of the Canadian Army that took place at the beginning of the first great conflict. The 16th

Battalion, consisting of the Seaforth Highlanders of Canada, also included a company of the Gordon Highlanders from Victoria. In due course, my father left for Valcartier Camp and then Salisbury Plain in England, where additional training took place. The First Canadian Infantry Division entered the theatre of war in Flanders, where they won laurels for having "saved the situation" at Ypres, to use the words of Sir John French, commander of the British Expeditionary Force from 1914 to 1916. They experienced the first poison gas attack launched by the Germans, the brunt of this novel assault falling upon the Third Canadian Infantry Brigade commanded by Brigadier-General (later Lieutenant-General Sir) Richard Turner, vc, a hero of the South African War. My father, Major G.B. Hughes, was his brigade major and for this and subsequent operations was awarded the Distinguished Service Order (DSO).

By this time my mother and I, accompanied by my paternal grandmother, had followed my father across the Atlantic to England in a neutral ship, the ss *Philadelphia*. My grandfather had secured this enviable passage, having no intention of risking his wife, his daughter-in-law, and his only grandson in waters beginning to be infested by German submarines. My mother, a chronic victim of seasickness, found the passage far more terrifying than any enemy threat could be. It was her only transatlantic crossing, for my parents and I remained in England until my mother's death thirteen years later. My father and I would return to Canada just in time for the Great Depression. I would not again revisit my native province for almost thirty years thereafter.

British Columbia remained remote for me for an additional reason. My roots were all in Ontario, the old district of Canada West, earlier and otherwise known as Upper Canada. My paternal great-grandfather, John Hughes, was an Ulsterman who immigrated to Canada in the late 1840s, no doubt a victim of the potato famine that spared no part of Ireland. The famine produced a flood of emigration from which the population of Ireland has never recovered. John came from the neighbourhood of Fintona in County Tyrone, the least fertile of the six counties of Northern Ireland as at present constituted, only exceeded in barrenness by Donegal among the lands of the ancient province of Ulster. Hughes is a common Irish and still commoner Welsh name and points to a Celtic origin, although the family in this case was of determined Protestant bent and liked to believe in a Scottish origin, a belief that must be ascribed to a sentiment rather than to any actual connection. Sir James O'Connor refers to an offshoot of the O'Neill sept by the name of O'Hughes, which reinforces my view that the Hugheses of Fintona were of Irish blood.

John Hughes and Caroline Loughlin (Lachlan?) had four sons and six daughters after coming to the Midland District of Ontario and settling in what was known as Durham County until the modern-day devastation of regional government. I shall have occasion to refer to the wide connection of relationships thus engendered, but for now I trace in a purely introductory sense the line from which I am descended. Their second son, always known as Sam, was born in 1852. Like his father, he was a man of powerful physique, an amateur athlete of some note, a teacher at an early age, and a militia man by preference at all times. It is well to remember that the militia of Canada, particularly in the older provinces, filled the role of social activity and recreation much as golf clubs do today. On its serious side, it was called upon to defend the country against the ever-present threat of absorption by the United States as represented by the terrorist activity of the day in the shape of Fenian raids. These incursions were not recognized by the government of the American republic but were enthusiastically supported by Irish immigrants of the Roman Catholic persuasion.

Canada West had both Protestant and Catholic Irish settlers; but the Midland District was largely settled by Protestants, many of whom were Orangemen, in whose ranks the Hugheses found themselves arrayed. Then as now, the Orange Order eschewed political affiliation in Canada, but Sam Hughes was to contract an alliance with strong Liberal party leanings after the death of his first wife, Caroline Preston. His second wife, Mary Emily Burk, was the daughter of Harvey Burk, a prosperous farmer of Darlington Township, subsequently a Liberal member of Parliament for West Durham. Burk was himself the grandson of John Burk, who had come to Upper Canada in 1791 as a somewhat belated Loyalist from Orange County, New Jersey, in company with two families, the Trulls and the Conants, as the first settlers in Durham County as it afterwards became. The journey from New Jersey, which had been almost reluctant, was fraught with difficulty. The family stock was driven into and across the swift-flowing Niagara River and eventually around the head of Lake Ontario to the vicinity of Frenchman's Bay. The approaching winter barely allowed time to cut feed for the stock, but not to erect any form of habitation. The conditions under which a child was born under canvas in the middle of a Canadian winter can better be imagined than described, and indeed were only laconically referred to in a contemporary letter.

They had to make their peace with the native people of that day, and John Burk was well equipped to do this. Being a man of great physical strength, he was often called upon to discipline refractory natives who tried to disturb the infant settlement.

Perhaps because they were simple farmers and not part of the gently bred Loyalists who preceded them, this group of settlers tenaciously held to their opinion as Reformers and not Tories. Sam Hughes in his courtship of Nellie Burk no doubt walked delicately in expressing his political opinions, which eventually made him a follower of Sir John A. Macdonald.

A schoolteacher since his teens in various parts of rural Ontario, by the time his eldest child was born in 1880 Sam Hughes was head of the English and history department of the Toronto Collegiate Institute (now Jarvis Collegiate). He was renowned as a disciplinarian and admired as a lacrosse player of prowess like his older brother James, also a schoolmaster and subsequently inspector of schools for the City of Toronto. Although never a regular student at the University of Toronto, Sam attended lectures, presumably in the summer, and accumulated a library which testified to the catholicity of his reading and to his interests in history and literature. It is curious that those who attempted to recreate his life, including for the Canadian Broadcasting Corporation, portrayed this man as a sort of hillbilly. Like his father, who was ineffective as a farmer and who taught school at Sonora and presided at public political meetings all over the countryside, Sam Hughes developed a marked didactic quality through his years of teaching. He always sought to change things and to persuade other people to conform to his ideas of what such change should be. As they are today, the classroom and the debating society were training grounds for later activity in courtroom and legislature.

Sam and Nellie's first child was born on Homewood Avenue in Toronto. He was named Garnet Burk and he in due course became my father. Shortly afterwards Sam Hughes took a momentous step and moved to Lindsay, where his brother-in-law, Dr John MacAlpine, had already settled after conducting a rural practice in the area south of Lake Scugog. With the doctor's financial help, Hughes bought one of the local newspapers in Lindsay, the *Daily Warder*. In the beginning and doubtless for years to come, he composed all the letter press himself and subsisted on revenues derived more from advertisers than from subscribing readers.

The town of Lindsay, then only recently respectable, had once been a boisterous centre of lumbering activity (northward to what became the provisional county of Haliburton), infamous for the number of brothels and saloons which the trade fostered. Now the county town for Victoria County, it was flanked by prosperous farmlands to east and west, by Durham County to the south, and to the north by the beginning of the lakes, forests, and granite countryside known as the Canadian Shield. All of this has been described with loving detail by Dr Watson Kirkconnell, son of the famous principal of the Lindsay Collegiate Institute and himself later president of Acadia University in Nova Scotia, in his history of Victoria County published early in his life but revised and republished as a centennial project of the county council in 1967.

The local lumberman John Carew had become a prosperous leader in the town, and he as well as Dr MacAlpine assisted the fledgling newspaperman. Sam's position as editor, sufficiently precarious as it was, was gradually supplemented by activity in the militia, represented by the 45th Regiment, and by politics in the shape of the Liberal-Conservative party, whose journal was the *Daily Warder*. Ranged against it was the *Lindsay Daily Post*, the considerably more prosperous Liberal party organ.

Sam Hughes's political activities in Victoria County (divided electorally into North and South Victoria) were associated to a considerable extent with his activities in the Orange Lodge. This was reflected in editorials in the *Warder*, provoking attacks on both its editor and premises, the one by attempted murder and the other by attempted arson. Although it was in South Victoria that Sam Hughes made his living, it was in North Victoria that he preached his political beliefs and became a familiar figure on platforms and at social gatherings. The northern part of the county and the undeveloped territory of Haliburton had been largely settled by the English Land Company – in England known as the Canadian Land Company. The large tracts of rocky, unfertile land acquired by the company became home to farming people from the English counties of Surrey, Sussex, and Kent, often described as the garden of England. These intelligent, industrious people with names like Austin, Hobden, Roberts, and Hodgson found themselves transported to an inhospitable countryside with a bitter climate, facing impoverishment and isolation such as they had not known for countless generations. Sam Hughes always referred to them as the "free men and women of North Victoria," and from all accounts he became their idol. He became the Conservative candidate for the north riding in 1891, the year of Sir John A. Macdonald's last election, and was narrowly defeated by his Liberal opponent, whom he then proceeded to unseat on charges of corruption, a practice much more resorted to then than now. He never lost another election and remained the member for North Victoria and subsequently for the combined constituencies of Victoria and Haliburton until the day of his death in 1921.

My own didactic qualities, honestly inherited, make me dwell upon these family origins in the conviction that most modern-day readers either have forgotten or never learned of the early struggles of the settlers of the well-named Midland District, and indeed of the province of Ontario as a whole. I must continue to dwell upon the principal episodes in the life of the man whose name I have borne for over eighty years and to whose memory and reputation I owe so much more than the echoes and distortions of controversies can ever take away. The quarrel with General Hutton, the British officer who was chief of the General Staff in Ottawa (it being the custom always to have this much imperial control exerted in matters of defence), which deprived my grandfather of a combatant's role in the Canadian contingent that went to the war in South Africa, led to his accompanying the contingent as a civilian at his own expense and then becoming a national figure through his spectacular exploits in the field as a British officer. The long years in opposition between 1896 and 1911 under the wand of Sir Wilfrid Laurier, whom Sam Hughes greatly admired and who always acknowledged the younger man's tireless work on behalf of the militia of Canada, and the latter's friendship with Sir Frederick Borden, Laurier's minister of militia and defence, gave an aura of statesmanship to someone who had been a local partisan.

When in 1911 Sir Frederick's cousin R.L. Borden became prime minister, Hughes was the logical man to be minister of militia and defence, and he quickly put into practice many of the things he had been urging from his seat on the opposition benches. Unprecedented activity now occurred. Armouries were built or refurbished across Canada; rifle ranges appeared in profusion; and all of a sudden the minister, himself a colonel on the active militia list, became a trainer of troops, exerting his authority day and night, often in uniform, always with vibrant energy and enthusiastic speeches. All of this was considered excessive by the unenterprising section of the Canadian population that usually predominates in political affairs. But as the year 1914 came closer and the aims of Germany were revealed at least in outline, the minister's urgency became more significant and more acceptable.

I return to the small theme of my own existence in 1915 and 1916. My earliest recollection was of the first daylight air raid on London in the latter year when my mother and I were living in St John's Wood. My mother was shopping in Bond Street and I was with her. I remember the explosions that accompanied the bombing of Selfridge's in Oxford Street and I remember clearly that the taxi from which we were hastily removed had yellow facings on its doors. My mother and I were hustled into the basement of a shop where we would undoubtedly have been in great danger had the building been anywhere near a bomb blast; but the incident passed off as a demonstration that daylight bombing by aircraft could be practised alongside night bombing by Zeppelin. By this time my father, who had earlier gone with Sir Richard Turner to the staff of the Second Canadian Infantry Division, had been promoted to command the First Canadian Brigade in the First Division, commanded by General Currie. In his new command he fought in the grim battles of the Somme until the end of the year. He was then promoted to major-general and to command the Fifth Canadian Division, which was assembling in England for training and preparation to proceed to France, where it was expected to form part of a second Canadian corps. Because of his seniority Sir Richard Turner was to have the three-division corps and Sir Arthur Currie the two-division corps, a plan which produced considerable intrigue and eventually frustrated the hopes of my father and his division that they would reach France as a unit.

My father's return to England to command the Fifth Division led to my mother and me moving from London to at least two different houses not far from Witley Camp in the pleasant county of Surrey. One was in the town of Godalming, where I remember being taken by my nurse from the house on Frith Hill to watch the great fire which consumed Charterhouse School; and the other was the vicarage at Haslemere, which I remember as a very pleasant place with a large garden.

In the meantime much had happened in Canada. My grandfather's path in office had not been easy. In spite of enormous activity and achievement (placing four divisions and a complete corps in the field in France; organizing the munitions industry in Canada; and defending his department's role from constant attack by factious opposition in Parliament), the almost universal applause which had greeted his administration in the opening months of the war had become tempered by allegations of corruption in the letting of munitions contracts and by the controversy surrounding the use of the Ross rifle by Canadian troops. As to the first, a royal commission consisting of the chief justice of Ontario, Sir William Meredith, and Mr Justice Lyman Duff, of the Supreme Court of Canada, exonerated the minister and discredited the prime mover against him in the House of Commons, one Kyte.

The Ross rifle, however, was a vexatious and poorly understood issue at the time and has been the subject of distorted, even hysterical, objurgations ever since. The rifle was the regular issue to Canadian troops and had been commissioned in 1902 by the Liberal government under Sir Wilfrid Laurier because British army contractors had refused to supply the Lee-Enfield to Canada. Its distinguishing feature was that its bolt action was so constructed as to allow the handler to pull straight back, instead of folding over and pulling back as the Lee-Enfield weapon required. As a colonel and Opposition member of Parliament, Hughes had been a member of the Militia Council that had approved the adoption of the Ross rifle for manufacture in Canada and issue to the Canadian militia. He had no personal interest in its adoption other than that resulting from his own well-known marksmanship and his approval of the weapon born of experience in the South African War. The rifle was exceptionally accurate, but the mechanism which actuated the bolt and gave it an automatic character turned out to be too delicate for the rough usage it was exposed to in the mud of Belgian and French warfare, particularly in the hands of much-tried and often exhausted troops. The minister was particularly disturbed and often incensed by the criticism of Canada's only personal infantry weapon, knowing as a trainer of troops that any impairment of their confidence in such a weapon put them at a serious disadvantage. He deeply resented criticism suddenly springing from communities that had been perfectly satisfied with the arming of Canadian troops until political capital could be made out of the difficulties encountered by the rifle in France and Flanders. Hughes, perhaps unwisely, continued to defend the rifle even though some sections of the army were bitterly opposed to its continued use. In due course, the Lee-Enfield rifle was substituted, although the Ross continued to be used by the navy and in training; and indeed I and many others in the Second World War were trained on the Ross rifle.

When I told Professor Desmond Morton of the University of Toronto, a recognized expert in the history of the early twentieth century, that the Ross rifle was Laurier's rifle he looked at me in blank disbelief.

The Honourable Leslie Frost, formerly premier of Ontario and himself a veteran of heavy fighting, has dealt judiciously with the subject of the Ross rifle in articles which appeared in the *Lindsay Daily Post* and the *Evening Telegram* in Toronto. These were subsequently transformed into pamphlets entitled "The Record of Sir Sam Hughes Set Straight" for distribution in the Victoria and Haliburton counties, which Frost represented in the Ontario legislature from 1937 to 1963.

In my view, the criticism devolving upon Sam Hughes's head alone was grossly unfair: the words "Ross rifle" were and are used against him much as the words "Gallipoli" and "Dardanelles" were used against Winston Churchill to his disadvantage until swept away by the glorious achievements of his later life.

The minister's resignation was actually brought about by the problem of the control of overseas military forces of Canada. This problem had simmered since the middle of 1915 and had resulted in a good deal of experimental and confused military administration.

In South Africa the simple function of supplying troops to the imperial authority had presented no problems. In 1914 the British War Office had lost its battle to continue to exert full authority and could no longer prevent a commander of Canadian troops from reporting directly to his government at home rather than to the War Office itself. The principle having been established, the administration took time to develop, but by 1916 Sir Sam had set up the Acting Sub-Militia Council in London in order to supply a continuous line of authority and consultation to himself from the commander of Canadian troops. The Militia Council in Canada was like the Army Council in England, the minister's consultative body, and the extension of its activities to England and France would have preserved his authority and incidentally provided some relief from parliamentary criticism and curiosity.

Sir Robert Borden, who had given his minister of militia and defence much support and latitude since the beginning of the war, drew the line at this development, and the year of the minister's knighthood (not the usual KCMG given to colonial ministers but a resounding KCB) was also the year of his fall. After refusing to compromise, Hughes was forced to resign. The Canadian government then attempted to bring the position under parliamentary control and appointed a minister for overseas forces, who then proceeded to set up his own staff in London and to conduct control even more independently of Parliament and the minister of militia and defence than had been envisaged by Sam Hughes and his Sub-Militia Council. From a purely military point of view, the solution to the control of overseas military forces was found during the Second World War with the establishment of a military headquarters in London that had direct contact with the senior combatant officer overseas and with the minister himself, who was reported to by both of the former. This system worked only as long as perfect confidence subsisted. The recall and replacement of General McNaughton exposed many imperfections.

The Canadian government's decision to dismiss Sam Hughes affected my father's career in the army seriously and he never returned to the theatre of war, being given command of the defences of London in a non-combatant capacity. He had added the CB and the CMG to his DSO and at the time felt relieved that he did not receive the knighthood that the commanders of the four divisions fighting in France received in due course. He could not believe that going back to Victoria and riding downtown in the streetcar would justify the title, but later, in retrospect and considering how knighthoods were broadcast at the end of the war, he may have had second thoughts. In any event, I had at one time, and have since mislaid, a letter from General Currie in his own hand urging my father not to accept command of the Fifth Division but to wait until the First Division command became available, assuring him it would be his.

At the end of the war, the prospect of returning to Victoria was precluded by an offer from Henri and Camille Dreyfus to become managing director of the British Cellulose Company, accepted by my father to the intense pleasure of my mother, who was determined to remain in England if possible. We moved to Derby and in 1919 were all stricken by the terrible influenza epidemic that swept over Europe in the wake of war. We lived in a house in the heart of Derby, and I remember leaning out of my bedroom window and watching the horse-drawn funeral cars queuing up for entry into the cemetery of All Saint's Cathedral in the bitter winter weather. In the course of my father's treatment, a local doctor made a pointless effort to help him by extracting three of his teeth.

Shortly afterwards we moved out of town to a charming Georgian house, called the Homestead, in the adjacent village of Spondon. This would be my mother's favourite residence, which she embellished by restoring the original oak panelling, stripping it of layers of paint, and excavating behind the hideous gas fire in the drawing room to uncover a cavernous eighteenth-century fireplace. When the house had been restored to its pristine state and the garden to an appropriate elegance, my father, distressed at the decision of the Dreyfus brothers to water the company stock, resigned his position, leaving the board in company with Sir Harry McGowan (later Lord McGowan and chairman of Imperial Chemical Industries). To rid himself of the association with the cause of his complaint, he sold his substantial shareholdings in the company at some two shillings a share. The company, of course, went on to change its name to British Celanese and to participate in the success of the Celanese Corporation of America, its stock becoming considerably more valuable.

I do not think my mother ever really recovered from the consequential move away from her gracious Georgian house. When my father decided to practise as a consulting civil engineer in London, we moved to a house outside Guildford in Surrey situated near the junction of the London road and the road to the village of Merrow. Enduring fame was conferred by the appearance of Merrow Down in Rudyard Kipling's *Just So Stories* (1902). The house was large and not memorable architecturally but there was a magnificent garden with a tennis court (grass, of course), nursery garden, greenhouse and stables, and a wonderful acre of woodland devoted to huge trees and wildflowers.

My parents considered the practice at that time prevalent in England of sending boys of tender age to preparatory boarding schools as barbarous, and for two years I enjoyed the ministrations of Emma McLeod Carey, a governess of great ability and unusually mannish dress and general appearance. She gave me, and for a brief period my first cousin, Aleen Green, rigorous lessons in English, history, Latin, mathematics, and French. When I eventually went to my preparatory school, Stoke Park on the west side of Guildford, at the age of ten, I was reasonably well equipped and highly competitive. The school, which had ample playing fields and property extending downwards through woods to the River Wey, has been long defunct and Guildford Cathedral now occupies a part of the original property. Looking back, I think the teaching was of a high order, particularly so in the person of a schoolmaster of near genius, D.A. Tatham-Thompson, a man who had taken only casual lectures at London University and whose health had been greatly impaired by the malignant form of malaria prevalent in British Guiana. This man took infinite trouble in enlarging the minds of his pupils, lending them his books and even-handedly teaching them Latin and mathematics with the result that, three years after my arrival, I was one of three successful contenders for a public school scholarship.

My father conducted his practice as a civil engineer in chambers on the south side of Piccadilly near the Arcade. He was a warm and, as I now realize, a very conscientious father. In addition to showing a keen interest in my education, he took me to play

billiards at his club in London and golf on Merrow Down. At school
I developed a keen interest in cricket and became a bowler of some
skill, and he would diligently turn up for parents' matches,
although I am sure he found the game a poor substitute for
baseball. In the days before he had settled in Victoria, he had built
reservoirs at Monterey in Mexico for the great Canadian contractors Mackenzie & Mann, the promoters and managers of the Canadian Northern Railway. It was therefore not surprising that a good
part of his practice was now devoted to reservoir work, which he
undertook first of all in the area north of London and latterly for
the equally enterprising and more durable construction firm of Sir
Robert MacAlpine & Sons in and about the Pireus at Athens. This
activity produced many trips abroad and many fascinating presents
for his young son on returning.

But on this happy childhood, of which I have many sunlit memories, stole the shadow of domestic discord, and I saw and heard
with growing distress that the father I loved and the mother I
adored were growing apart. Although they did their best to conceal
the breakdown of their marriage from their son and to make
immense sacrifices of their own feelings for mine, the grief of an
only child in these circumstances is difficult to describe and painful
to remember. In later years this experience weighed heavily with
me when as a judge I had to preside at the frequently interminable
trials of matrimonial disputes and to observe the callous disregard
to which the children of broken marriages were too often subjected
by the self-centred litigants who had brought them into the world.

My father's character and my mother's beauty brought many
visitors to our house, but I shall refer to only three because of their
critical importance in my life and their relationship with my family.
The first was my maternal grandmother, Harriet Parker Newling,
who came from Victoria to live with us shortly after we moved into
the Guildford house, bringing her belongings in crates of British
Columbia cedar that filled the house with a gorgeous scent. My
father used the wood to carve the swords and spears and other
devices stimulating to the imagination of a small boy being showered by his mother with mythology, poetry, and history. My grandmother was a fascinating woman of parts who as a single parent
had raised her daughter through diligent employment in the civil
service of Canada. She also smoked cigarettes, an unusual habit

for an elderly woman even in the Roaring Twenties, and I used to be allowed to buy them for her on walks into town. They were of Russian manufacture and, like many cigarettes and pipe tobaccos of the time, could be bought in bulk. Of course, in those unregenerate days nobody complained, and although I do not remember my mother ever smoking, my father was a steady pipe smoker all his adult life. When I in my turn came to contemplate smoking tobacco, my father sternly warned me against cigarettes and offered me the free run of his tobacco jar, thus making me a confirmed pipe smoker until my late seventies when old age and health-care propaganda and sense induced me to desist.

Then there was my glamorous aunt, Aleen, my father's much younger sister, returning from a safari in East Africa where she had met James Freeman Clarke, a Bostonian war veteran similarly engaged and soon to be my uncle by marriage. Later, at our next house, she turned up with a lion cub, which she had determined to raise after shooting its mother on another expedition of the same kind. She too was a committed smoker of cigarettes and alas, as we must now admit, may have paid the penalty for it because she died of cancer in her mid-forties.

The third visitor was Lieutenant-Colonel Cyril Douglas Hughes MacAlpine, whose father and mother I have referred to, who had been a senior staff officer in the Canadian Army in England during the war and had been awarded the Order of the British Empire. Years later he would regale me with stories of this period and accounts of my mother's accomplishments. At the time of his visit he had, virtually in his hand, options to acquire the property near Rouyn, Quebec, from which the great Noranda mine would be developed by other hands. In vain he tried to persuade my father to become an investor and again, as in the case of British Cellulose, my father deflected prosperity. The sybils of high finance were never to make him a third offer and Cyril MacAlpine saw his title deed snatched away; but to him, as it turned out, the sybils were kinder.

One memorable journey, the first of my sixteen transatlantic crossings, was made in 1921, when my father took me to Ottawa to see my dying grandfather. Although he died in Lindsay, it was in his Ottawa house that he was receiving numerous blood transfusions, arm to human arm as was the practice in those days. I noticed fearful changes in his physique since the days, only a few months before, when he had visited us at Guildford and I had taken his hand to walk into town to the barbershop for his daily shave. But he was no less buoyant than he had been on those occasions, when he had been able to persuade a roomful of reserved Englishmen to put down their newspapers and join him in conversation and anecdote. The deep voice and compelling eyes had had the same effect as on the "free men and women of North Victoria" so many years ago.

When he died a few months later and was laid to rest in the Riverside Cemetary in Lindsay, after serving in Parliament for thirty years, the press of Canada broke out in an acclamation of his services in the Great War. He had been a journalist and the source of much news and comment in his lifetime. When I held his hand at his bedside in Ottawa, I thought he must be a very old man. He was sixty-eight.

After my parents separated, we left the big house with its cook, parlourmaid, housemaid, and gardener, and my mother and I went to live in the village of Calverton, on Watling Street, a scant two miles from the town of Stony Stratford. In that broad valley of North Buckinghamshire, the Great Ouse flowing eastward across England to the Wash at Kings Lynn, the grim Duke of Gloucester had met his young nephews to conduct them on their last journey to the Tower of London. Calverton Cottage, as our house was called, was on a small scale but had a pleasant walled garden.

In spite of the new circumstances of his marriage, my father would regularly come for weekends except when I joined him in London for a season of theatre-going or my mother took me on a similar expedition. I remained as a boarder at Stoke Park for at least a year, until the time came for me to go to Stowe. For two summers we took our holidays at Flamborough Head in Yorkshire, that fascinating promontory at one time almost severed from the land by what is still visible as Danes' Dyke. There I learned to swim, not very easily, in the heaving waters of the North Sea.

Stowe School was a new establishment quartered in the great palladian palace of the Temples and the Grenvilles in North Buck-inghamshire. I was thirteen when I left Stoke Park and went to

Stowe. The examinations for the six entrance scholarships offered each year were held at Stowe's grand premises and the candidates lived in the infirmary during the week-long tests. I returned to Stoke Park to await the results, and I shall never forget the feeling of triumph and relief when the headmaster of my preparatory school announced that I had won an entrance scholarship. By the skin of my teeth, I had managed to secure number six. It meant only half fees for my beleaguered father, as well as a wonderful translation to magnificent architectural surroundings in six hundred acres of gardens, woodland, and classical monuments to the taste of Stowe's eighteenth-century creators. And, *mirabile dictu*, the school provided excellent food at a time when English boarding-school food was almost scandalously inadequate.

The headmaster of Stowe, J.F. Roxburgh, was a teacher and leader of genius. He had been a housemaster at Lancing (see Evelyn Waugh's *A Little Learning*) and knew the names and first names of the some five hundred boys at the school. At least once a month each form was taught for a period by the headmaster himself, either in Latin or French. He would bring into the classroom a satchel full of copies of Latin or French texts in book form and would deal these out to all corners of the room, the air filling with flying volumes. When the dust settled, he would indicate a victim and say, "Page so-and-so, translate." These were "unseen" translations, and this process was the very essence of language education in England. At Stowe "set books" were derided. Roxburgh, a tall, handsome Scot, had been a notable athlete at Cambridge and held a degree from the Sorbonne and the Military Cross for his exploits during the war. His life and influence upon the public schools of England have been fittingly recorded by Noel Annan, also a scholar in my year and afterwards provost of King's College, Cambridge, and a life peer.

The accepted way of entering either Oxford or Cambridge University in those days was by obtaining the Oxford and Cambridge School Certificate through a public written examination in Latin, mathematics, English, French, and history. Oxford required a credit rating in all five, while Cambridge was satisfied with four. Entrance scholars at Stowe were admitted to a form halfway up the school, commonly the fifth form, the members of which were expected to complete the School Certificate in one year and spend the rest of their time reading for university scholarships. Most of us, and certainly the scholars, did this, and competition in the classroom was intense. At regular intervals – two weeks if I remember correctly – the class gathered in the great marble saloon of Stowe House and our form master, under the eye of the headmaster, called out the names of his form in order of performance for the period. This was called a "stance," with classic punning of the name of the school. I remember the feeling of exaltation that swept over me when after several weeks my name was called out first and I took my place at the head of a long line of boys who were individually complimented or admonished by "J.F."

In due course, my School Certificate with the requisite five credits for Oxford was secured and I was gazetted a member of the sixth form the following year. My father and I again crossed the Atlantic to see the Clarkes in Boston, the Greens in Toronto, and my grandmother, Lady Hughes, in Lindsay. My mother was in indifferent health when we left, and while we were away she suddenly died. The shock to an adolescent son may be imagined. The distance that lay between my mother on her deathbed and us in Canada would nowadays be easily reduced, but in the days of ocean travel of necessity, even transatlantic telephone calls were not available to the public. My grandmother had to face this tragedy alone. My mother was buried in the rural churchyard of the village of Stowe, in the belief I am sure that I would return to school and be close to her.

It was not to be. My father and I returned to England but only to settle my mother's affairs and to make provision for my grandmother, who did not wish to return to Canada. The year was 1928 and the Great Depression had begun to seep over Europe ahead of its onset in North America. The year was still one of great prosperity in Canada and my father decided to return. My career at Stowe had lasted only one wonderful year, the result of which was for me a qualification to enter any university in the British Empire forthwith. But I was still only fourteen years old. The University of Toronto, no doubt one of many, would not admit an undergraduate under the age of sixteen. What was to be done with me? With this problem weighing more heavily on my father's mind than mine, we sailed for Canada.

CHAPTER TWO

A Toronto Education

Canada as a whole was bathed in prosperity in 1928. I suppose the experts could have detected the onset of difficulties but they kept silent. Nevertheless, the euphoria that had admitted wartime generals to high place at the beginning of the decade had evaporated by its end. Still, my father lived in high hope and fair promises. At first we lived at my uncle and aunt's house on Balmoral Avenue in Toronto and with my grandmother in Lindsay. My uncle by marriage, Lieutenant-Colonel Byron Green, was manager of the Royal Bank of Canada branch at Bloor and Yonge Streets and had done well in the spectacular rise in value of shares quoted on the Toronto Stock Exchange. He was in fact if not in name administrator of that portion of my grandfather's estate that had gone to his widow and to his daughter Roby. My grandmother lived in some style in the large house she owned on Glenelg Street in Lindsay. She had a chauffeur who taught me to drive.

Here it was decided that I should go to the Lindsay Collegiate Institute to supplement, if not complete, my schooling. Of course, co-education was a complete novelty for me and I am sure this was a temporary expedient so that my father could find his feet in the city of his birth. I had spent more than a year out of school, no doubt illegally but hardly in a state of truancy. It was not long before Dr Kirkconnell, principal of the school and a man of discernment as well as learning, took my father aside and pointed out that I was not suited to the new environment and unhappy to boot, suggesting that he should see W.L. Grant, principal of Upper Canada College in Toronto, to settle my future.

I went to Upper Canada at the beginning of the winter term of 1929, gradually shedding my English accent and making many good friends. In September of that year I began to study systematically for the upper school examinations (later grade 13), which as I have explained I did not need but the pursuit of which allowed me to become familiar with the Ontario of those days and to reach an age which would allow me to proceed to a university in the normal course. I was not a star as my friend Robertson Davies wrote in a book about the college to which he contributed, but I found some of the standards required lower than in England; others, mainly in mathematics, somewhat higher.

Upper Canada College was and is a remarkable institution. While I was there in 1929, it celebrated its centennial, and at this writing it is 170 years old. It has in consequence the most deeply rooted and most numerous Old Boys' organization. This was dramatically proven when it was found necessary, after the Second War and an unfavourable report on the foundations of the college's second premises, to demolish the imposing building which my generation was familiar with. The herculean efforts of the Old Boys and their many business and professional friends produced a magically swift replacement of the long front of the school buildings, including the tower, the special donation of four Old Boys as I have been told.

In my youth I used to hear constant reiteration of the fatuous boast that Ontario had the best system of public education in the world. No one now pretends that it is any longer a good one. But the debt owed by Ontario to its private schools is enormous if not incalculable, although indeed the provincial government does not acknowledge this by contributing anything to their support. The principal in my time was of course the gifted and statesmanlike W.L. Grant, son of the famous Principal Grant of Queen's University and son-in-law of a predecessor principal, Sir George Parkin. His brother-in-law was Vincent Massey, head of the Massey Foundation, Liberal politician, diplomat, and finally governor-general of Canada, a benefactor of taste and discernment whose benefactions included the elegant quadrangle of the school. To these two men I owe a great deal.

My time at Upper Canada was necessarily short – one term and one school year (1929–30), since I was determined not to squander the advantage gained at Stowe and wanted to enter university as soon as possible. As it turned out, I had no difficulty with the senior matriculation examinations, but to the college I had contributed almost nothing. I played no cricket and occupied only a subordinate position on the editorial board of the *College Times*. One agreeable encounter was with Robertson Davies on the same board. In the competition for the Beatty reading prize, I was outclassed by this accomplished and indeed precocious young man, then full of promise for what would be a brilliant future. At least I obtained a handsome volume of *Macaulay's Essays* for the second place, which still graces my shelves.

The Faculty of Arts of the University of Toronto, if ever it was thus called, was split between the university itself and the federated colleges. The university taught history, economics (political science, commerce, and finance), law, and philosophy, the federated colleges having almost exclusive jurisdiction over English and other languages ancient and modern and, of course, religious knowledge and relevant philosophy.

In the sphere of the arts there was a major division between those who sought an honours bachelor degree and those content with a pass degree. For the former, much was provided, particularly a selection of specialized honour courses, for example, Modern History, Political Science and Economics, Commerce and Finance, Law, Mathematics, and Mathematics and Physics. These courses were vouchsafed over four years of largely specialized study. For those who wished to obtain an honours degree in three years, an accumulation of upper school matriculation credits might enable them to avoid the first year of an honour course. There was also a general course with honours status. For the rest there was a pass course of great variety and little focus, of a size in comparison with the honour courses never disclosed. Honours were divided into first, second, and third classes, and first class began with an average of 75 per cent, which illustrates the economy of marks awarded in those days compared to the inflated awards of contemporary fashion.

The strength of Trinity College lay in its large residential component of the total enrolment of undergraduates. It consisted of men and women from towns and farms outside Toronto in the main, and in many cases from countries around the world. The college either owned or rented a venerable apartment house on the southwest corner of St George and Harbord Streets to house its male undergraduates and a number of houses north of Hoskin Avenue and on the east side of St George Street, constituting St Hilda's College, for Trinity women. Residents and non-residents alike wore gowns to lectures, meals, and worship within the precincts of the college, unlike any other students in the university. Although it would have been normal for me as a Torontonian to live at home, I decided to live in residence at what was then called Trinity House. While this imposed a considerable sacrifice upon my father during the Depression years, which exactly matched my own attendance at the university, from 1930 to 1934, we never regretted it and I made many lifelong friends across Canada.

Student affairs in those days were in the hands of the Trinity College Literary Institute, a debating society with considerable funds and responsibilities to be managed by its "government." This government could enjoy the support or endure the disapprobation of the members of the institute in the course of weekly debates. Two defeats in a row would unseat it and an opposition slate would assume office. Since this society met only in Trinity House and with unfailing regularity on Friday nights, it possessed a permanence and a following which no other debating society in my experience enjoyed, with the exception of the Oxford Union Society.

For the university men as a whole there was Hart House, the splendid benefaction of the Massey Foundation which with the Soldier's Tower, a graceful war memorial with a matchless peal of bells, offered an impressive example of collegiate gothic architecture at the heart of the university campus. Hart House then was for men only, but these were the days before the word "discrimination" was wrenched from its ordinary meaning to become a tool of invective. The house had a noble debates room, a library, music room, squash courts, and swimming pool, crowned by a magnificent Great Hall in conscious imitation of those of the best-endowed Oxford and Cambridge colleges. The debates at Hart House were more formal and less frequent than those at Trinity College and were presided over by the secretary of the Debates Committee, who acted as Speaker of the House, arrayed in full evening dress with the two leading speakers on each side of the question wearing dinner jackets. There was always a special guest who wound up the debate, often a cabinet minister from Ottawa and on two occasions in my time the prime minister of Canada himself.

I was a member of the Debates Committee of Hart House fairly early in my undergraduate career, and in my third year I was secretary. This brought me into close contact with the famous warden of Hart House, the late J.B. Bickersteth. He was the son of a canon of Canterbury Cathedral, an Oxonian and the holder of a Military Cross. His civilizing influence through the medium of Hart House was enormous and his life as a bachelor in this all-male society was happy and successful. Burgon Bickersteth had impressed Mackenzie King when King was prime minister before 1930. King had indeed tried to lure the warden to Ottawa to set up a cabinet secretariat on the English model, but the prime minister throughout my undergraduate days was R.B. Bennett, a dominating figure and powerful orator whom the warden and others were anxious to invite to a Hart House debate. Bennett had refused all previous invitations and I was urged to use my position as a leading student Conservative when I became secretary in 1932–33. Mr Bennett did not fail me and accepted the committee's invitation. The excitement in the university mounted quickly. Here was the arch-Tory in the middle of a deep economic depression about to expose himself to the slings and arrows of radicals ranging from sentimental socialists to active Communists. By the time the day came, my friend Sydney Hermant had succeeded me as secretary and consequently was in the chair. I do not now remember the subject for debate nor most of the participants, but I do recall that Gordon Skilling was leading for the radical groups with many eloquent supporters while I was on the other side, with the prime minister of Canada winding up the debate.

I was apprehensive of a debate that might prove offensive to the prime minister, especially after all the cajolery employed to induce him to come to Hart House. At this stage of the Depression and of his term in office he was no longer a popular figure. As the debate drew on, with many barbs and pointed questions hurled in his direction, Mr Bennett sat with his eyes closed. Only the occasional

movement of a foot revealed that he was conscious of the vigour
of the opposition attack. Those who had launched it were confident
they would command a majority in the house. I need not have
worried. When the time came, the prime minister, towering above
his opponents, answered every question, repelled every attack, and
without a note swept his detractors away by the force of his eloquence. Only a handful of a large throng voted against him and
long lines formed to pass through the "government" lobby. It was
a great victory and a sound lesson for an eighteen-year-old and
faint-hearted debater. Even the ranks of Tuscany could scarce for-
bear to cheer.

The debating style at Toronto in those days was relaxed, extem-
poraneous, and untrammelled by judges and laurels. The sole
reward was the support and approbation of the audience. In this
spirit Sydney Hermant and I went to Montreal and debated successfully in the McGill Union. But this is anticipation.

In September 1930 my friend W.D.S. Morden and I entered the
honour course in Modern History. Bill Morden had won the Herbert Mason Gold Medal at Upper Canada and his brother, Ken
(later a justice of the Ontario Court of Appeal), had preceded us
and as it were had broken the trail. It was my good fortune,
sustained by enthusiasm and a good deal of hard reading, to stand
first in this course in the final examinations of each of its four
years' continuance, with first-class honours in the second, third,
and fourth years. The course was not a large one compared to the
honour course in English and History, much frequented by aspirant teachers. It was conducted on the tutorial system in vogue at
Oxford and Cambridge for which small numbers, the writing and
discussion of essays, and a relaxed attitude towards attendance at
lectures were well suited. The teaching was excellent and reading
in the stacks of the university library a satisfying experience, but
the accumulation of knowledge took second place in interest to
association with the faculty of the history department.

On October 30, 1994, at the University of Western Ontario,
under the sponsorship of the Joanne Goodman Foundation, I gave
a lecture in the Department of History on "Canadian Historians I

Have Known" and of necessity the early experience was confined to those of the University of Toronto except in the case of Principal Grant of Upper Canada College, a Canadian historian whose credentials were not dependent at all upon his great work as headmaster of a boys' school. Grant, known as "Choppy," presumably a corruption of the English diminutive "Chappie," had taught both at Toronto and at Queen's University in Kingston, which owed so much to his father, Principal George Grant. He had been Beit Lecturer in Colonial History at Oxford University for six years before the war of 1914, and although his written work was mostly editorial, his prestige in the field was substantial. I shall relate in its proper place how his interest in history affected me.

The university's history department was headed by Professor Chester Martin, at the time of my arrival only three years translated from the University of Manitoba, a very different man from George M. Wrong, his predecessor. Martin was the author of *Empire and Commonwealth*, a book of critical importance dealing with relations between colonial governments and their masters in London. As far as I know, the book was the first to reveal elements of statecraft in the Quebec Act of 1774 inconsistent with the popular view that the act was a measure of unrequited generosity to the French inhabitants of Quebec. Not only an accomplished author and historian, Martin was a brilliant lecturer and presided with good-tempered urbanity over the affairs of the department. Other members of the department included Ralph Flenley, the author of a remarkably useful text on European history from the beginning of the nineteenth century; George Brown, who concerned himself with and taught mostly Canadian history; George Glazebrook, who shared Brown's interest and subsequently became an influential member of the Department of External Affairs; and Dick Saunders, an American historian and also a specialist in European history. All of these men I greatly liked and admired, but I must concentrate for a moment on those who influenced me most.

In my first year I was fortunate in encountering an experiment which had the purpose of familiarizing us with elementary medieval constitutional development in England, or in other words, Stubbs's *Charters*. The experiment was conducted by an assistant professor called Rothwell, late of the Victoria University in Manchester, and as a preliminary to the introduction of a study of medieval history, it was not considered a great success. Indeed, until the arrival on the scene of Professor Bertie Wilkinson, also from Manchester, the project lapsed. But I greatly enjoyed it, and since the only really serious work in medieval studies was being done by the Pontifical Institute in St Michael's College – I suspect more in the field of philosophy than in that of history – not really accessible to declared students of modern history, I was fortunate.

Thereafter there were three men in particular whom I admired, all from my university, all with subsequent membership in Balliol College, Oxford: Donald J. McDougall, Donald Creighton, and Frank Underhill, all very different except in their intellectual capacity. McDougall, a young hockey player of proven ability, had come to Toronto early in the Great War from the far north of Ontario – from the town of Kapuskasing – to enrol in the School of Practical Science and become an engineer. Then he joined the Canadian Army and in 1916 was blinded by shrapnel in the terrible Battle of the Somme, the battle the Germans called the "Bloodbath." Sidelined from the war, he made the momentous decision to study history. He learned Braille and how to use a specially designed typewriter, engaged friends and undergraduates to read to him, and trained his memory to serve him with great exactness. He went on to obtain first-class honours and a specially awarded Rhodes Scholarship to take him to Balliol. There he had great success and again obtained a first-class honours degree with a congratulatory *viva voce* examination, where all the examiners stand to shake hands with the candidates earning the highest distinction. Returning to Canada, he became by far the most eloquent lecturer of my experience in any university. He built up a substantial library in which he could direct his students to the position of a volume on his shelves and even to a page reference. Needless to say, the exercise of this feat of memory gave him the greatest pleasure.

Donald McDougall was an avid pipe smoker as was I, and the charm of his conversation on the occasions when we indulged in this once-respectable practice was intense. He specialized in British sixteenth- and seventeenth-century history, but I felt that his heart really lay in the Middle Ages where the civilizing influence of his own church was at its height. His precise knowledge of the Puritans and all their thoughts and all their works in the age of persecutions was always judicious; later in life he became immersed in Irish history and had he lived longer I am sure he would have produced a definitive work. He was a great teacher, and mainly because of his influence, and indeed on his recommendation, I applied to Balliol and was accepted.

It is difficult to imagine Donald Creighton as an eloquent lecturer also in the field of British history because of his subsequent eminence as an exponent of the history of his native land, but such he was in my time. He had been some three years a member of the Department of History when I first knew him and he was a forceful and imaginative teacher. In due course, he was to be strongly influenced by the opinions and writings of Professor Harold Innis, a member of the Department of Political Science and Economics and an economic historian of note. Creighton's first major work was *The Commercial Empire of the St. Lawrence,* very much a work in Innis's field but infinitely more readable than the important work of Innis himself owing to Creighton's style of writing. His writing bloomed more fully in *Dominion of the North* and reached its ultimate resonance and authority in his two-volume life of Sir John A. Macdonald. The ties which had seemed to bind him to economic history were clearly cast off. When I first knew him, he had not found his predestined path but his style both written and verbal was exciting.

By contrast, Frank Underhill was then at the height of his powers. Before the war he had at Oxford achieved a "double first" in classics and history, a feat rarely accomplished. Years later one of my tutors, Vivian Galbraith, told me that he did not think Frank had been happy at prewar Balliol, with all the potential proconsuls. In most ways, he was still the pride of Markham High School, modest in manner and unexpectedly vigorous in speech and action. Wherever Frank taught, he became involved in local politics, and his experience of teaching history in Saskatchewan governed his activities in Ontario. Although a founding member of the Co-operative Commonwealth Federation (CCF), Canada's first organized socialist party under the leadership of J.S. Woodsworth, he was more a philosophic radical than a socialist, and in the evening of his life he became a dutiful Liberal as custodian of Laurier House in Ottawa.

Nonetheless, in the years of which I write and which I consider to have been his prime, F.H. Underhill was a formidable debater and writer, particularly in the pages of the *Canadian Forum*, a respected magazine with a reputation for intelligent journalism and, generally speaking, for its devotion to left-wing causes. In an earlier age Underhill would have been a notable pamphleteer. As it was, all his political activity did him harm: first, it circumscribed his activities as a teacher; and second, it brought him into collision with those who governed the university and with the province's Department of Education, which supplied the university with the greater part of its funds.

My relations with Frank Underhill were cordial. I recognized him as a brilliant teacher and admired his academic record and service as a soldier in France. For his part, he used to single me out in lectures and tutorials as the classic Tory, often using me as a butt of the ironical comment of which he was master. But I was content to be singled out on any terms by this great controversialist. When we were charged with the duty of writing a summer essay at the end of our second year, I presented him with one on the Great Reform Bill of 1832, a work of considerable length and full of sententious comment. Frank thought well of it. He gave me the unheard of mark of 86 per cent and illuminated it with his comments, creating a document I treasure to this day.

When I entered the university, it was presided over by the respected but somewhat remote presence of Sir Robert Falconer. He died not long afterwards and was succeeded by the Reverend Canon H.J. Cody, the eloquent rector of St Paul's Church whose hour-long sermons enthralled a large congregation and many beyond by the help of radio. Canon Cody had been briefly minister of education in a Conservative provincial ministry, and when the university appointment was made, clamour rose from the ranks of the radical left, particularly at the university of which he had become president. This accession did not escape the acidulous observations of Frank Underhill, and in an age when left and right were more sharply divided than they are today, his academic career at the University of Toronto appeared to be in peril.

Few will remember the strong appeal made to intelligent men and women by what was known as the Popular Front, presented as the gathering together of all the forces which could be deployed against the rise of fascism in Europe. Stalinist Russia was considered the natural ally and indeed protector of the Popular Front, and the shock to its supporters, mainly people of goodwill and devoted to democracy, when the Russo-German Pact of 1939 was reached and revealed, was profound. But in the years of the Depression, plain speaking was perilous and honest controversy was often regarded as seditious. Frank Underhill had reason to fear for his job. And yet, as he told me many years later, it was the despised Tory clergyman who saved it for him. As Dr Cody became acclimatized in the office of president, he was able to interpose a strong shield over Frank Underhill and avowed Communists like Felix Walter, and fight the battle of academic freedom against Liberal and Conservative alike. Frank freely admitted to me that had it not been for Cody he could not have maintained his position as professor of history at Toronto.

Midway through my four years of enjoyable study of history, some of my friends, thinking I should strengthen my position as an aspirant for a Rhodes Scholarship, persuaded me to try for the position of coxswain of the university eight, then vacant. This brought me to the attention of Lieutenant-Colonel T.R. Loudon, always known as "Tommy," a professor of engineering and a famous coxswain in his day. At that time the Rowing Club boated three crews: heavy, 150 pounds, and 140 pounds. These rowed at local regattas, such as the ones in Toronto Bay on Dominion Day and at the Royal Canadian Henley in St Catharines, but only the heavy eight went to Montreal in early October to row against McGill on the Lachine Canal, a two-mile race emblematic of the intercollegiate championship. This race, held immediately after the McGill-Varsity football game at Molson Stadium, attracted a considerable crowd along the banks of the canal. Competition for the coxswain seat in the heavy boat was keen, and after a prolonged trial period I outlasted my competitors and secured the prize.

   The Toronto climate was not good for rowing. Dreary weeks were spent on rowing machines in Hart House in the beginning of the year, and as soon as the ice was out of the bay in the early spring, the crew got its oars in the water at the Harbour Police station at the foot of John Street. We rowed at six-thirty in the morning and six-thirty in the evening or thereabouts, Sundays I think excepted, and to sustain this program we had to have summer jobs. A Henley course of one mile and five-sixteenths distance could be achieved by starting well off the easterly shore of the Toronto Islands and finishing at the end of the turning basin canal at Ashbridge's Bay. At the end of this course, the smell of oil from the tanks in the neighbourhood made breathing on a hot summer day, already shortened by extreme physical effort, an agonizing experience, one the coxswain could not share.

Rowing on Toronto Bay was not without its hazards. It seemed to me remarkable that a sixty-foot craft bearing nine men at a uniform pace should have to give way to the frivolous motions of a dinghy containing one or two people, but such is the maritime rule. An eight-oared shell cannot be halted abruptly or easily diverted from its predetermined course; and yet in order to steer it safely among sailing craft, power boats, and ferries, a coxswain must decide upon a course well in advance. The concerted drive of eight oars militates against manœuvre. All of this I found very stimulating, and my interest in rowing and oarsmen has continued to this day.

In the first race that I steered against McGill, our heavy crew, rowing against a head wind, easily won by several lengths. This was the fourth victory in consecutive years and only the first two races had been won by McGill, coached by the well-known but eccentric Belgian oarsman Urbain Molmans. Molmans liked a light crew, believing that when well trained they could master a heavy one even at a distance of two miles; but his repeated failures led Tommy Loudon to fear for the continuance of the race. In my second year as cox, hoping to make the race more competitive, Tommy selected a much lighter crew, stroked by Jack Cameron instead of the towering Henry Gibson. Larry Skey, the lightest member the year before, was now the heaviest number seven. The bow oar was David Woods, little heavier than myself. Fortunately, I held my place and after a hair-raising two miles we beat the McGill crew by a canvas. Alas, even this narrow loss was too much for the temperamental

Molmans and our intercollegiate rivalry lapsed after eight successive annual races.

In those days, before the qualifications for Rhodes Scholarships
established by the great imperialist had been purged by latter-day
trustees of the slightest taint of racial or sexual bias, it was common
knowledge that the all-rounder was the preferred object of Cecil
Rhodes's bounty. Not consciously but out of sheer high spirits, I
had become at one time and another president of the Historical
Club, president of the Foreign Affairs Club, a member of the
students' administrative council representing Trinity, and a
member of the university's Athletic Directorate. With my debating
activity, big "T" for rowing, and scholastic record, I felt reasonably
sure of getting one of the scholarships for the province of Ontario
at a time when the University of Toronto frequently captured both.
The trustees were known to be anxious to get younger candidates
and when the examination (and interview and essay) took place
in the autumn of 1933, I had barely turned twenty. But it was not
to be. The examiners considered me young enough to try again
the following year, giving for the first time in history one scholarship to a McMaster University man, J.R. Baldwin, later to have a
brilliant career in the civil service of Canada, and the other to my
contemporary Gordon Skilling. When I left the interview, I heard
a receding voice, presumably a member of the board, say, "That is
a very shrewd young man." Perhaps I had overplayed my hand.

When the news of my failure was given me over the telephone
by my friend Marvin Gelber, I was disconsolate. The idea of waiting
another year and pursuing a lackadaisical master's degree did not
appeal to me for two reasons. In the first place, in the year 1933
my father was barely holding his head above water financially, and
in the second, like most young people in those stressful years I felt
that there was no time to lose. But before night fell on that day of
disillusion, a wonderful consolation was offered to me. Principal
Grant of Upper Canada College had heard the news and was
indignant at what he felt was an injustice. On the telephone he
startled me by saying that if I still wanted to go to Oxford, the
Honourable Vincent Massey would award me a Massey Scholarship

provided I submitted myself for an interview. At that interview I was brash enough to suggest to Mr Massey, who had just been appointed national organizer of the Liberal Party of Canada for the impending general election, that his party was in danger of following in the footsteps of the Liberal party in England, which was then beginning to shrink into insignificance. He received this fatuous observation with good temper and I came away with the scholarship in my pocket.

The benefactor was either Vincent's father Chester Hart Massey or the Massey Foundation under Vincent's direction, and the scholarships were to be available for candidates proceeding to the American University in Washington. At the time of the benefaction, the American University existed only on paper, and between the two wars Vincent Massey had a free hand. In my time, at least two scholarships were awarded every second year. Many subsequently well-known Canadians were helped by this cultivated and far-sighted statesman, including Lester B. Pearson, who became prime minister; J. Tuzo Wilson, the world-famous geophysicist; Carl Pollock, electronics manufacturer; and Lorie Tarshis, economist, who went to Cambridge and was a pupil of John Maynard Keynes.

In 1934 I was accompanied to Balliol by another Massey Scholarship recipient, Max Patrick, who became an authority on seventeenth-century English poetry and lectured in the United States. I am sure we had successors but I cannot now name them. In any event, after the Second World War the American University rose into concrete existence and the period of the scholarships' diversity was at an end.

My father's companionship and intellectual stimulus were meanwhile generously given to his son. As early as 1926, when we were at Flamborough Head in Yorkshire, he decided to show me something of the battlefields with which he had been familiar only a decade before. We boarded a small freighter at nearby Hull, crossing the North Sea in foul weather to Antwerp. I was desperately seasick and the calm waters of the Scheldt with its leisurely and serpentine approach to the famous city were an enormous relief. Antwerp, Brussels, Bruges, and Ghent were full of historic treasures stirring to my bookish mind. Finally, Ypres, with the ruined Cloth Hall rebuilding and the Menin Gate leading to that portion of the old front line at Hill 60 – the Railway Cutting, Poperingh, and Zillebeeck Farm – that was carefully protected by the Belgian government in its original state of devastation, provided ample authoritative reminiscence for a small boy's endless questions.

Two years later, before we left England for good, my father decided that I should see Paris and that we should travel by air, a thing he was used to but a rarity for most people and a complete novelty for me. We flew from Croydon to Le Bourget in one of the huge Imperial Airways triplanes with eight engines. I believe the cruising speed was about eighty to a hundred miles an hour with an elevation of perhaps two thousand feet. The company provided passengers with a route map that pointed out prominent features on the ground; but shortly after crossing the Channel, the clouds enveloped us and the airsickness to which I was then prone enveloped me. In Paris we stayed at the old Chatham Hotel, now I think defunct, and for the first time I became familiar with landmarks like Notre Dame, the Opera, and Les Invalides. No doubt there were many adolescent emotions stirring within me in the famous city, but one I remember most vividly was the realization that I was actually taller than many of the adults I passed on our walks.

Later, after settling in Toronto in a comfortable apartment building on St Clair Avenue, immediately adjacent to the Badminton Club and separated by only one apartment house from the new Granite Club, my father and I made many trips by car into eastern Canada, New York State, and New England. Long drives in the Ontario countryside were commonplace, even over indifferent roads, and summers were made fragrant and memorable by annual visits to my grandfather's summer house on Eagle Lake in Haliburton, still in existence as a hotel under the name of Sir Sam's Inn in largely unspoiled surroundings. It was then isolated in almost uninhabited country full of lakes and covered by the great deciduous forest of the region. In the fall the sense of isolation was heightened by the howling of wolves and the melancholy calls of loons. The area was almost never visited by tourists, being defended by a sparse network of infamous roads. When we visited Eagle Lake, we broke the journey at Lindsay, staying overnight to begin the long trip to Haliburton village at daybreak. Even Lindsay was not reachable on a paved road, although the gravel roads of the day were excellent enough in the first stage of the journey. North of Fenelon Falls a wonderful adventure began on what was not much better than tracks over the rocks and through the swamps of a landscape unchanged since the days that my grandfather had travelled in a horse-drawn buggy to visit the free men and women of North Victoria.

CHAPTER THREE

Hawk Lake and Oxford

When I came to the final examinations in my fourth year in Modern History, I had the flattering experience of reading my own paper to Donald McDougall, perhaps because of the difficulty his readers had with my handwriting but I prefer to think that this was a compliment paid to me by the man to whom I owed most academically and on whose initiative I was admitted to Balliol College, Oxford. I was also happy to get a first class from Harold Innis in Canadian Economic History. But I did not stay in Toronto to hear these results or to have the chancellor, Sir William Mulock, dub me Bachelor of Arts.

Previously all my summer jobs had been at the Department of Education in the Parliament Buildings in Toronto, the locale dictated by rowing requirements. Now I had a job in the Ontario bush.

My uncle Byron Green had spoken on my behalf to George MacNamara, who with his brother Howard had ascended from fame as hockey players – the Dynamite Twins – to renown and wealth in the construction business. They, along with other contractors, had been awarded a contract to complete a difficult section of the Trans-Canada Highway near and around Hawk Lake some forty miles east of Kenora. The highway project, which was under the jurisdiction of the Ontario Department of Northern Development (DND) from the French River northwards in Ontario, was subsidized by the Bennett government in Ottawa as an unemployment relief scheme paying some ten cents an hour. To this point, it had made little progress.

In the spring of 1934 this lethargy was dispelled, and many students such as I found employment. My father had given me many tips culled from his long experience working in the bush. He bought me a pair of "shoe-packs," heavy leather boots with a half pound of hobnails driven into their soles and heels. He had not reckoned on the modern invention of the sneaker, so easily discarded when worn out, which I would find that most people wore when walking over rocks, but which were not so effective in muskeg.

I took the Canadian Pacific Railway's principal transcontinental train as far as Port Arthur, staying the night there and resuming my journey the next day on a slower train that could be prevailed upon to stop at Hawk Lake. After descending to the small platform on a sunny evening, I watched the train go round the bend and felt the silence "surging softly backwards," with the tiny noises of insects making the only disturbance of it. After about an hour a wagon drawn by a pair of horses clattered out of the bush, disclosing a makeshift tote-road. The driver relieved me of my baggage and my feeling of loneliness and in due course deposited me at Camp I of the MacNamara Construction Company. I bunked in with the bookkeeper and paymaster, Duncan McDonald of Sudbury. I was now a little over a thousand miles from Toronto by rail. No connecting road was then in existence.

The MacNamaras operated five camps to build the stretch of road under contract, and a word should be said to try to bring back the north country traditions of construction camps and more generally lumber camps. There were no caterpillars driving impressive excavators and earth movers; everything was done by teams of horses, and each camp had a mile of stables at least. On road-building jobs, the grade was made by stoneboats and scrapers drawn behind a team of two horses and controlled by a teamster of impressive skill and dexterity. It is pleasant to dwell upon the origins of the labour union which James Hoffa raised to power and infamy. I cannot remember any of the hundreds that I met in the course of that summer that I did not like, drawn from all over northern Ontario and Manitoba and beginning to feel the effects of an improving economy and a renewal of hope. The essential complement to the builders of the grade were the levellers of the path upon which it was laid: the blasters of the rock and the ditchers, particularly in the muskeg, who made sure that the road

did not dissolve into sinkholes. The making of rock-cuts and
ditches was in the hands of what were called "station gangs,"
subcontractors who generally contracted to perform their work for
a sum certain within a specified time. If completion were on
schedule or, better still, early, they pocketed this amount. If, as was
often the case, they were unable to complete in time because of
delays in delivery of compressors, jack-hammers, and so forth, they
lost, as it were, their wager and were paid on the basis of twenty-
five cents an hour for a ten-hour day, however long and hard they
may have worked to complete the job on time.

Since I was the timekeeper for our camp and had continuous
contact with whatever was going on along the grade, I became to
a greater extent even than the foreman a personification of the
company. In this role I received many complaints before dissatisfaction became widespread and commanded the attention of
senior officials. On one occasion I was chased to the top of a high
rock by a Swedish station gang, among whom I had friends, that
had failed by a slim margin to complete their formidable rock-cut
by the prescribed time. In their drunken state they could not reach
me, but I did not dare to move until after nightfall and sleep had
descended. In the course of that long season I learned at the
tender age of twenty a good deal about life in the bush. I was able
to accept more and more responsibility for both payrolls and
materials and acquired the ability to get along with men in a setting
where the absence of women was palpable. Over and over again I
reflected on how my father had spent ten years of his youth in a
similar situation, suspended in the far north in an enterprise
infinitely lonelier, since his few companions were either native
people or Métis.

The provincial Department of Northern Development was
largely staffed by young engineers, many of them from the University of Manitoba. The MacNamara Company had its own experienced hard-bitten engineers, usually innocent of any academic
qualification; these engineers were constantly at loggerheads with
those of the department. The DND would soon be humbled for
having shut its face against the representations of Peter Heenan,
Liberal-Labour member for the federal constituency embracing
Kenora. Heenan would soon became a member of the Ontario
cabinet of Mitchell F. Hepburn, who defeated the Depression-

haunted Conservative government of George S. Henry in an election which introduced a new type of blatant political patronage to the provincial political scene. Vulgar and raucous as he undoubtedly was, Mitchell Hepburn had in full measure one quality essential to political success in Canada: the ability to make his auditors laugh with him rather than with his opponents, whom he generally succeeded in making look ridiculous. His Sam Slick extravagance of speech and action had a tonic effect in those Depression years. The Department of Northern Development disappeared, but the construction companies remained to trample upon the last remnants of the policy of government make-work relief instituted by R.B. Bennett, soon to suffer almost annihilating defeat at the hands of Mackenzie King in 1935. By then my personal circumstances had suffered a dramatic change.

For those familiar with Oxford University in the two decades between the great wars, or perhaps with what such autobiographers as Anthony Powell and Evelyn Waugh have written about it, no descriptive observation might be necessary; but for those who know it only in its postwar evolution as a largely post-graduate organization, a reminiscent word or two will not be amiss. Before this transformation, Oxford, like Cambridge, was for nearly all purposes an undergraduate community ruled by teachers (quaintly known as dons) content to pass useful, even distinguished, lives wearing only the academic hood of a master of arts, which represented an honours bachelor of arts convertible upon payment of an appropriate fee. If one wanted to pursue a diploma or a doctorate "learning more and more about less and less," one was free to do so – but not to attract more than polite acknowledgment. For Oxford, the glory was in its Examination Schools; for Cambridge, the Tripos. Graduates of universities abroad by and large happily repeated the undergraduate experience at these two universities, appreciating their casual approach to lectures and intense concentration on tutorial teaching. Competition among the colleges for academic distinction in the Schools was fierce, but it was recognized that since students were in a state of pupillage, a light rein was desirable where the rules of ancient foundations permitted.

The high spirits which placed a chamberpot on top of the Martyrs'
Memorial and robbed many an Oxford policeman of his helmet
were innocent enough in a mainly adolescent student body, by no
means sobered by the nascent female element.

Traces of medieval turbulence still remained. The ferocious town
and gown warfare was a thing of the past, but colleges still required
their student members to be inside college premises by midnight
on pain of rustication, or as the phrase had it, "being sent down"
for a term, a year, or for good. The college servants, known as
scouts, so deferential and helpful to undergraduates in the normal
course, were bound to report any absence from bed and board to
the college authorities. The sole exception to the midnight curfew
was, as I remember, Christ Church, where legend had it that a
medieval gownsman pursued by bullies of the town had been
stabbed to death as the great doors of the college were closed in
his face; hence an additional half hour had been allowed to the
belated undergraduates. Gowns were worn at all hours both in and
out of college, short gowns for commoners, long ones for scholars
and exhibitioners. The university proctors and their "bulldogs" or
"bullers" patrolled the city and imposed penalties on those undergraduates found in public houses or in questionable female company. The result of the curfew was to promote some extraordinarily
daring climbing of castellated college walls and church steeples by
alpine clubs or societies which proliferated among the fashionable
youth of the day, accustomed to real alpine activity in Switzerland,
France, Austria, and Italy.

In early October 1934 I made my way from the granite wilder-
ness of northern Ontario to the "fair and floral air" of the great
university. Balliol College, into which I was admitted, contended
with University College and Merton College for the title of oldest
there, as if it really mattered after seven centuries of continuous
collegiate existence with Wycliffe as an early master. Nevertheless,
Balliol had suffered severely at the hands of nineteenth-century
reconstructors who had left only a small portion of the original
quadrangle, substituting a Scottish baronial edifice and adjacent
buildings; these formed a much larger quadrangle of satisfactory
proportions and agreeable appearance if only because of its diversity of architectural styles.

My rooms were in Kenneth Bell's staircase just east of the Hall, and my scout was Nelson, who had been Billy Bishop's batman during the war. These rooms, consisting of a bedroom and sitting room, were quite luxurious by Balliol standards and much too expensive for me, particularly since the Massey Scholarship was paid in American dollars at a time when it took slightly more than five of these to equal one pound. However, Nelson's attentions and the surroundings generally were in such startling contrast to the cabins at Hawk Lake that I lunched in my rooms and dined in Hall in the grandest style until "chill penury" stared me in the face and I was forced to seek refuge in the humbler levels of the residence building known as "Dicey," named after the great constitutional lawyer, however descriptive of my financial condition at the time the move was made.

Kenneth Bell was one of the three teaching fellows at Balliol who had charge of me for the next two years. He had won a Military Cross during the war, had been briefly on the staff of the history department at Toronto, and then had established at his old college in Oxford a reputation as a first-class tutor and a "hearty" pipe-smoking supporter of the college Boat Club. The heartiness was only skin deep. He was a learned, sensitive scholar with tragedy awaiting him in the years ahead. I was lucky enough to be a victim of his shock tactics, having prepared a thirty-page essay for him, quite acceptable in Toronto, and having received gruff instructions to boil the paper down to six pages and resubmit it. Thus I learned in timely fashion the secret of the Modern History School, which was to train its students to write answers to examination questions to be encountered in the Schools. Incidental casualties were wool-liness and pomposity, and although I felt I had been thrown into the deep end with a vengeance, I was grateful.

My next tutor was V.H. Galbraith, a Manchester medievalist who would become Regius Professor of Modern History at Oxford. To say that he shed light upon the medieval history of England would be a wholly inadequate statement. With his natural eloquence and enormous energy he literally blew understanding into the minds of his pupils.

My third tutor was Humphrey Sumner. Handsome in an ascetic way, he looked more than anyone like a medievalist, although his field was Russia and adjacent lands. He was a man of great learning, reserved to the point of impassivity, but his occasional smiles were magnetic. He later became warden of All Souls, where he had once won a prize fellowship. He would be meanly criticized by A.L. Rowse of that college for having successfully promoted the appointment of Vivian Galbraith to the Regius Professorship. Rowse had contended that the holder of that office should be not a medievalist but a modernist, conveniently ignoring the (post-classical) scope of the Modern History School. I was fortunate indeed to have been able to sit at the feet of these three great men; they filled my academic horizon and judiciously steered me to attendance at a few but memorable lectures.

I confess that the task of getting a first class in two years (the limit of my scholarship) was beyond my reach, something I did not dare to tell my father, who had made such conspicuous sacrifices to supplement the Massey stipend. Perhaps the prospect of an additional two years of studying history at the undergraduate level, even at Oxford, had begun to lose some of the excitement with which it had been embraced. And then, steadily encroaching upon my studies, there was the river – the fabled Isis – with its year-round call to oarsmen and steersmen alike to battle floods in the winter and soak up the perfect summer weather in athletic endeavour. These were still the days of the college barges, ranged mostly on the left bank of the river where it passed Christ Church meadow. Brightly painted, they were apparently copies of the luxurious craft which once plied the tideway in London, and their great stern cabins contained a club room and changing room. Each college boat club employed a boatman, most of them masters in the lore of the river. I listened carefully to the wise representative of this group who served Balliol for many years, and I had no difficulty taking my place as coxswain first of all in the first Torpid and subsequently the first eight.

It is hardly necessary to say that both Oxford and Cambridge had made a virtue of the necessity of racing eight-oared shells on very narrow waters by developing the bumping race. The boats started one behind the other in several divisions from stakes at predetermined points and raced away at the sound of the starter's pistol. The object was to overtake the boat in front and "bump" it. If this were accomplished – no easy feat with wily coxswains using their tillers to frustrate the bump – the successful pursuer would start the next day's race ahead of the boat it had bumped. The Torpid races were in clinker-built boats, but in Eights Week, which occurred in high summer, thin-skinned racing shells contended over the same narrow waters. It was all very exciting for the contestants, more mildly so for the spectators; but those who were young and female flocked to the tow-paths and then to the college balls which filled the evening and early-morning hours. Why do I say the early-morning hours? In fact, the dancing lasted all night and was concluded by an ample breakfast; even those who had fallen by the wayside and retired to their rooms would emerge, sheepishly but with a hearty appetite, to join the rest.

There was at this time a strange controversy that divided the Oxford oarsmen and secured for Cambridge an annual victory in the university boat race. The Oxford University Boat Club (OUBC), majestically ensconced in a land-based building on the right bank of the river, probably influenced by its Etonian recruits, held to the "fixed pin" method of securing the sweep oar in its outrigger position. A button on the leather binding of the oar fitted into a thole pin, making a satisfying clunk at the end of the stroke. This device, which had been the glory of nineteenth-century university rowing, had long outlived its usefulness and had been replaced by the "swivel," a revolving rather than a fixed gate. A large proportion of the Oxford college boat clubs, including that of the head of the river at the bumping races of Eights Week, Oriel College, and Balliol amongst others, had adopted the swivel, which was certainly the universal choice in North America. Intransigent colleges like Christ Church, Magdalen, and a few others clung to the fixed pin and in consequence were the sole providers of oarsmen for the university eight. This strange situation – a self-inflicted wound on Oxford rowing – was resolved in favour of the swivel after I had gone down. I think I was one of the last to appreciate the comfortable sound of the fixed pins in perfect unison when I was asked to go downstream to Goring and Pangbourne to cox trial eights and, on another occasion, to cox in practice the university eight itself – apparently the OUBC felt that the rough edge of a Canadian coxswain's exhortations was necessary. But alas, I was clearly over-weight for what was required in a coxswain by the OUBC.

Nevertheless, the years of experience in Toronto Bay, at Port Dalhousie, and the Lachine Canal sufficed to secure me the tiller of the Balliol first Torpid and first eight in 1935. In the previous year Balliol had finished Eights Week in third position, while Oriel rowed over as head of the river (if you were not bumped and did not bump the boat ahead of you, you were said "to have rowed over"). It is a measure of my main preoccupation in 1935 that I cannot remember who was immediately ahead of us, my chief concern having been the charging boat of Christ Church immedi-ately behind us. Every night during Eights Week the three leading boats rowed over the course without being bumped. Balliol was coached in the final period of training by R.C. Sherriff, author of among other distinguished works the wonderful play *Journey's End.* I cannot resist telling what is no doubt well known, that this play, set in a dugout in the front line of a Great War battalion, was written for the Kingston Rowing Club, which never produced it because of the lack of any female parts. It was rediscovered some years later and made its author's reputation.

Our eight was in a way characteristic of the college itself. Our captain was an Etonian from Dublin with the decisive name of John Brown, a good tough oarsman; our stroke was a skilful middle-weight from Yale, Arthur Gordon; Tom Mendenhall, also from Yale, rowed five or six; my particular friend Peter Corbin either four or two. My memory fails me as to the names of other members of the crew (my photographs were all destroyed in a flood in Welland in the postwar years), but I well recall that we rowed over the course every night in Eights Week, neither catching nor being caught. Because of the prevailing custom that the Oxford and Cambridge eights and trial eights and the first three boats on the river in Eights Week at Oxford and May Week at Cambridge were asked to be members of the Leander Club at Henley, I managed to enjoy this distinction by the skin of my teeth, being the last man in the last boat of the last group of qualifiers for 1935.

The secret of Oriel College's dominance in this and other neigh-bouring years was its boat club's adherence to the swivel oarlock and to the style of rowing introduced at Jesus College in Cambridge by the famous Australian coach Steve Fairbairn. The classical style of rowing associated with the fixed thole pin, so long adhered to between the wars, emphasized the dropping of the blade of the oar at the beginning of the stroke followed by a strong pull and a long drawn-out finish in which the oarsmen would be well down on their backs. This long fluid motion precisely executed by eight men was a beautiful thing to see. The Fairbairn method, in contrast, required the blade of the oar to be rowed into the water accompanied by a powerful drive with the legs and a sitting-up finish, not nearly as stylish to watch. But, in fact, dropping the blade in at the beginning of the stroke tended even in expert hands to stop the forward motion, whereas rowing the blade in, like bowling a hoop, was calculated to increase it at every stroke. Fairbairn also had convictions about mileage, and his crews and those of his adherents would go for long distances over the rivers and canals of the English Midlands developing those all-important legs. Eventually – I think before the outbreak of the Second World War – the Oxford University Boat Club capitulated to these renovations and after that war (there being no races during it) began to win the boat race with almost monotonous regularity.

The Isis course posed problems for coxswains, particularly at the Gut, a narrowing of the river that produced a strong head-on current. Making a mistake in negotiating the Gut could spell defeat for your crew. Fortunately, I never did this in an actual race, and during the 1935 Eights Week my captain said that I steered the best Gut of his experience on the river, which certainly made my week. Then again, the cox is sitting some fifty feet behind the bow, with eight oarsmen with their flashing oars obstructing his view of it, but he is expected to be able to judge when his boat is in a position to overlap the stern of the boat ahead of him and complete a bump. British coxswains are not generally held in the high esteem, sometimes amounting to reverence, that prevails in North America, but those who labour successfully on the Isis and the Cam at Cambridge should take a back seat to no others (except of course their own oarsmen!).

My absorption in rowing in my first year at Oxford threatened successful completion of the serious work ahead in my second and final year, so in 1936 I did only a little coaching and emergency steering and read for dear life. In one last fling at steering an eight-oared shell under racing conditions before returning to history, which after nearly a year of neglect brooked no further delay, I and most of the Balliol first eight enjoyed the fabled river at Henley with an entry in the regatta competing for the Ladies Plate. We occupied an agreeable house, by what lease or licence I know not, with a balcony from which we could dive into the deep water above the weir, and we kept our boat at the Leander Club. The famous course, running upstream from Temple Island for one mile and five-sixteenths, presents a serious steering problem because it is as straight as an arrow lying between booms and accommodates two eights rowing abreast with little room for errors of judgment by the coxswain. Moreover, the churning of the oars when eight-oared shells are rowing side by side can create a vacuum that causes a drawing together, which, if not carefully watched and gently corrected, can result in the overlapping of blades and immediate disaster. No disaster occurred but neither did we win. In these idyllic surroundings, to have rowed at Henley at all was reward enough.

Three terms, each of eight weeks duration, leave a lot of time for vacation, a problem for undergraduates far from home and without a legion of relatives to visit. I was able to revisit Cornwall and Paris, having last seen the latter with my father when I was a schoolboy and where I now found my friend J.K. Thomas, a contemporary at Trinity College, and his delightful New York fiancée, Harriet Tomkins, known as Hallie to a devoted generation. France, having been a refuge for the impecunious in the postwar years, had by now accumulated most of the gold that was not in Fort Knox and was expensive; it was also torn with bitter political strife between the Popular Front and totalitarian sympathizers, such as the Croix de Feu, and nursed an intimidating rate of exchange. Those of us who depended upon dollars had to be very careful. France was even more expensive than England, and the French, bad-tempered as usual in seasons of prosperity, affected to patronize those they had once fawned upon. Firewood in small bundles of sticks was occasionally available at a stiff price for much of the population of a city famous for gaiety and enlightenment. When I was there, it rained relentlessly. But companionship was warm and wine was cheap, and with an effort those of us who looked askance at the Anglo-German Naval Treaty of June 1935 eschewed the vacation allurements of Germany and Austria.

It became obvious as the summer of 1935 approached that I would not be able to maintain myself in England or any other European country, so I made arrangements to ship as supercargo on a freighter leaving Swansea for Montreal. I had the agreeable experience in Swansea of entering the bar of a public house where everyone was speaking Welsh, whereupon as I timidly asked for a pint in English, they all stopped and started talking English too. Here was an example of bilingualism in perfect balance and a Celtic language very much alive. Courtesy and good humour, in marked contrast to Paris, was the prevailing atmosphere in this South Wales town nestled between the mountains and the sea and partly built on the slag heaps of its tin-plate industry. I boarded the freighter unaware that we were faced with a fourteen-day voyage to Montreal against persistent headwinds and without the use of one of the ship's boilers, shut down since the onset of the Depression.

I arrived at home to find my father deeply involved in the general election of 1935, having undertaken the nurture of five of the midland Ontario ridings for what was still known as the Liberal-Conservative party under the general provincial chairmanship of Denton Massey. The latter, a cousin of my benefactor and a man of great gifts and eloquence, had an established reputation as leader of the York Bible Class and, in the teeth of that disastrous Liberal sweep that reduced the Conservative membership in the House of Commons to thirty-nine, found a place among that number. R.B. Bennett paid the penalty of being at the head of affairs during the worst depression of modern times. Mackenzie King, with his astonishing good luck in politics, began a reign of fourteen years in placid and prosperous beginnings, stretching into the convulsions of a second great war and beyond until a year before his death.

I greatly enjoyed being with my father in this long vacation of 1935, but I could not fail to see how the weary years of the Depression, further embittered by the defalcations of a trusted member of the family that had impoverished all of us, had undermined his magnificent constitution. Had I been able to look ahead and realize that he was entering upon the last two years of his life I doubt if I would have returned to Oxford at all. As it was, I did with a troubled conscience and a determination to economize and work hard, two activities not noticeable in my first year. Having set out the previous year in the beautiful *Empress of Britain* from the ship's historic base at Wolfe's Cove below the Plains of Abraham in Quebec (the great ship itself having only a few years left before it fell victim to German aircraft in the northwest approaches), I hastened back to England in a forgotten ship from a forgotten port.

I moved out of college into diggings at Iffley with Michael Richardson. It is a peculiarity of England's two great universities that at Oxford one spends one's first year in college and thereafter generally in lodgings, but at Cambridge the reverse is true. I must say the Oxford practice is kinder to young undergraduates going to the university for the first time. I was happy at Iffley and able to work. Every effort was now directed towards the Schools final examinations in Modern History. These are a physical as well as a mental test, and in those days amounted to two three-hour examinations a day every day for two weeks excepting the weekend. It was customary for tutors to send their charges away for at least a fortnight's holiday free from study before the onset of this formidable trial, but having been too prodigal of my time the year before to benefit from this ideal approach to an academic test, I continued to read up to the last day. At the end of Schools I was exhausted but felt able to write an examination paper on any subject under the sun, for the sweep of the Modern History course at Oxford was wide enough to test one's ingenuity as well as one's learning.

In the result I had a fairly perfunctory *viva voce* examination – a bad sign – and got a good second class upon which, to my mortification, I was congratulated by Humphrey Sumner. My father was very disappointed and said he had been expecting a first because I had always been able to manage one. I had now to think about employment and getting back to Canada as soon as possible, although 1936 was not a propitious year.

Before embarking on recollections of that stage, I must acknowledge the efforts made by many people to make life in England agreeable. The Vincent Masseys – he was now high commissioner for Canada – were unfailingly hospitable and I dined more than once at their London house in Portman Square. I was also entertained through the organization started by Lady Frances Ryder, which was greatly expanded during the war under Celia Macdonald of the Isles. And I had a no doubt characteristic interview with Lord Beaverbrook, whose London residence was then Stornoway House, hard by St James's Palace and subsequently destroyed by German bombs. He sat in the immense chair frequently depicted by the cartoonist David Low, and around his feet were arranged perhaps a half-dozen telephones which rang almost incessantly. In conversation we got no further for a while than a question about my father's health. Finally he said he would send me a railway ticket for Cherkley, and we were then interrupted by the arrival of his daughter Janet. I took my leave and walked back through the rows of desks occupied by Lord Beaverbrook's secretaries and was about to lay my hand upon the doorknob leading to the outside world when a thunderous voice from the inner sanctum door rasped, "Open the door for Mr Hughes!," whereat I was almost knocked over by the rush to assist me. The ticket to Cherkley was forgotten by both of us.

CHAPTER FOUR

Back to School

I made my twelfth sea crossing of the Atlantic in no very sanguine mood. Whereas a first class in Modern History should have made my entry into university teaching a certainty, I was aware that my second would meet some stiff competition. The prospects were worse than I thought. Six years of depression had darkened everyone's horizon, tightened every purse string, and chilled the spirit of enterprise so often celebrated by Canadians in the past. Deflation of a magnitude never to be experienced in subsequent years was still the order of the day and now is mainly remembered for providing tall stories of what in those days could be bought with a dollar.

On my arrival in Canada I bought a second-hand car, and a modest one at that. I lost no time in seeing my friends in the history department at Toronto University (in those days it was often called that or even just Varsity). I was given a warm welcome but not encouraged to seek employment. I sought out President Cody, who was charming and expatiated on the need for the development of medieval studies in the department, a situation far from contemplation when I had left for Oxford. There were fewer universities then in Canada and the few seemed to be fully staffed and not looking for me. C.P. Stacey has described a similar impasse a few years before which drove him to Princeton and ten years' distinguished exile in the United States (*A Date with History*). But Stacey had a specialty that over time became dominant. He was one of the few students of military history in his day. My path of early modern European history had been too well trodden.

Nevertheless, out of the blue came a telephone call from Dr H.C. Griffith of Ridley College in St Catharines, one of Canada's leading private schools. Some guardian angel had told him that I was available to teach history, and after an agreeable interview in his office I was engaged at a salary of $1,300 a year to teach all the history in the Upper School and a little English literature on the side.

I had a pleasant apartment on the top floor of Merritt House, the most modern of the school buildings, and everything was provided, so that the modesty of the salary in those days was more apparent than real. In 1937, when Jack Pickersgill left his eight-year stint as a lecturer in history at Wesley College at the University of Manitoba to work for the Prime Minister's Office, I was advised that I might be his successor if my salary tender was acceptable. I suggested $2,000 per annum if there were no provision for board and lodging. I had priced myself out of a thin market, but by this time I was receiving enough from Ridley to congratulate myself on a narrow escape from self-immolation.

Teaching boys at the secondary school level is not for the faint-hearted. In spite of warnings from my new colleagues of what might happen after the classroom honeymoon was over, I thought that I had made a promising start and that discipline would be no problem. I was rudely undeceived after about a three-week period when signs of testing my nerve began to appear. On one occasion I could smell cigarette smoke, however faint, but not a muscle on several ranks of faces betrayed the perpetrator. When a class gets out of hand through inattention, it is useless to admonish it as a whole. I found, as legions of my predecessors have found, that it was generally necessary to pick on one offender for my comments if only to secure the attention of the rest. All went well in the end at the cost of keeping most of the school hockey team in class on a Saturday when they were meant to be playing at Appleby in Oakville. This move shocked the headmaster ("Not the way to become popular, Sam") but, since the second team was able to take the place of the first and win the game, proved remarkably successful. From then on my crisis was over. But I have seen how deadly the test can be. In one case a colleague, well trained and enthusiastic, who later gave his life as a bomber pilot over Germany, was driven from teaching in the space of a year.

I thoroughly enjoyed my colleagues at Ridley, most of whom were devoted to the education of boys and were prepared to give their lives to this work. Pre-eminent among these was J.R. Hamilton, universally known as "Hammy," a gifted teacher of physics and chemistry, housemaster of Gooderham House, and held in the highest and most affectionate esteem by colleagues and boys alike. There was an interesting and characteristic story about what had happened to him a year or two before I arrived at Ridley. One of his pupils, whose father was a senior official of the Eastman Kodak Company in Rochester, New York, had spoken to his family so warmly about Hamilton that his father offered him a position with the great company on such terms as to make it immediately irresistible. But in spite of the challenge and increased prosperity of this new endeavour, the Hamiltons pined for Ridley and teaching and returned joyfully to St Catharines. Thus, it was foreordained that Russell Hamilton should become headmaster of Ridley in succession to H.C. Griffith, although not until after a painful period of supporting the latter in his long decline before he eventually released his hold on the headmastership.

Dr Griffith had been a famous quarterback at Ridley and Toronto University early in the century and had become the second headmaster after a triumphant return as teacher and particularly as coach of the cricket and football teams. When I arrived, his interest and effectiveness in teaching had declined, but it was otherwise with cricket and football, and Ridley's reputation in these sports was fearsome. Only once in the course of conversation did I raise the prospect of using the Royal Canadian Henley course, the magnificent stretch of water over which we looked, for instruction and competition in rowing. The conversation ended abruptly, rejection of the idea complete. Many years after my connection with Ridley was over and Dr Griffith had ceased to be headmaster, the school was allowed to dip its oars in water renowned throughout North America and the result was astonishing. Ridley's reputation as a rowing school of international importance has now completely overshadowed its prowess in other sports. With typical generosity the late Hamilton Cassels ("Laddie" as Canada knew him in war and peace) said to me not long before his death: "It was your idea." This laconic tribute was treasured but undeserved, since several of the leading Ridley athletes at the time urged me to press the headmaster harder.

Griffith's last years at Ridley were I think unfortunately prolonged by the loyalty of Russell Hamilton, without whom he could not even keep order and whose own period as the third headmaster was tragically shortened by the exhaustion this effort imposed.

I was only twenty-three when I began to work at Ridley, not much more than five years older than many of the senior boys. My colleagues without exception were kind and considerate, and I owed much to the maternal solicitude of Helen Boyd, the matron (a Bobcaygeon Boyd). Two at least were old friends, John Page of my vintage at Upper Canada, who was to play an important part in my life during the Second World War, and John Guest, a year ahead of me at Trinity College and a fellow resident, who, with his wonderful wife, Cosie, as Ruth Rigby of St Catharines had been known since childhood, was unsparing in friendship and hospitality in the agreeable surroundings of the Lower School. Terance Cronyn, who taught English and a little history (it is difficult to separate the two and make sense), was a stimulating member of the famous London family whose avocation was writing novels which were unfailingly rejected by publishers and articles which were eagerly sought by them. Cronyn became perhaps the most familiar and revered figure in Ridley history, outliving his activities as a teacher to become a goodwill ambassador for the school with worldwide connections. Roy Wainwright, who came to Ridley in my second year at the school, taught "business" subjects and mathematics. After distinguished service during the war, he returned to Ridley as housemaster of Gooderham House before moving to Ottawa as head of the mathematics department at Fisher Park Collegiate. Finally he retired to my native city of Victoria with his wife, Margaret, also a native and of great charm. All of these became lifelong friends. Many months slipped pleasantly away in the company of these and others until in April 1937 I lost my father.

His prospects had improved in 1936. He was able to return to the scenes and occupations of his youth in Alberta, where he had once located the Canadian Northern Railway. The Turner Valley had for many years been a source of natural gas, but in 1934 R.A. Brown, manager of the Calgary Street Railway, gambled and won

by bringing in a discovery well of crude oil. He and his son Bobby
formed a company called Turner Valley Royalties and became
prosperous; but not unnaturally they sought expansion and turned
to the east for capital. Cyril MacAlpine and his friend Brigadier-
General Donald M. Hogarth were interested and commissioned
my father to go west and make a report. The first journey to the
valley sufficed for his report, prepared in Calgary where he suffered
chest pains, not at first disclosed to me or to anyone; Calgary's
elevation had given him a warning. The second journey led to an
inflamed appendix and constipation, which he treated characteristically with castor oil. When I met him at the train in Toronto,
he looked ghastly. An immediate operation was advised and successfully performed, and I returned to Ridley.

Two days later I was telephoned by Colonel Sodden Irwin, the
officer commanding the Irish Regiment of Canada. He had been
in touch with a nurse in the Toronto General Hospital who had
seen my father's chart and considered his convalescence precarious. In my state of panic, an attempt to drive my ancient Buick at
full speed from St Catharines to Toronto would have been suicidal.
I do not know by what strange process my friends at Ridley heard
of the crisis. I do not remember appealing for help, but Cosie
Guest offered at once to drive me in her husband's spanking new
Ford convertible and she broke and more than broke every speed
limit on the old road to Toronto (Highways 8 and 2). When I saw
my father in the hospital, he appeared weak but relaxed. No urgent
movements were observable among the medical and nursing staff.
I thought it desirable after some conversation with him to secure
lunch for me and my heroic driver. On my return to the hospital
he was propped up in his bed, his face fallen, dead from heart
failure. He was within a week of his fifty-eighth year.

One of the remarks made by him while I was at his bedside was:
"Don't let them bury me in my uniform." I had made some depre-
catory response, not wishing to countenance what he clearly
thought was inevitable. Fortunately, I did not have to feel bound
by this injunction because his great friend Colonel Baptist Johnston
took all arrangements out of my hands and the Department of
National Defence ordered a full-scale military funeral for the senior
major-general in Canada. While this was in train, he lay in state in
Christ Church on Heath Street for two days as veterans and friends

paid their respects. The funeral service was held in the University Avenue Armouries, since demolished and replaced by the graceful Metropolitan Court House. It was conducted by the chaplain of the Toronto Scottish Regiment and attended by the lieutenant-governor of the province, Colonel the Honourable Herbert Bruce, an eminent surgeon and family friend from Durham County. As I sat beside him, stunned and miserable, I could not help feeling my spirits lift at the noble words of the burial service established in the Book of Common Prayer and was struck by the sense that death was more endurable for the bereaved in this disciplined military setting.

As the cortège passed out of the Armouries and up University Avenue led by the band and a company of the Toronto Scottish Regiment, followed by the gun carriage, the riderless charger, Carl Webber as junior subaltern carrying my father's medals on a cushion, then myself in a plain blue suit as chief mourner, this feeling intensified. Up University Avenue and around Queen's Park we went at a slow march, to be received in front of the Royal Ontario Museum by a guard of the Royal Canadian Regiment, then one of three regular infantry battalions in Canada. The coffin was removed from the gun carriage and transferred to a motor hearse, and flanked by Ontario Provincial Police motorcyclists we drove at speed the seventy miles to Lindsay. Here another gun carriage awaited the dead soldier, and the local 45th Battery and other troops marched along Kent Street, crowded on both sides, and out to the Riverside Cemetery for interment. That night I shared a room in my grandmother's house with my Bostonian uncle Jim Clarke.

Not long after my father's death, I qualified for and was accepted as a marker of the upper school examination in Modern History, then conducted by the Department of Education of Ontario as a public examination and not, as in these degenerate days, by the schools which had taught the course. I was in for a severe shock from which my opinion of the much-vaunted school system has never really recovered. Those of us chosen for marking these papers were paid ten dollars a day, a satisfactory supplement to one's ordinary stipend; but the process was humiliating. We were each issued with a marking scheme which provided that at the mention of certain prescribed names of people and events and dates a large "1" was to be marked on that portion of the page. For example, one mark for Waterloo, one for Wellington, one for Napoleon, and perhaps one for 1815. No objection was taken to illiteracy, which was frequent, or even to a series of jottings with no connecting language. When I sought to make what I considered appropriate additions or deductions for style and organization of an answer, I was told by the chief examiner that I was marking history papers not English Composition.

I returned to Ridley after this first experience sadder and wiser and determined that my classes would be forewarned about this puerile practice. Of course, the marking scheme was designed to impose uniformity and it was in this sense justifiable; but it was clear that the marking job could have been done better by departmental officials than by teachers invited to come to Toronto and act as so many rubber stamps. The attitude of the Department of Education, as wooden in this case as it was eight years before when my contemporary at Upper Canada Stanley Ryerson was given zero for writing his English Composition paper in blank verse, convinced me that my days as a secondary school teacher were numbered. Other signs and portents marshalled on the horizon. For one thing, I was not good enough to want to devote my whole life to such a serious and often unrewarding task. For another, I was not moved by the great challenge of my profession – devotion to my pupils. I was disconcerted to find that living at close quarters with adolescent boys was not especially agreeable. I feared that as the years passed I would become, to use a theatrical expression, typecast.

Every vacation brought me into touch with people who seemed to be part of a greater and more exciting world. I was, for instance, becoming interested in politics, and in 1937 I spent a large part of a summer vacation campaigning for Leslie Frost in support of his second, and first successful, run in the provincial riding of Victoria and Haliburton. I not only formed a lasting friendship with the candidate but also encountered in this constituency that had sustained my grandfather in Parliament many relics of his own day and many people who remembered him intimately. At an annual meeting of the Ontario Conservative Association (no longer Liberal- or yet Progressive), I was elected to the executive, then presided over by Cecil Frost, who predeceased his brother Leslie by many years. But a more important consideration must now be recorded.

In my second year at Ridley I had met and been captivated by Helen Spencer of the neighbouring town of Welland. Welland, as is well known, is an industrial city situated on the famous Welland Ship Canal connecting the Great Lakes Ontario and Erie. It was the scene of early industrial development because of its proximity not only to the canal but to the unique producer of hydro-electric power where the Niagara River falls in thunder. In the years before the great war of 1914, Lynn Bristol Spencer had brought his bride from Collingwood to Welland and practised law with a long-established native of Welland County, Colonel L.C. Raymond. "L.B.," as Spencer was generally known, was energetic and resourceful. As a student he had completed his final year at the University of Toronto and his first year at the Osgoode Hall Law School in the same calendar year, a feat requiring mental and physical energy of a high order, including hectic transportation by bicycle from one institution to the other. In Welland he became a dominant figure, not without arousing jealousy. On one occasion a letter addressed simply "To the Leading Lawyer, Welland" found its way easily to his desk. In those days Buffalo, New York, loomed much larger in the Niagara Peninsula than did Toronto, and it was through earning the confidence of large Buffalo trust companies and law firms that the practice of Raymond and Spencer grew in importance and prosperity. In due time the firm secured Robert Brown Law from Ottawa, a war veteran and tax expert, and Stewart S. MacInnes, a native of Vankleek Hill in Prescott County. It was thus constituted when I turned my steps towards Welland.

When I first knew him, L.B. Spencer, KC, was general counsel for and a director of Atlas Steels Limited, a comparatively recent addition to Welland industry and the first maker of tool steels in Canada; its principle product was high-speed drill steel for pneumatic drills ("jackhammers"). He was also one of the founders of the Peace Bridge linking Buffalo and Fort Erie across the Niagara River and was its general counsel for Canada. At this stage of his career he had largely relinquished an abundant practice in the courts to cultivate his commercial and municipal business. His formidable professional reputation disguised a warm heart and sensitive nature. I felt myself drawn to him when bereft of guidance and wisdom after my father's death.

As an additional mercy, the day after that death my cousin Cyril MacAlpine's wife, Lena, had led me away from the apartment I had shared with my father on St Clair Avenue and carried me off to her capacious house on Warren Road to the midst of her family. Thereafter, whenever I was in the city I stayed there, and I divided my vacation time between the MacAlpine house on Sturgeon Lake and Boston, home of my Clarke relatives, which in the summer meant their house on Great Hill above Tamworth, New Hampshire, overlooked by Mt Chicorua. The Clarkes had bought the interest of my father and my aunt Roby Green in Eagle Lake and I was welcome there too. All these members of my family combined to make life pleasant and easy for me, and the star rising over Welland increasingly shed happiness on my labours and recreation alike.

In the summer of 1938, while I was staying at Sturgeon Lake, a leadership convention to select a successor to R.B. Bennett was summoned in Ottawa. I attended with Helen and her father, delegate as I was. At this gathering in Lansdowne Park, the former leader and prime minister Arthur Meighen, eloquent as always, delivered an address entitled "The Defence of Canada." When he pronounced in that electrifying staccato voice that whenever we had looked for support and defence we had always looked to one country (Great Britain) and asked when we had ever looked in vain, the crowd rose and shouted their acclaim – with one group being a significant exception, the delegates from Quebec sitting stonily in their seats to indicate their displeasure. The impact of Meighen's speech was so great that an influential section of the Conservative party carried him off to the Chateau Laurier Hotel and sought to have him allow his name to be put in nomination. This was indeed a tribute to his great oratorical powers, particularly since his own prime ministership had ended in rejection as a result of his attempt to placate the French Canadians. I happened to be on the fringe of the discussion in the Chateau Laurier and thus observed the disappointing, but no doubt sensible, action of the former prime minister, who said he would like to consult Sir Edward Beatty, president of the Canadian Pacific Railway (CPR), by telephone before making a decision. There was no time for delay, and it was painful to see the enthusiasm of his supporters evaporate; the anti-climax was complete.

We elected the Honourable R.J. Manion, formerly minister of railways and canals in the Bennett government. Earlier, he had been one of those devoted Liberals who had turned away from Sir

Wilfrid Laurier on the issue of conscription and joined the Union government under Sir Robert Borden in 1917. Manion was able, a distinguished veteran of the Great War during which he was decorated for bravery, and the first Roman Catholic leader of the party since Sir John Thompson; but he was unlucky and, in 1940 after the beginning of the Second World War, failed to convince the country of the necessity for a national government. Mr Mackenzie King, perhaps the antithesis of Dr Manion, secured a great triumph.

I also spoke at the convention, briefly but passionately, on the defence question and emphasized the threat to Western civilization presented by the now rampant National Socialists in Germany. Because of my name and the memories it conjured up, my intervention snatched a late headline. The congratulations which overwhelmed me at Lansdowne Park produced a mental lapse I have never forgotten. I had asked Helen to dine tête-à-tête at the Chateau Laurier, and she came back from visiting friends on the Gatineau River in response to this invitation. I failed to show up. Later that night, distraught as I was, I was forgiven and we breakfasted next morning together in the Grill Room happily enough. I had learned two things from this fiasco: I was in love and so was she.

As we drove back westwards along the tortuous gravel road then newly developed as Highway 7, wherever we happened to stop we were greeted with marks of displeasure for having selected a Roman Catholic leader for the Conservative party (then renamed the National Conservative party). This will make strange reading for those who are aware that for the past thirty years neither the Liberal nor Conservative party has produced a leader of any other faith, and they may welcome the dissolution of ancient prejudice on this issue.

In this intensely personal narrative I must record the momentous international developments at this period of our lives. The situation in western Europe was threatening every institution dear to the English-speaking world. For one thing, it meant aerial warfare and bombardment in a form and an intensity never before experienced, if the Spanish Civil War was a reliable indicator; for another, few people had any confidence in the defensive preparations of either Britain or France and most tended to measure Soviet Russia's ability to wage war successfully by the Russian catastrophe of twenty years before. The apparent attitude of the majority of people in the United States was a willingness to advise but a determination not to join hands against the dictators. More disturbing still was a growing split between those who relied on negotiation, leading apparently to appeasement, and those who had made up their minds to resist the German aggression even if it meant war. This issue divided families and households across Canada and in Britain, too. I felt it in my own family, and I was warned not to show hostility to Neville Chamberlain. To deplore Godesberg and Munich was to go far beyond the scope of polite argument and to risk permanent estrangement. When in August 1939 the Russo-German Pact revealed where Russian interests and sympathies evidently lay, the sense of disillusion and foreboding fell heavily upon all men and women of goodwill. Open war would be better than this; and so indeed it was.

My admiration for the great opponent of appeasement, Winston Churchill, never flagged and may well have begun when at the age of ten I inscribed, on my father's birthday in 1923, the first volume of *The World Crisis.* I would read all four volumes, as well as *The Aftermath,* the four volumes of his life of Marlborough, and anything else, books or speeches, that his pen produced. In 1931, I recall, the year of a U.S. lecture tour during which his life was almost ended by a New York taxicab, I went to hear Churchill speak at Maple Leaf Gardens in Toronto, then a new building for professional hockey with a capacity for some thirteen thousand spectators. On the occasion in question it was full and the ice space was also occupied by listeners. When Churchill began to speak, noisy interruptions were heard high up in the grey seats, repeated whenever he tried to resume. The police were uneasy in these Depression days and they moved upward to investigate. It then became evident that the amplifiers, intended to carry the speech from a lapel microphone to every corner of the building, were hung too low and that the upper levels could hear nothing but confused noise. Churchill thereupon removed the microphone from his coat and with his bare unamplified voice, lisp and all, held the vast audience spellbound for one and a half hours. Television for me has never produced anything like the excitement of that evening. I remained a devoted follower. I thought the slurs about his defects of judgment and the refusal to heed his warnings simply the product of those who were "adamant for drift."

Although I vividly remember this occasion, it is only right to say that neither in his own historical works of an autobiographical nature nor in the official biography is there any mention of a side visit to Toronto during Churchill's 1931 lecture tour of the United States. Nevertheless, I stand by my story, although what I describe may be chronologically misplaced. Moreover, my colleague the Honourable Mr Justice John Osler has the same recollection of this event.

Increasingly my thoughts turned in one direction, marriage and a home. But I was an unmarried schoolmaster in a boarding school, a highly desirable commodity from the point of view of the authorities, and the headmaster was not prepared to let me live in town. A long postponement loomed ahead. Helen, who had lost her mother at the same time as I lost my father and before I could have known her, was her own father's hostess and the mistress of his household. In that summer of 1938 she was prudently spirited away to the Canadian Bar Association's convention in Vancouver and thereafter explored California with her father. She returned with unshaken resolve but not prepared for the conditions imposed upon my continued tenure. There was, however, a solution and her father proposed it to his partners in Welland. I wanted to be a lawyer and had, before circumstances steered me into teaching, long contemplated the bar as my ultimate goal. Mr Spencer now proposed that I in my turn should go to Osgoode Hall Law School and offered financial help. Moreover he did more: he offered employment in his firm. I completed my last year at Ridley teaching history, happy and easy in my mind. Arrangements to enter the law school were quickly made and I was articled to my family's solicitor and long-time friend, T.H. Stinson, KC, of Lindsay and incidentally a friend of L.B. Spencer, KC, of Welland.

In those days a student took two lectures a day at Osgoode Hall, the site of the Court of Appeal and Supreme Court judges chambers as well as the law school conducted by the Law Society of Upper Canada. In the other hours of the day one worked, and in most cases fairly hard, for a law firm necessarily in Toronto, perhaps varied by working out of town in the long vacation. Through

the intervention of my cousin Cyril MacAlpine, I was apprenticed
to P.C. Finlay, KC, of the firm of Holden, Murdoch, Walton, Finlay
and Robinson, at that time the most prominent in gold mining
circles and having as clients both Hollinger and Noranda. In their
hands were all the MacAlpine interests as well as those of the
numerous families connected with and dependent upon their corporate clients. But before I go too far along this path of recollection, I should say that before I set foot in the echoing halls of
Osgoode we all found ourselves – a week after September 3, the
day of Cromwell's "crowning mercy" – at war with Germany, following Mackenzie King's cautious insistence on summoning Parliament to make Canada's own declaration. The surge of public
feeling across Canada effectively drowned out the oracular voices
of the East Block, at least for a time, at the end of summer in 1939.

CHAPTER FIVE

Qualifications

When I went to Osgoode Hall in 1939, five years after my contemporaries at the university who if so-minded had preceded me, I found a system very different from what prevails today. Legal education in Ontario was entirely in the hands of the Law Society of Upper Canada. One had to produce a degree from a recognized university and sign various undertakings to become a student-at-law and an articled clerk, in the latter case giving articles to a practising solicitor. No exposure to legal studies in a university made the slightest difference or offered any advantage to an applicant for enrolment; in spite of many academic sniffs, the reputation of the law school was high across common-law Canada and attracted many extra-provincial candidates, especially from the western part of the country. Whereas most provincial law schools relied heavily on local practitioners to lecture, Osgoode Hall could boast that its lecturers included such distinguished academic lawyers – academic in the sense of non-practising teachers of law – as Dean Falconbridge, A.D. McRae, Cecil A. Wright, my university contemporary and rowing friend Bora Laskin, and Professor Clute, who owed his position, so it was said, to narrowly defeating the dean in some long-forgotten examination in their youth.

For university graduates, the course lasted three years; for those who had no degree, it was necessary to take the first-year course, serve in a law office under articles for the next two years, and complete a final two years of study at the law school, thus making the qualification period last for five years. This latter practice is not now authorized but it once admitted such celebrated lawyers as W.N. Tilley, QC, a famous treasurer and advocate, and John Cartwright, QC, finally chief justice of Canada. These arrangements constituted the only game in Ontario, and successful candidates received the "degree" of Barrister-at-Law, being called within the bar after graduation by a judge of the Supreme Court of Ontario and enrolled as a solicitor of that court. To these distinctions were added the functions of notary public and commissioner of oaths.

Three goals now presented themselves with varying claims for swift achievement: marriage first of all; a place in the army (the navy and the air force being unattainable for one who had been a lifelong wearer of spectacles); and qualification as a lawyer, soon to be doomed to postponement. Being once more a student led me back to the hospitable house where Zeta Psi had claimed my allegiance as an undergraduate. There I was happily introduced to a whole new generation of Zetes: George Renison and Edward Dunlop, already caught up in their famous regiments, respectively the 48th Highlanders of Canada and the Queen's Own Rifles of Canada; Hugh Henderson, with whom I shared a flat all too briefly before he went on active service in the navy; and Jed (officially Walter) Lind and Ron Bennett, both from McGill, with whom I shared the next flat. The last three were at various stages at Osgoode Hall, as was Albert Shepherd, with whom I shared thereafter many transactions of interest and importance.

The difficulty of studying in May of 1940 when "the heavens were falling" may well be imagined. I had already paid a heavy forfeit by taking six weeks off to campaign for Cyril MacAlpine in the federal riding of Victoria and Haliburton in the election of 1940. I threw myself into this enterprise with infatuated enthusiasm and thoroughly enjoyed it, failing in only one examination in the spring, Criminal Procedure, the easiest subject in the curriculum. The lectures on this subject were given by the then crown attorney for Toronto, who spoke with a heavy Ulster accent, and the typescript, which a few of us had commissioned a stenographer to prepare, was unpunctuated and in any event unreadable. I was, however, to get a second chance.

After the initial rush to the recruiting stations and it becoming clear that the upshot would be disappointment and delay, an unexpected lethargy seemed to descend upon military authorities. Of course it was going to be different this time they averred, nothing like the chaos which accompanied the efforts of Sam Hughes in the first war. This approach was indebted to the "phony war" period, without which there would have been chaos in dead earnest.

The decision to keep the established militia units with all their loyal but superannuated personnel in place was a popular one in militia circles, which had resented the constitution of new units for an expeditionary force in 1914. Fortunately, the permanent force was able to supply sufficient experienced instructors and trainers of troops to avert breakdown, and the long pause between the autumn of 1939 and the spring of 1940 was used to advantage.

Quite apart from an atavistic preference for the army, I realized, as I have said, that having worn spectacles since early childhood, I stood little chance of successful operation in any other fighting service. Accordingly, I joined the University of Toronto Canadian Officers' Training Corps detachment, transferring to that of Osgoode Hall as soon as it was constituted under Lieutenant-Colonel Bobby Langford as chief instructor. Langford was a tragic figure, his military career in the Royal Canadian Regiment and in the army generally having been blasted by his involvement, giving aid to the civil power, in the Stratford strike, the professional death warrant of so many soldiers engaged in this kind of activity. But then Bap Johnston came to the rescue. He had been appointed to command the 2nd Battalion of his old regiment, the Queen's Own Rifles, the 1st Battalion having gone on active service to Newfoundland preparatory to its incorporation in the Third Canadian Infantry Division and a date with destiny on the beaches of Normandy. He offered me the chance to complete my qualifications as an infantry officer with the rank of second lieutenant in his battalion, and this was by far the most agreeable and most rewarding way of getting into uniform, even if only for parade nights, and waiting to go on active service.

The Queen's Own was the oldest regiment in the country with a continuous record of service as such. As a rifle regiment it had all the glamour of the quick light infantry pace, the rousing regimental march and drill peculiar to light infantry regiments in the British army. Its unofficial motto, "Once in the Queen's Own, always in the Queen's Own," had been a reality for generations in Toronto. In the 2nd Battalion we were a mixture of veterans of the first war and neophytes in military matters. My fellow subalterns included Donald Fleming, almost twenty years away from being minister of finance of Canada, and Kenneth Morden, about the same distance from being a judge of the Court of Appeal of Ontario. R.H. Sankey, an Irish Guardsman in the previous war, was our second in command; Alan Telfer, the second in command of my company, had seen service in India between the wars. And so it went, a number of the younger officers and an even larger number of other ranks moving on to join the 1st Battalion as vacancies occurred, and to lose their lives in or survive the experience of battle.

Helen and I were married in St Andrew's Presbyterian Church in Welland on the 27th day of July, 1940. Her uncle, the Reverend R.A. Spencer, a veteran of the Great War and a minister of the United Church of Canada, performed the ceremony. As a sign of the times for which no apology will be made, we decided to dispense with Wagner's pompous wedding march with its teutonic cadences in favour of a composition by Edvard Grieg, a famous member of the subjugated Norwegian nation. The organist, wiser than we were, played a bar or two from "Lohengrin" to alert the congregation to what was about to happen and then swung into Grieg's sprightly measure. This antithesis of solemnity called for explanations at the subsequent celebrations, where tented on the Spencer lawn and laced with champagne, members of the wedding party made the appropriate speeches. And then, following the decent custom of the day, the bride and groom were allowed to "go away" before the final festivities began at the Lookout Point Golf Club, to begin their pilgrimage of over half a century alone at last. This transition was eased by the ingenuity of the best man,

Bill Roberts of Dutton and Zeta Psi, and his coadjutors who had concealed an uncluttered automobile free of slogans and rice in the unfrequented purlieus of Fonthill.

These were days which while memory serves will never lose their lustre. I have mentioned the difficulty of studying for law examinations while ancient states were being subverted and overthrown, when the famous French republic itself, once the terror of Europe, was being broken and divided into a conquered territory, when the coasts of continental Europe from the North Cape to the Pyrenees were in the hands of German despoilers and the world watched with panic and foreboding for the day when, to use General Weygand's venomous phrase, "England's neck will be wrung like a chicken's." Yet a greater phrasemaker than Weygand was by ruthless action and electrifying words dispelling fear and restoring hope. Let no one forget that Churchill's speeches served notice that Britain would not only never surrender but would never negotiate and would with her possessions and Commonwealth allies fight the common enemy, to use their maker's words, "if necessary for years, if necessary alone." The world was to see the greatest air onslaught in history repulsed by the Royal Air Force, with many volunteers from those realms and territories where the raising of men and women and the manufacture of munitions of war were their prime concern, to be devoted first of all to defence and thereafter to destruction.

In the meantime the Union of Soviet Socialist Republics, still a year away from attack, was gorging itself on the Baltic states and expecting a swift victory in Finland; as an ally of Germany it was, and with truth, deemed to be hostile. The United States of America, a neutral country not for the first time, was a year and a half away from attack, benevolent but correct. Where to go for a honeymoon without risk of internment? We had no knowledge of when the trumpet would sound for my call to active service, and thus we were fortunate in being confined to our own country and being introduced to the delights of the Maritime provinces, which in those days had completed a program of road improvement converting most of the gravel main roads to tar macadam. We traversed these along the Saint John River Valley and, after an interval of exploration in New Brunswick and Nova Scotia, returned by that of the Matapedia.

In Moncton, staying at the old Brunswick Hotel, I received a telegram from Colonel Johnston requiring me to have a medical examination for the army forthwith. We prevailed on a doctor to leave his dinner table, take a long look at me, and pronounce me A-1. This was to create difficulties later on because categories such as A-1 and B-2 and so forth were converted into the Pullems Scale, each letter of which represented an extremity or function for which I received a first class, including the E for "eyes." Such a result was far from accurate in the case of eyesight and would later call for explanation.

In the Matapedia Valley, huddled under blankets in an uncomfortable but unfrequented motel, we listened to the troop trains thundering southward through the night. The next morning we swam in the cold, rapid river, clinging to rocks for a foot- and handhold to the disgust of some leisurely salmon fishermen downstream. In Saint John the Admiral Beatty Hotel made us comfortable, as did the Lord Nelson and the Nova Scotian in Halifax. We spent a night at Indian Harbour, not far from Peggy's Cove, in a boardinghouse where the landlady, after a quick look at Helen's ring, admitted us to her confidence and told us that she hated the sea that had robbed her of two sons. She gave us mutton instead of fish for dinner. We slept soundly in a huge double bed innocent of springs and with a deep trench in the middle. No matter.

This was the first and most memorable of several trips to New Brunswick, Nova Scotia, and Prince Edward Island over the years, and it wonderfully widened my horizons. In those days the railways still dominated industry and recreation in Canada. We enjoyed staying at the Canadian National system's Pictou Lodge, where the staff sedulously swept the beach of the intrusive jellyfish which spoiled so much of the shores of the Gulf of St Lawrence. Of the quite new Nova Scotian Hotel in Halifax and that noblest of all railway hotels, the Chateau Frontenac in Quebec, the Canadian Pacific Railway's flagship for a century, we had only pleasant recollections.

My immediate concerns after returning from this idyllic journey were the army, the law, and a habitation in Toronto, whence the army and the law beckoned. For the first, the 2nd Battalion of the

Queen's Own had a very civilized summer camp at Niagara-on-the-Lake on the spacious and unspoiled grounds long since donated by the Department of National Defence to the Niagara Parks Commission. For years these lands had been the scene of militia camps in the summer, units being transported from Toronto among other places by the pleasure steamers that plied between the city and the mouth of the Niagara gorge at Queenston. I was in command of the infantry-carrier platoon and was introduced for the first time to military tracked vehicles. The training was otherwise not suggestive of war, but included much marching, martial music, and musketry. For the second concern, I was to have addressed the lace by taking an unannotated copy of the Criminal Code of Canada on our honeymoon so that I could take a second jump at what was regarded as a fairly easy hurdle. Although the Queen's Printer had cut the book's pages, it was otherwise unblemished and undisturbed, but the examiners were kind and I succeeded at the supplementary test in criminal procedure. As for the third concern, Helen found a modest third-floor apartment at the foot of the Avenue Road hill. To this unpretentious abode I grandly ordered some of my father's furniture out of storage and returned one afternoon from the office to find my young wife perched on a pyramid of cartons full of books, on the verge of tears.

Serious work now began both in the lecture rooms at Osgoode Hall and in the offices of the Holden Murdoch firm in the Royal Bank building, where I was beginning to learn about real property in a practical sense as accumulated by the families and friends of the Hollinger and Noranda pioneers. My instruction was directed with that of other students by Mrs Vida Grover, the widow of John B. Holden's first partner, George Grover, who had returned from the first war to find himself displaced by James Y. Murdoch. Shortly afterwards Grover had died, but his widow, herself a capable lawyer, was given salaried employment.

There appeared to be no release from this apprenticeship in sight, no vacancies occurring in the 1st Battalion of the Queen's Own or anywhere else. Then one day we spotted in the *Evening Telegram* a Canadian Armoured Corps advertisement for recruits. Those interested should report to the headquarters of the Ontario Regiment, a tank unit suitably located in Oshawa, where most of the automobiles and trucks in Canada were manufactured. I travelled to Oshawa and my name was taken by a young officer without ceremony. This expedition was soon forgotten and life continued divided between the Queen's Own and Osgoode Hall throughout the winter of 1940–41, but on the eve of the final examinations of the second year, Dean Falconbridge announced at the conclusion of his lecture that he would like to see Mr Shepherd and Mr Hughes forthwith. In his chambers he told us that we were improperly dressed and should be in uniform and at the depot as soon as possible. Albert Shepherd had followed the same route as I, having been an officer in the militia unit of the Algonquin Regiment, and we both went on active service with the armoured corps on the same day.

As the culmination of a lot of waiting, this development was received with relief and a good deal of celebration from which Helen noticeably withdrew. I then realized that its true significance was not lost on her and that it foreshadowed a long separation, perhaps a permanent one, and more sensitivity on my part would be appropriate. But there was still precious time to be shared and savoured, the immediate result of mobilization being a posting to the Officers Training Centre at Brockville. I had always liked Brockville and liked the town even more when we rented a semi-detached house on Pearl Street. I was still in the uniform of the Queen's Own Rifles as a second lieutenant. Since we were only the increment constituting the second course to be mounted at the training centre, we escaped the later regime when every candidate was an acting sergeant and lived in barracks. By then it was obligatory to live in barracks at night, but we, as commissioned albeit unqualified officers, were allowed to live outside the camp as long as we were within its boundaries by six o'clock each morning. For young married men this was a precious privilege.

The work at Brockville was chiefly aimed at getting the candidates into good physical condition and helping them gain an aptitude in such subjects as map reading, reception, and transmission of messages in the Morse code, and in the use of the radio sets provided for infantry, artillery, and armoured vehicles. Drill on the square was an unexpected pleasure, since it was administered by permanent force instructors from the Royal Military College; under their tutelage one's conduct of parade ground manœuvres became flawless in a comparatively short time. Musketry (with the Ross rifle of course) and marching were the remainder of the curriculum, and these laconic words do not do justice to the long marches in battle order which hardened our feet and strengthened our shoulders, agonizingly but in the end rewardingly. There were no tanks and perhaps the only tracked vehicle at the time of this second course in the area was an infantry personnel carrier. Nonetheless, my friend Gerald Levenston did his best with lucid and uncomplicated lectures on armoured fighting-vehicle tactics, and he took every opportunity of expressing his envy of our chance of going overseas, believing he was destined to be a lecturer to officer candidates. In fact, he became the senior armoured corps staff officer at First Canadian Army before the war was out.

Brockville was an enjoyable experience, providing pleasant surroundings and a hospitable society. In addition to my friend Albert Shepherd, there were other members of Zeta Psi in the armoured corps wing, particularly Bill (inevitably Bing) Crosbie and Doug Crashley, both already wearing the uniform of the Governor-General's Horse Guards, a cavalry regiment only recently mechanized and given a reconnaissance role. Helen and I made friends with Tim (David S.) Beatty and his wife, Ann Elise, who had secured a cottage on the banks of the St Lawrence River. This was an enduring friendship, as was that of my comrade in the Queen's Own Douglas Jennings, a rising lawyer in Toronto, older than most of us, who had much to lose professionally as an infantry subaltern but who lived to command the Queen's Own in peacetime.

The serenity of life in spring by the great river changed at the end of June for translation to the sandy plains but more sophisticated installations of Camp Borden. I had pleasant memories of Brockville, as might any young soldier having not yet completed a year of marriage even had the surroundings been unpromising; as it was, our departure was made more memorable by my selection to command the armoured corps wing in the passing-out parade.

The training at Camp Borden was "special to the arm" and the work was a concentrated introduction to the tactics and maintenance of armoured fighting vehicles. As it happened, there was only one tank in the camp and that was kept on display like a precious jewel in a vehicle shed. It was a Valentine armed with a two-pounder gun. Even then the two-pounder gun was not impressive, and when it was later installed in the much larger and more powerful Churchill tank it was ludicrous. The explanation was simple. Lord Beaverbrook, after galvanizing the aircraft industry, had been put in charge of tank production in England, and his energy had far outstripped that of those producing guns.

At Camp Borden we were again able to live in some comfort, billeted with the Beattys and Dick Squires and his wife at T.P. Loblaw's farm on the road between Alliston and the southerly gate of the camp. Dick was a Newfoundlander, the son of Sir Richard Squires, the last prime minister of Newfoundland as an independent dominion. He was a subaltern in Lord Strathcona's Horse, and morning after morning I used to ride into camp behind him on his elaborate Harley-Davidson motorcycle. Fortunately, it was high summer. Here also were hurdles to be jumped, such as convincing the eye examiners that I could see and finding a regimental connection in the armoured corps. Both were surmounted, the second thanks to my friends in the Governor General's Horse Guards and the sudden decision to ship the Fifth Canadian Armoured Division overseas ahead of schedule. The six armoured regiments in the division all rushed to fill up their complements of officers, and I considered myself fortunate to be chosen by the Horse Guards. Albert Shepherd was selected by the 8th Princess Louise's New Brunswick Hussars, where he was immediately happy and became a fighting squadron commander and incidentally a keen horseman.

Long before the final course of instruction and tests thereof were reached, Canada's First Armoured Division was being lifted by train to the port of Halifax and the harsh reality of separation from home and family was confronting its soldiers. As our train moved slowly through the North Toronto station of the Canadian Pacific Railway, coming to a halt amid a crowd of relatives and well-wishers, one soldier ventured to step off his car to embrace his girl. He was immediately placed under arrest by the second in command, Major Ian Cumberland. This example of discipline, amounting almost to inhumanity, had its effect: on arrival in Halifax the regiment was congratulated by the authorities for having turned over a troop train with no serious damage – not even a broken window – in marked contrast to the destruction visited upon many of its predecessors.

The regiment, indeed, had been a centre for recruitment of mechanics and motorcycle riders because of the early propensity of the British War Office, transmitted to the Canadian Department of National Defence, for copying the war establishment of German units that had fought so successfully in France in 1940. The motor-cyclists of the German reconnaissance units had ridden almost unopposed around the French countryside, acquiring a reputation impossible to maintain against well-informed and well-trained troops. A moment's reflection would have convinced a dispassionate observer of their extreme vulnerability. In fact, even the dispatch riders in areas such as the south of England, completely out of contact with the enemy, could not be protected from the perils of a blacked-out landscape. Those of the First Canadian Division were almost all dead at the end of a year. But this eccentricity of the planners had produced recruits of a high order, and the gradual transformation of a cavalry regiment into a mechanized unit had raised the level of intelligence of its members.

The higher the general level of intelligence in any unit, the easier it is to train citizen soldiers. This was especially true in the complicated technical apparatus of a regiment now converted into one of tanks and scout cars, with wireless networks operating on frequencies ranging from regimental to tank troop level, with guns performing in closed turrets, all requiring a training of a higher order than ever encountered before in the history of the army. With all of this in prospect and in sober mood the Fifth Canadian Armoured Division detrained in the historic port of Halifax and immediately repaired to their transports moored at quayside. This manœuvre took the Horse Guards less than half an hour and the whole operation impressed me as a credit not only to the embarking troops but to the Army Service Corps personnel and conducting staffs involved.

The convoy we had boarded in Bedford Basin on that October day in 1941 was composed of half a dozen passenger ships that were relatively fast when compared with the workaday freighters carrying food and munitions that gave so much anxiety to the Royal Canadian Navy at the start and the Royal Navy in their home waters. We had a remarkable voyage, running north as far as Iceland and thence southeasterly to the northwestern approaches, a dangerous area but the only one available to Great Britain, since Chamberlain in 1938 had incontinently given away the Irish treaty ports. But none of these reflections crossed the minds of at least one happy ship's company consisting of the 3rd Armoured Regiment

(Governor General's Horse Guards) as it had now become in the comfortable RMS *Warwick Castle*, with all ranks in staterooms, no hammocks necessary, and wine, spirits, and tobacco (all from South Africa) duty-free. Only those who remember transatlantic troop ships at a later date when General Eisenhower had assumed overall command, with their crowded hammock-slung decks and dry canteens, can appreciate the good fortune we enjoyed. We reached the Mersey, waiting on our decks under arms while the Luftwaffe bombed the Liverpool docks, and eventually passed scathless into the long meandering train which took us by novel routes in the blackout across rural England to our camp on the Marlborough Downs near a village called Ogbourne St George.

The train had taken us as far as Swindon and there we were met by trucks and an advance party commanded by a Black Watch officer, none other than Ron Bennett, whom I had not seen since more than a year earlier, when the Lind-Bennett-Hughes establishment had broken up and we had both married and joined the army. It was a pleasant reunion and he said that whenever we could put two short leaves together I should go with him to Juniper Hill to stay with his uncle Dick (now Viscount Bennett of Calgary). I never saw him again. All the preoccupations of training and movement to and fro in the south of England kept us apart and he was later killed at Fontenay-le-Marmion on a day when the Black Watch was simply cast away by headquarters of the Second Canadian Division, their valour expended in vain against prepared German positions of superior strength. Ron's brother Harrison was, I believe, killed the same day in the artillery at another place. Their uncle Dick never recovered from the double blow.

CHAPTER SIX

Training and Transition

I first met Farley Mowat at Brockville and we met again in Italy near Campobasso in 1943. He was then known as "Squib," no doubt because of his restless energy. To his experience as an infantry and intelligence officer he added a discerning eye, and of all the regimental histories written in Canada his *The Regiment* about the Hastings and Prince Edward Regiment (the famous Hasty P's) must be the most distinguished. No one has shown more or indeed as much insight as Mowat into the essence of regimental life, the regiment as home. The recognition of this quality is much intensified when the regiment serves abroad in training or in action, where all its members are "single men in barracks" and regimental custom and discipline fortify the fighting man.

But life on a bald landscape in a red-brick "Belisha" barracks equipped with a modest quantity of small and inefficient cast-iron stoves, snowbound in the freezing winter weather of 1941–42, was no bed of roses. The cooks went on courses to learn how to cook on Mr Hore-Belisha's stoves; in the meantime the food was not only unfamiliar but spartan. The mechanics who had left their cherished kits of stainless steel wrenches in Canada were issued a couple of hammers and a few files; incredulous and disgusted, it was not until they took courses on how to make their own tools that they felt the world right itself under their feet. Moreover, the isolation of the Marlborough Downs added to a general feeling of depression difficult to dispel. An example within my experience will suffice. On New Year's Eve Ian Cumberland returned to the mess after a brigade headquarters party to find that all the lights were out and all the officers had gone to bed. He immediately dispatched two men to rout us out of bed, and at his instigation we then had a riotous and enjoyable party well into the small hours. Things seemed to improve when we moved to the cavalry barracks in Aldershot where our First Armoured Brigade was already installed, with divisional headquarters in the Royal Pavilion.

I have vivid recollections of that period because I was acting technical adjutant of the regiment pending the arrival of the permanent incumbent, Jack MacEachren. Our training had not yet advanced to the point where we could with profit be equipped with tanks, but wheeled vehicles we desperately required. Consequently, I found myself proceeding to the Royal Ordnance Corps depot at Bordon in Hampshire, from thence to lead convoys of trucks from the depot by the shrouded country roads of Hampshire and Berkshire, mostly by night, past Basingstoke, Hungerford, Newbury, and Marlborough, to our camp on the downs. This was good practice for map reading, particularly when driving at night in blacked-out conditions. On one occasion I lost my command of these excursions to a captain of another regiment. This individual seemed to enjoy putting me in my place when I offered advice as to what roads to take. To my secret delight he got hopelessly lost and had to be conciliatory towards me, a rare experience for a very junior subaltern. Later on, when we emerged from Aldershot and were encamped between Farnham in Hampshire and Milford in Surrey around the village of Elstead, we drew tanks on a training scale and sampled the American General Stuarts and General Grants and the Canadian Ram, designed initially by our General Worthington, a tank expert. I saw no British tanks at this stage; most of them were in the western desert, or scheduled to go there, and in Murmansk, since convoys were beginning to take much of the tank production to Russia.

I have now to recount an act of folly which almost finished my stint in the army. Every member of the regiment – officers, non-commissioned, and troopers – was given landing leave as soon as possible after our arrival in England. Somewhat over 60 per cent went to relatives in Great Britain, a remarkable proportion and a great saving of money. Because I was a very junior officer, my week's leave did not fall until well on in the winter. I had no English relatives or friends upon whom I could impose but had made an arrangement to spend the week with my cousin Rod MacAlpine in London, or such other place as we might decide after our reunion. I made a reservation at the Park Lane Hotel on Piccadilly, at that time a great haunt of Canadians in the services. I duly deposited my kit in the room reserved for me, but after meeting Rod I discovered that he had been recalled to proceed that evening to Chichester for a commando exercise or operation, so all we could look forward to for our joint leave was a few drinks in Victoria Station. Rod had begun the war in the artillery and had recently transferred to the Stormont, Dundas and Glengarry Highlanders in the Third Canadian Division, then deployed in the defence of the south coast. He had much to tell me. Drinks were indeed consumed and all the more quickly when it became clear that the departure of his train to Chichester was imminent. In an evil hour he persuaded me to board the train with him to say goodbye and we found ourselves in a dimly lit railway carriage with the shrouded lights revealing a ghostly company hatted and capped and reluctantly making room for a pair of junior officers who had reached a stage of amiability they did not share. All of a sudden whistles were blown and doors were slammed shut and I realized with shock that unless I got out of the carriage at once I would be bound for Chichester while my kit remained serenely in the Park Lane Hotel.

The contest was thus clearly between two Canadian officers excitedly disputing as to whether one of them should leave the train and return to his hotel or accompany the other to Chichester, unofficially and without equipment. I tried twice to leave and was hauled back by Rod, breaking the black-out when I opened the carriage door and causing the train to stop. At this point a shadowy figure in the corner of the carriage next to me said, "Make up your mind whether you're coming or going." This was no doubt a very reasonable remark, but to me it seemed monstrous that anyone should misinterpret the nature of our dispute and not realize that I was desperately trying to leave and was being restrained. So to this figure, obviously military but with rank badges covered by a

raincoat, I addressed exasperated words, with appropriate expletives, telling him to mind his own business, at which he rose, left
the carriage, blew a whistle, and summoned the Military Police. I
was at once put under arrest, upon which Rod MacAlpine jumped
out of the carriage and said, "You can't do this to my cousin."
Predictably he was also put under arrest by the blower of the
whistle, who turned out to be a British lieutenant-colonel and a
staff officer of Southeastern Command, then in the hands of the
vigorous and feared General B.L. Montgomery. We spent the night
in the cells at Victoria Station, our only communication being a
grating near the ceiling between our adjoining cells. Through this
opening Rod was able to pass a succession of cigarettes until sleep
overcame us both.

The next morning I was driven to my hotel, where I reclaimed
my kit and paid my bill for one night's lodging. From thence I was
taken to Waterloo Station with appropriate instructions from Canadian Military Headquarters to return me to my unit. I was delivered
by my escort to the railway transport officer, a veteran Guardsman
who invited me to tea with his wife and himself and treated me
with friendly courtesy and ironic congratulations on the amount
of money I was saving by the swift termination of my landing leave.
On my return to the Horse Guards I was also treated with a
sympathetic kindness by my seniors and some hilarity by my contemporaries for which I was and am grateful to this day. But after
a week of tranquil resumption of duty, the word came down,
regretfully explained by the adjutant Mark Auden, that I was to be
placed under open arrest. This was accompanied by a list of
charges which began ominously with the most serious of all –
"conduct unbecoming an officer and a gentleman" – for which the
penalty upon conviction was cashiering or dismissal from the army
with ignominy. A field general court martial was clearly in the
offing and our quartermaster, Captain K.B. Stratton offered to
represent me. I accepted with relief and he began to make representations on my behalf.

I did not resent the actions of my accuser in placing me under
arrest at Victoria Station, where I had behaved badly; but I did
resent the report given by him on which a charge of using obscene
language had been laid. The language in question was the lowest
form of the English barrack-room variety and may well have been

more characteristic of him than of me. The summary of evidence was taken in the Royal Pavilion at Aldershot, our divisional head-quarters, and I was there treated with marked consideration, which I probably did not deserve, a consideration not extended to the officer who had laid the complaint. He was received with cool correctness and provided with a drink by the general's ADC, Arthur Reid. The summary of evidence was taken from me by Captain R.A. Ritchie, an artillery officer who afterwards became a close friend when he was a judge of the Supreme Court of Canada in Ottawa. Another officer whom I had not known beforehand was Captain Neil Fraser of the Ontario Regiment, then assistant deputy judge advocate of the Fifth Division, who agreed with Ken Stratton's representations. As a result, I was allowed to plead guilty to the reduced charge of "conduct to the prejudice of good order and military discipline."

In due course I was escorted into the presence of Major-General Sansom, commanding the division, and severely reprimanded. My commanding officer, Colonel Sharp, was in attendance, and after the accused and escort had been marched out of the general's presence, he addressed me very audibly with the words "Hughes, I believe your story," a thunderous tribute from a mild-mannered and compassionate gentleman. Thus, a court martial was avoided, and since courts martial are frequently directed from on high to reach a verdict consistent with policy rather than with the princi-ples which prevail in the regular courts, I think I was fortunate. I had, however, accumulated a mountainous file at headquarters which subsequently played a malignant part in my affairs.

There is no question that the precipitation of the United States into the conflict in December 1941 was an important influence on the morale of the fighting services of the British Commonwealth and Empire. Hitherto "Thank Soviet Russia for quiet nights" had to suffice, but the German campaign in Russia had promised to be as short as it was sharp.

At home Helen had been able to volunteer for the Mechanized Transport Corps (MTC), a deservedly famous British volunteer unit of women which had won its spurs in and around the London docks and other areas smitten by the Luftwaffe. Only my consent was necessary to enable her to come forthwith to England and take part in the heroic work being done by the MTC. I was reluctant, for at this time we were still carrying anti-gas respirators; invasion, though remote, still seemed a possibility, and the resumption of heavy bombing at night was hourly expected. I refused my permission accordingly and made by telegram a sententious observation about my wife not being a sacrifice I was prepared to make, which not unnaturally infuriated her.

In the regiment, training in tanks, wireless operation, gunnery, and driving was in full swing both on courses in South Wales and other parts of the country and in the pleasant part of Surrey where the regiment found itself deployed. It was difficult not to feel pangs of regret at the destruction of carefully cultivated greens and fairways on the golf course at Elstead by heavy tracked vehicles, but spring was in the air and optimism triumphed over the discontent of winter.

It must have been at this time that the role of the regiment was changing to one of armoured reconnaissance, for I was put in charge of a number of Daimler armoured scout cars. This assignment gave me great pleasure and a sense of usefulness. But it was not long before it was explained to me that my need to wear spectacles at all times was problematic, especially in tanks, and that whatever talents I had would be more suitably employed on the staff than in armoured operations. To what extent this conclusion was facilitated by my disastrous landing leave I have no idea, nor was any indication given that it had played a part. I was sorry to leave the regiment and have nothing but the warmest feelings of comradeship towards all its ranks.

In due course, I was posted as a staff learner to headquarters E Group, Canadian Reinforcement Units, at Blackdown barracks near Sandhurst. E Group, consisting of the reinforcement and holding units for the Canadian Armoured Corps, was commanded by Colonel S.A. Lee, a professional soldier with a Military Cross from the previous war. Colonel Lee had been commandant at Camp Borden and second in command of the Second Armoured Brigade, a position which I think was being eliminated from the war establishment. Always known as "Garry" because of his association with the Fort Garry Horse, he was an experienced administrator and an accomplished gentleman with a wide knowledge of the Canadian Army. He had three staff learners, one for "G" (operations), one for "A" (personnel and administration), and one for "Q" (supply and transport), representing the three main branches of the staff of the army. I was "Q" and I was busy.

I thoroughly enjoyed this attachment and learned a good deal about staff procedures (not to be confused with "staff duties"), and I also learned to ride a Harley-Davidson motorcycle, an eight-hundred-pound monster only good for intimidating ordinary traffic on the nicely maintained highways and byways of the south of England. During this work I took my second seven-day leave, going as far west as I could to Penzance in Cornwall. Devonshire and Cornwall were remarkably empty at this time, before the great concentrations of American troops which eventually filled them, and all sorts of bargains could be found in the cellars of hotels and public houses. The hotel in which I stayed longest was the Queen's Hotel on the seafront in Penzance, and the wine waiter took some pleasure in producing for me some of the treasures of his house. One day I decided to go to the local cinema after lunch but my ally persuaded me to delay my departure and sample a bottle of hock. The sampling was generous and eventually I decided to forget the entertainment and have an afternoon nap, in the course of which a pair of Focke-Wulf 190's flying low and unperceived demolished the theatre, killing some three hundred people. Thoroughly chastened, I returned to duty in Surrey.

CHAPTER SEVEN

The Intelligence Phase

In June 1942 my old friend and Ridley colleague John Page, now GSO 2, Operations and Intelligence, at Canadian Military Headquarters on Cockspur Street in London, asked that I come and write the intelligence summaries that were distributed throughout the Canadian Army in Britain, down to lieutenant-colonels' commands. It soon became clear that there was more to this request than met the eye. The appointment was to a position of general staff officer third class or GSO 3, with liaison duties at the British War Office and direct communication with National Defence Headquarters in Ottawa of intelligence of the most secret character. Of course, I worked into this enviable position by degrees and a captaincy was not long delayed.

Military intelligence in the British and Canadian armies was divided into "Ia," or information about the enemy, and "Ib," or field security, a more active branch at this stage of the war. Operations was the least active branch of our section in view of the static and defensive role of the army. It mainly involved liaison with the active formations in the field and maintenance of an accurate order of battle.

But if information about the enemy was not vital to the operations of the Canadian Army Overseas so far, the recruitment and training of intelligence officers and other ranks who could speak German and Italian against the day when contact with the enemy would begin were of the first importance. The Canadian Army did not have the same resources in this respect as had the British; in Great Britain the commercial contacts with Germany had always been numerous and close. Most of our immigrants could speak their native language, but mostly in a form of dialect that would immediately betray them as semi-literate. This was particularly the case for the Italian language, whose dialects are legion and vary from town to town, but all those who pretend to literacy can speak the *lingua Toscana nella bocca Romana.* One experience of the U.S. Army was well known. The army had recruited from New York's east side alleged Italian-speaking interpreters who in fact spoke only Neapolitan or Sicilian dialects and were thus received in 1943 with hilarity. We listened respectfully to the British intelligence community, as the Americans could not always bring themselves to do, and avoided many pitfalls in the constitution and training of intelligence personnel overseas; but in Canada many mistakes were made, including the constitution of a Canadian Intelligence Corps in imitation of the British Intelligence Corps but with a distinctive uniform, which in Britain was generally regarded as a backward step, intelligence officers and other ranks not being anxious to be identified. Although in Canada we had followed the British closely, we were able overseas to wear the badges of our original regiment and perform our duties discreetly.

To return to my early days in Cockspur Street, it was clear that the writing of an intelligence summary for distribution to unit commands was only a marginal activity. At the highest echelons of the army in Canada the appetite for secret intelligence was voracious. Obtaining this information was a delicate matter. I had a pass admitting me to the "war room" in the War Office in Whitehall, and here maps with pins and flags showed the reported and reputed positions of all the divisions, Allied and enemy, in territories occupied by the latter and in theatres of war in Russia, the Far East, the Pacific, and North Africa. On all these fronts our fortunes had reached a critical stage, only Italian reverses from time to time relieving the desperate pressure applied by the Germans and Japanese.

The war room was staffed by civilian ladies, exquisitely helpful and polite, but there was an iron rule that nothing observed upon its walls or heard in conversation should be committed to paper. A tremendous strain was thus put upon the memory of the observer, and I would return swiftly to my headquarters to unburden my memory and indite a "most secret most immediate" telegram to the chief of the General Staff in Ottawa. Needless to say, when the Americans arrived, the pleasant function of polite conversation without any written record had to be abandoned to accommodate more literal minds. As a result, pieces of paper covered with confidential information turned up in shirt and trousers pockets and in the hands of launderers and a new security problem was created.

Much of the information thus collected was derived from various visits paid to intelligence sections in the confines of the War Office buildings. Not being a breezy, thick-skinned type of interviewer, I found that the liaison visits to the offices of the hardworking staff officers, informal and unscheduled as they were, required tact and good humour; but I was treated sympathetically and generously and soon was on friendly terms with most military intelligence sections. A section that collected information on the Russian front, sometimes through enemy sources because of the complete lack of effective liaison with the Red Army, was staffed by three officers of exceptional ability and charm. The officer in charge was a Major Tamplin, who had been with Bruce Lockhart, the British agent in Moscow, in the first war, and his colleagues were two Canadian captains, both Russian born and Russian speakers: Nicholas Ignatieff of Toronto, afterwards warden of Hart House, and Nicholas Vandervliet of Vancouver. These two officers were both in the Canadian Army, and I felt that their service by attachment in the British army to some extent repaid the debt which in general we owed the British for information and training. This was a very happy section, and the conversation was frequently in Russian as much as in English.

But we were in for a shock. I was summoned by the brigadier General Staff, Elliot Roger, and told that there was a complaint from the War Office about the sensitivity of the information I had been sending to Ottawa.

"But that means —"

"Exactly. They have broken our most secret cipher. As for your cables, they are not killing Germans, are they?"

"Not yet."

"Let's cut them out then."

Needless to say, a strong protest about the activities of British code-breakers who had nothing better to do than monitor the transmissions of their allies went forthwith to the War Office. Only a fortnight passed before National Defence Headquarters demanded to know what had happened to the cables that we had decided were not killing Germans, and I went back to dispatching them as before. Could it be that the code-breaking was merely an exercise, a *jeu d'esprit* that had gone astray? Amateurism had taken over somewhere.

John Page had long since gone to the Cossac planning staff in Norfolk Square and had been succeeded by Hugh Halbert, a Montrealer from the Black Watch. My arm had been strengthened by the addition of Lieutenant J.K. Starnes, also from the Black Watch, who had a speaking knowledge of French and German, but at this time was concentrating on the security side, which had become more and more critical as invasion plans matured. Starnes was to become after the war well known as an ambassador, director general of the security service in Canada, and a gifted writer of espionage novels.

Then the accomplished Felix Walter appeared on the scene, also as a subaltern. He was an old friend from Trinity College days and had taught French and German to my contemporaries. Soft-spoken but forceful with a capacious mind, he was destined to supersede me and become deputy director of military intelligence for the Canadian Army Overseas as a full colonel. In addition to a mastery of the French and German languages, he was fluent in Spanish and Italian and had a working knowledge of Russian. In his youth he had sown the wind and become a member of the Communist Party of Canada. Yet Walter was one of many who, upon learning of the infamous Nazi-Soviet pact of 1939, abruptly changed course and went down to the Armouries in Toronto to enlist as a private soldier in the Royal Regiment of Canada. Deep in the councils of the intelligence community, and in an atmosphere where Soviet Russia was an important ally, he passed and deserved to pass the most rigorous security tests. Then, virtually at the end of the war, he was called back to Canada to become director of military intelligence. He reported to General Murchie, chief of the General Staff, only to be told that the American FBI had filed a report about his Communist connection and that the appointment would not be his. After expressing amazement that an American agency appeared to be dominant in Canadian affairs, he left the general. Earlier Lester Pearson, then under-secretary of state for external affairs, had suggested to Walter that he would have work for him in the department after the war was over. Walter now repaired to the East Block, told Mr Pearson of his difficulty, and reminded him of his promise; but the under-secretary of state took a grave view of the FBI report and said he doubted if the State Department would look favourably upon a diplomatic appointment for a former Communist. A temporary solution was reached by Walter's appointment as second secretary at the Canadian embassy in Buenos Aires, where the Peron regime was considered to be unlikely to corrupt him. He must have found this exile unendurable because he left the diplomatic service, became a broadcaster for Radio Free Europe in London, and died shortly after, doubtless of a broken heart.

However that may be, at this time Walter's star was in the ascendant and mine was declining, although pleasantly enough. Having already been on a German army recognition course at Cambridge University, I was now sent on the highly regarded War Intelligence course at Matlock in Derbyshire. I was successful and greatly enjoyed both the course and the spectacular scenery of the Peak District. The Canadian Intelligence Corps was formed in October 1942, and although I was shortly afterwards to move out of intelligence work, I joined as one of the first members and remained with the corps until I left the army. In early 1943 security began to tighten around the military operations of all our units in England.

Hitherto, raids of the commando type, always British led, had been undertaken by small units; then in August 1942 the largest, and Canadian led, had been launched against Dieppe, a most unpromising site of cliffs and shingle beaches, launched in the teeth of every reasonable security precaution, and the planning of which had aroused bitter opposition by Major Nicholson, the GSO 2(I) at First Canadian Corps headquarters. The misplaced self-confidence, amounting to arrogance, with which the corps staff had planned the Canadian landing of units of the Second Canadian Division was exemplified by Brigadier Churchill Mann appearing at headquarters in London the day after the operation and telling us how successful the raid had been and how this opinion was to be our "official line." The unfortunate Nicholson was never employed again in operations and his fate was one example of the malignity with which hostile critics of the Dieppe raid were for some time pursued. But in October Montgomery won his great battle at El Alamein; then the winter and the Russians fell upon the Germans at Stalingrad. A new hope was born. As Winston Churchill said, "A bright gleam has caught the helmets of our soldiers." It was time to see that Canadian troops had an opportunity for such reflection.

CHAPTER EIGHT

The Historical Section

Our headquarters in London, static like the War Office, was housed mainly in Oceanic House, situated beside and to the west of Canada House, previously the Union Club. Canada House, now superseded by the larger establishment in Grosvenor Square, then occupied a commanding position on Cockspur Street. Jutting out into Trafalgar Square, it had been familiar to Canadian tourists for decades and intensely so to Canadian servicemen and service-women during six years of war. In Canada House sat the high commissioner since 1935, destined to hold the position through-out the war, the Right Honourable Vincent Massey; in Oceanic House sat the senior officer Major- (later Lieutenant-) General the Honourable P.J. Montague, CB, CMG, DSO, MC, on leave as a judge of the Court of Appeal of Manitoba for the duration of the war. Montague was a distinguished veteran of the first war and a close associate of the commander of the Canadian Corps (subsequently First Canadian Army), Lieutenant General A.G.L. McNaughton, CB, CMG, DSO, who commanded the divisions and army tank bri-gades of the Canadian Army Active Service Force stationed, trained, and ready in the home counties. These dispositions must be referred to as prevailing in the winter of 1942–43. General McNaughton, as the senior Canadian combatant officer overseas, was at the summit of his reputation and was frequently the subject of speculation as the Allied commander of ground troops in the inevitable invasion of the continent.

In Oceanic House the established structure of the staff was the same as that already described in E group, where I was a staff learner, and basically the same as that throughout the army: "G" represented by sections dealing with training, operations and intelligence, and staff duties, which included planning for this and that, such as resistance to chemical warfare; "A," with administration and personnel; and "Q," with supply and transport. The Ordnance Corps were represented in Lincoln's Inn Fields, and Records were housed in Acton far away to the westward. But almost from the beginning and throughout the bombardment of England and the object lesson of Dieppe, there had been a keen and indeed committed observer in Oceanic House – the historical officer, Major Charles Perry Stacey, whom I had known, but at a respectful distance, since arriving at headquarters.

Although he had been alone as the champion of military history in the army overseas, and had been justified by the war establishment people as a mere collector of records that an eventual official historian would employ, it was by 1943 beginning to be plain that Stacey would himself have an important part to play in the enterprise of an official history. By this time he had been joined by Major George F.G. Stanley, another Oxford historian and a professor of history at Mount Allison University. These two were companionable neighbours next door to the offices of Operations and Intelligence, and one day Charles Stacey made a suggestion to me. The armies in North Africa were on the move, he said, and some if not all Canadian troops would soon be leaving England. This meant, he had been assured, that the Historical Section would expand and properly qualified historical officers would accompany each force, write reports from the field, and then return to contribute drafts for the use of the official historian. Was I interested in being the first of these?

My assent was instantaneous. The chance of getting to a theatre of operations was too good to miss and there seemed little possibility of my getting there as an intelligence staff officer without mastery of a foreign language. Moreover, there was no chance of being promoted to the second grade of staff employment (GSO 2) with the rank of major without taking the staff course at the Royal Military College (RMC) in Kingston and no vacancy there appeared to be coming my way. The prospect of Stacey's plan was otherwise exciting because the Historical Section would inevitably be able to collect and collate tactical information of importance in current operations, and thus play a role like the German army's *Historische Abteilung*, long in place in the enemy's military establishments. This was not the first time that I had found that a certain facility in writing had helped me find congenial employment, and I moved pleasurably into the field of military history. My one regret concerned what seemed a lost chance for an imminent reunion with Helen. For some months she had been in the Red Cross Corps as a driver mechanic and was transferring to the Food Division, the most promising of the corps' activities for those anxious to go overseas from Canada. It had seemed likely that she would soon be in England, even though she had embarked on a successful venture for the city of Welland, organizing the collection and marketing of salvage for that city.

Stacey had not confined himself to the role originally planned for him. The collection of materials in the form of war diaries of units could well be left to the officer in charge of records and indeed was ably done by Major C.J. Lynn-Grant, a barrister and solicitor from Saskatchewan. This delightful Irishman, who had been a member of the Royal Irish Constabulary (known and feared as the Black and Tans), introduced me to the complexities of his organization at Acton and we enjoyed several convivial luncheons in Shepherd's Bush. Later on when I expressed the intention of going on leave to Ireland, as many did in spite of its neutrality, he asked me if I would take a letter to his solicitors. I naturally asked why he did not consult his solicitors himself, at which he confessed that the commandant of the Civic Guard in Dublin – who was his cousin – would make it awkward for him because the last time they had met, Lynn-Grant had shot him in the hip, an unforgotten episode of the Easter Rebellion in 1916.

I was able to read many of the numerous reports Stacey had sent to Ottawa on the activities of the Canadian Army Overseas since its first arrival. George Stanley, for instance, was working on an account of the operations of the tunnelling companies of the Royal Canadian Engineers at Gibraltar. Their members, largely hard-rock miners from northern Ontario and Manitoba, were transforming the famous rock into an impregnable fortress able to withstand the threats of General Franco, who was urged on by the Germans to subdue this strategic outpost and close the Mediterranean to Allied convoys. As his main preoccupation, Stacey had undertaken a painstaking examination of the Dieppe raid, and it was well for the Canadian Army and its reputation that he did. He provided, as it were, a fortress of impartial research and measured analysis that has defied the efforts of journalists and revisionist historians to trivialize the efforts of the fighting troops, whatever legitimate criticism might have been directed against political pressure and defective planning. He had secured the confidence and support of General McNaughton, still at the height of his power and influence, not yet diminished by his failure in Spartan, the largest troop exercise to that point, which had pitted both Canadian corps as an invasion force against the troops of Eastern Command. Stacey's loyalty to McNaughton would remain steadfast. In spite of what followed and the fact that Spartan persuaded Generals Brooke and Paget that McNaughton was not the man to command a force to assail Fortress Europe, this loyalty did nothing to affect Stacey's reputation as an effective and impartial analyst.

CHAPTER NINE

The Road to Rome

I have referred generally to the tightening of security as the principal intelligence preoccupation at the beginning of 1943. Additional security was necessary because of the inevitability of the Allied army striking a blow at Germany's occupation of the continent of Europe. There was no point in trying to conceal from the enemy that extensive preparations were being made; only the time and the place of the operation had to be withheld from the enemy's knowledge.

Security precautions now intensified around training of the First Canadian Infantry Division in the western highlands of Scotland. With the First Canadian Army Tank Brigade, this division was destined to join the veteran Eighth Army under General Montgomery in the invasion of Sicily.

Major Stacey was determined that I should join this force. But there was a hitch. The new divisional commander, Major-General G.G. Simonds (successor to Major-General H.N. Salmon, killed in a flying accident), had a GSO 3 (Operations) whom he was anxious to replace in that role but equally anxious to retain in some other capacity, for his knowledge of the Italian language could be useful. This was Captain A.T. Sesia. Gus Sesia was a Montrealer whose designation as historical officer for the First Division did not depend upon any literary or historical qualifications but whose usefulness as an experienced member of the divisional staff was undeniable. My disappointment was great but a crowning compensation was in the offing. I was now able to reunit with Helen. She had spent many of the intervening months organizing the collection and marketing of salvage for the city of Welland with great success, but had abandoned a promising business career and arrived in England with the Red Cross Corps in July, around the time that the division was landing in Sicily. If I had been with it, I would have missed two months of reunion after a separation of almost two years. As it was, I missed the whole Sicilian campaign and did not join the division by way of a sojourn in North Africa until it was deployed in reserve around the Appennine town of Campobasso at the end of September.

Charles Fraser Comfort, a supremely talented landscape and portrait painter, muralist, and teacher, has in his book *Artist at War* vividly described our journeyings together from Aldershot to the First Canadian Division in Italy, the fourteen-ship convoy in which we sailed for nine days sweeping westward in the Atlantic to avoid the questing Condors, the blacked-out nighttime passage of the Straits of Gibraltar incongruously silhouetted against the bright lights of Tangiers, and the brilliant sunlit passage into danger in the western Mediterranean Sea. His presence as my companion was due to Stacey being entrusted with the military control of the Canadian war artists in the army, whose embodiment had been vigorously sponsored by High Commissioner Vincent Massey. Stacey's plan was to have a field historical section at each corps headquarters and presumably at First Canadian Army headquarters when this majestic body took the field, with historical officers and war artists at the divisional level. At this point in the war, however, the divisional level was the highest reached by the Canadian Army in contact with the enemy, and Comfort and I were on our way to replace the pioneers of the experiment at First Canadian Division, Will Ogilvie, a Canadian of South African origin and an artist whose reputation continues to grow long after his death, and Gus Sesia, already referred to.

In Algeria, hard by the town of Philippeville, we were encamped in the sand on the edge of a cork tree forest; indeed the smell of cork and the feel of sand were pervasive. We had experienced delays in leaving England and were similarly delayed in leaving

Africa. But in spite of our impatience, particularly that of Charles, who had already done a number of enchanting watercolour sketches of the convoy and the Algerian coast and was impatient to paint the battlefield, we made the most of inaction. A trip by truck to El Arrouch, where our No. 14 General Hospital was fully employed – under canvas in intense heat and on bare earth – with the wounded from Sicily, led to a visit even further south to the spectacular city of Constantine. This relic of Roman Africa was perched on a rocky eminence split by a river gorge that was bridged to join the French colonial city and the Arab town, otherwise completely separate in habitat and spirit. Here were to be found white-robed Moorish chieftains and elegantly caparisoned Spahi officers, peopling the hotels and restaurants and drinking the excellent coffee and the detestable brandy of the district in picturesque idleness as if no war had impended. The illusion of timelessness was dispelled on our return to the cork forest for a brief stay in coastal Africa, with its oranges, lemons, grapes, and wine, its hot clear days and cool starlit nights in bracing contrast with the intimidating weather of England, where neither an orange nor a lemon had been seen for years.

It must be remembered that at this stage of the Mediterranean campaign the tail of the Eighth Army, in which the First Division and the First Army Tank Brigade were under command, reached back to Cairo and the Indian empire for administration and supplies even though operational command was exercised by General Eisenhower in Algiers and his deputy, General Alexander. In this rather complicated transitional stage, my draft, consisting of No. 1 Provost Company of RCMP personnel, Charles Comfort, and myself, were fortunate to obtain passage to Italy on a U.S. Navy LSI (Landing Ship Infantry) from Philippeville to Taranto, in the heel of Italy. After a stormy passage, which sometimes made our decks slippery with vomit, we landed at Taranto to observe the wreckage caused by the Royal Navy's Fleet Air Arm in the naval battle at Cape Matapan. Here the beaches were occupied by serried ranks of Allied landing craft, under whose prows we disembarked. We were then carried by truck northward through a landscape overlooked on hills to the South by the ruins of Norman castles. These I struggled to identify in the pages of Gibbon, my only source of information in the absence of maps or guidebooks once available to tourists but now gathered up and impounded by the military authorities. But the stretch of road between Taranto and Bari was innocent of castles, being flanked by *latifundia*, the great estates, rising since Roman times from the limestone soil of Apelia olives, oranges, and lemons, the peasantry poor and dependent, the women and children barefoot as in coastal Africa, their dialect flavoured with Greek words redolent of a culture stretching back to the days when the heel of Italy was under the heel of Byzantium. I have written elsewhere (*From Pachino to Ortona*) of the way our Canadian soldiers and their allies invaded Italy, not like the barbarians and other oppressors from the north, but like the liberator Garibaldi "through the humble and neglected villages of the south." And indeed our path lay always in *Il Regno*, Garibaldi's principle target, that strange Norman creation so long joined with Sicily under the personal rule of foreign interlopers, leaving to the native born only brigandage as a road to distinction – *cosa nostra*, "our thing."

I confess that on this journey I suffered the lapse of interest in the present that all lovers of history experience when treading on historic ground. In the stifling autumnal heat of Foggia, dreary and depressing marketplace for the great pastoral plain on which its most famous resident had settled his Merino sheep, in Lucera where he built the fortress confronting the Appennines to house his Saracen troops, I mused upon Frederick II, excommunicated for recovering Jerusalem for the Faith without the approval of the Vatican. Eastward from the great plain, still the site of seasonal migrations and pasturage of thousands of sheep, were distant views of the Gargano, the mountain massif since time immemorial a refuge for saints and sinners, at the foot of which lies a town bearing the name of Manfred.

All these reflections were dominant as we passed under the walls of Frederick's fortress at Lucera and wound westward in our jolting trucks up the flank of the Appennines and along the road to Campobasso. Here the weather was clear and cool, a pleasant change, but signs of battle abruptly presented themselves in the shape of shattered farmhouses, Bailey bridges spanning the gorges, and defiles made impassable by German demolition. From time to time we halted along the mountain road to look at the white crosses beginning to appear. Here was one bearing the name of my old friend Jim McMullen, a handsome man and a gentle product of Trinity College School and Trinity College itself, cut down by machine-gun fire while leading his platoon of the Seaforth Highlanders of Canada. There, even more poignant, was one which read Lieutenant W.A. Wood, 48th Highlanders of Canada. Bill Wood was perhaps the brightest star of my truncated year at Osgoode Hall; he had been upset at my decision to join the army with the course unfinished and had strongly urged me to receive my call to the bar before going on active service. He had governed himself accordingly and had qualified as an infantry subaltern when the wastage in this category was high; I had found staff employment and was far in the wake of the fighting troops. As I sat on the roadside with a mess tin of hot tea, staring at this rough and ready monument to my accomplished friend, Frederick II faded from my mind.

Campobasso was a pleasant community consisting of the usual old quarter (this one dominated by a thirteenth-century castle), a modern suburb, and a ski resort area that took full advantage of the slopes of the surrounding mountains. It was also the capital of a province with the same name and sustained a local unit of the regular national police, the Carabinieri, and a local branch of the Fascist party. It had been the business of our security and military government forces to eliminate the latter's grip on local government wherever it was to be found in Sicily and southern Italy, to replace blackshirt officials with democratically inclined people who were held to favour the liberating armies. This effort had produced some very strange bedfellows, and I regret to say that in many cases the local Fascist officials had to be restored to their positions so that local government did not dissolve in chaos.

Campobasso had been entered after a relatively bloodless assault by the First Infantry Brigade consisting of the Royal Canadian Regiment, the 48th Highlanders, and the Hastings and Prince Edward Regiment, or, to use familiar abbreviations (which I shall henceforth do), the RCR, the 48th, and the Hasty P's. One of the first familiar faces I met at headquarters was that of Bill Cooper from Toronto, now in command of the First Field Security Section and a veteran intelligence officer on the Ib side. He invited me to join him and his section in Campobasso, which they had entered on the heels of the RCR to begin the process of dislodging Fascist officials and establishing trustworthy substitutes who supported the Badoglio regime. I spent that night on the top floor of the house that his section occupied in company with a couple of Carabinieri and one or two of these recruits, but sleep was postponed by a battery of German artillery shelling the town. It was the enemy's custom to slow down further advance from a newly occupied area by this means. This was my first experience of being on the receiving end of shell-fire, however distant and desultory, and it was clear from the reverberating crashes that this distance was diminishing.

As the explosions crept towards us, my companions raised their heads and seemed about to leave their blankets, but paused to look at me. I was terrified but kept my head down, resolved not to lead the way downstairs. After neatly bracketing their target, the German gunners inexplicably tired of what must have been a simple formality and stopped firing. We were undisturbed for the rest of the night, and next morning after a look around the town I was taken back to headquarters.

It had been Stacey's plan to have Comfort and me replace Sesia and Ogilvie at the conclusion of the Sicilian campaign to allow the latter pair to return to England and begin definitive work. Neither the construction of a narrative nor the production of paintings in oil would be attempted in the field. Making periodic reports and interviewing soldiers at all levels, particularly at that of command, were to be the staples of the historical officer's activities, while making watercolour sketches were those of the war artist, both being under canvas and able to move quickly and freely as operations developed. No one had counted on the Germans moving backward as quickly as they did, and it was not recognized until the Biferno River was reached by the Eighth Army and the Garigliano River by the Fifth. A very minor consequence of their rapid retreat was that our replacement schedule could not be met.

The members of the historical section lived and worked in a tent in the divisional headquarters compound. The section had a Humber staff car, weatherbeaten by its long journey from Egypt across the desert. This remarkable vehicle had four-wheel drive, map tables, and other amenities that had been offered to the divisional commander when the division inherited equipment from those units of the Eighth Army that had returned to England. The commander, it appeared, had declined such a drab conveyance, preferring the majestic Buicks that were shipped from Oshawa for the use of commanders of his rank. Nevertheless, the four-wheel drive made this leather-upholstered Humber a godsend the historical section was glad to inherit. In due course, I met Major-General Guy Simonds and his GSO 1, Lieutenant-Colonel George Kitching, both now having established reputations in the army owing, not only to their proven capacity, but also to the tragic accident which killed Major-General Harry Salmon and Lieutenant-Colonel Finlay on their way out to Africa. Shortly afterwards Simonds and Kitching left to join the Fifth Canadian Armoured Division when it arrived at Naples, to be succeeded at Campobasso by Brigadier Christopher Vokes to command and Lieutenant-Colonel Malem Harding as GSO 1.

I began at once to interview brigade and battalion commanders, taking my notes in a sort of longhand-shorthand script I had developed in countless hours of lectures. I sent the information back to Stacey in extended form without reference to any authority on the spot. These were invariably accounts of operations along with a brief narrative of my own movements and observations. There is a stark contrast between this freedom of communication and the inability of the Directorate of History at Ottawa decades later to get uncensored reports from its representatives at the Gulf War. Comfort painted masterly studies in watercolour, one of which depicted me interviewing Hamish McIntosh of the 48th, a pupil of mine when at Ridley, in a house in one of the many hilltop villages surrounding Campobasso. This work was reproduced later in Stacey's *A Date with History* as depicting the historical officer's functions, and later still became the whole cover of the paperback edition of that volume.

In that autumn weather in the open air of the mountains, life was invigorating and enjoyable. As always, association with the fighting troops was of the same order. Efficiency and avoidance of fuss were their principal characteristics, and in this respect soldiers were sustained at different times by the staffs of 30 and 13 (British) Corps, veterans of the desert campaigns who had long since ceased to exact receipts in quadruplicate for every round of ammunition expended. I must not dwell upon the details of operations more than is absolutely necessary to describe my own activities, but it is safe to say that during my ten months in Italy I only saw one action which could be described as a tank battle, that being in the Liri Valley in May 1944, which I will talk about later. The terrain simply prohibited the classic use of armoured fighting vehicles, and the First Army Tank Brigade, consisting of the Calgary, the Three Rivers, and the Ontario Regiments, was used in close support of the First Division's infantry brigades in country where any transport was frequently reduced to the use of mule trains. The Fifth Armoured Division had a similar experience, its two armoured brigades being reduced to one and its infantry component increased by one full brigade. It was under these circumstances that General Simonds took over the armoured division and his trusted staff officer George Kitching was given command of its Eleventh Infantry Brigade.

One of the rivers rising high in the Maiella massif of the central Appennines was the Sangro, which became a broad stream at its confluence with the Adriatic Sea. Fighting across this river line and exploiting northward was to be the last operation planned for the Eighth Army under Montgomery's command. It is interesting that he makes no reference to this operation in his memoirs, which are full of foreboding about the lack of a master plan for further operations in Italy by the Eighth and Fifth Armies and the administrative muddle in Algiers that had brought both armies to a virtual standstill. But before the Adriatic campaign resumed, the general expressed his interest in what our historical section was doing and particularly in the work of the war artists. Accordingly, Comfort, Ogilvie, and I, shepherded by Dick Malone, journeyed to Vasto (Histonium to the Romans), a little to the northwest of which was Montgomery's tactical headquarters. I have a vivid recollection of this occasion, and I do not blame Charles Comfort for failing to mention in his memoir that I was a member of the party. Indeed, I was fortunate to be there because it was clear that the wonderful work of these two artists was really what the general wanted to see. Nevertheless, I saw for the only time in my life the famous three caravans that were always with him, mounted on truck bodies, as were all vehicles of the type: one for sleeping, one for working, and one for housing the collection of tropical and exotic birds which various potentates had presented to him after the battle of El Alamein.

My impression of tea in Monty's mess and his inspection of the paintings differs from that of Comfort. He describes the general as being seated at the head of the table flanked by officers of the highest rank, but I have the liveliest picture of him carrying on a cheerful conversation with the young ADC and liaison officers while the handful of senior officers from Main Army Headquarters sat restlessly at the far end of the table, not particularly enjoying the experience. After a while I had the opportunity of explaining briefly what my function was in the Canadian Army, evincing a cool but polite interest in his unwavering glance. After tea had been consumed, he said to me, and I am sure included my colleagues: "You may smoke. I don't." I stammered an acknowledgment of this courtesy and my intention to decline the invitation. The general then said he had work to do and retired to his caravan.

The first week of December 1943 was spent by the First Division in forcing the Moro River and securing a desperate hold on its left bank in steady and sometimes torrential rain, fighting forward through a tangle of vines, olive trees, and gullies staunchly defended by the remains of the 90th Panzer Grenadier Division with mortars and machine guns. Until our engineers, under heavy bombardment, had succeeded in repairing at least one of the two bridges demolished by the Germans, it was very difficult to support the scrambling advance up the steep left bank of the river; but eventually the road running between Orsogna and Ortona was reached and the axis of the advance turned in the direction of the latter. Ortona stood on a high promontory with the usual fine medieval cathedral, romanesque embellished with baroque, and a castle with massive walls which laughed at modern artillery. The enemy had transformed Ortona into a fortress, blocking its narrow streets with the rubble of demolished houses. The town was defended by German paratroopers in the most bitter fighting experienced by Canadian troops, or any troops for that matter since the Italian landings.

My friend George Renison, brigade major of the First Brigade, conducted an important study of the street-fighting tactics employed by both sides in the capture and defence of the town, particularly the house-to-house fighting known as "mouseholing," in which partition walls were breached inside houses and furious hand-to-hand fighting was the order of the day. This study, widely circulated throughout the Allied armies, was the first to throw light on a phenomenon which might be expected to occur with frequency in any invasion of northern Europe. The story of how the Seaforth Highlanders of Canada had their Christmas dinner in one building while fighting in another in relays is well known. I saw the bodies of dozens of the paratroopers killed in this type of fighting, some still clutching hand grenades, most of them stiffened in attitudes of menace. The old town was in ruins, the cathedral having lost half its dome and presenting Charles Comfort with a favourite subject for work in both watercolour and oil. Seven-point-two-inch howitzers, mothballed since the first German war, were eventually employed against the castle with some success, but the paratroopers made a fighting withdrawal and successfully defended positions on the next river line to the northward, staying there till they were moved southward to confront the Allies in the defence of Cassino. Dust and the smell of death shrouded Ortona until mercifully dispersed on New Year's Eve by the snows of an Adriatic winter.

I must be careful not to confuse the functions of memorialist and historian. Here I do not seek to give an authoritative account of operations I have described in another place. Reading over what I wrote in *From Pachino to Ortona*, I am satisfied that what there appears is a clear and readable narrative of what transpired. I have also reread with care the memoirs of Field Marshall Viscount Montgomery of Alemain and have failed to find any allusion to the execution of the operation which he had undoubtedly planned. The month of December for him was one of saying farewell to the Eighth Army preparatory to his departure on December 31 for England to take over command of 21 Army Group, to review and in important aspects to reverse the work of the planners for the invasion of Normandy. Although his departure elicited an emotional response from him and from his soldiers, it is clear that he disapproved of the failure of the high command at both Allied Force Headquarters in Algiers and the headquarters of the Allied Armies in Italy (AAI), established at Caserta in the massive palace of the Bourbon kings, to come up with a plan to exploit the gains of 1943. Indeed, the direction of the campaign in Italy had thus far had a quality of aimlessness, fortunately concealed from the fighting troops.

On New Year's Day 1944 misery and frustration prevailed. Slit trenches, the natural refuge and even sleeping place for soldiers in combat were full of water. George Renison, now GSO 2 at divisional headquarters, and I took a bottle of Scotch whisky to the command vehicle of the First Brigade, now commanded by Dan Spry of the RCR. (Dan's predecessor, Howard Graham, had been invalided out after winning a bar to his DSO.) Dan, later to command the Third Division in France, was sitting in his long underwear and gas cape with the brigade staff, similarly attired and in considerable discomfort, while a Balkan storm howled across the Adriatic Sea. The bottle, which went only once around the company, was a reminder of the celebrations of other days and its like had not been seen for weeks.

The weather of course improved but the situation of the mighty Eighth Army did not. An attack by the Eleventh Brigade, north of Ortona, was a failure, revealing inadequate patrolling and insufficient persistence on the part of one of the attacking battalions (this particular battalion had won a reputation for wrecking pubs in the south of England). One positive result was achieved. The brigade's commander and General Simonds were able to return to England equipped with "experience" sufficient to justify their promotion to major-general and lieutenant-general respectively in contemplation of their new roles in the invasion of Normandy.

During the succeeding months of stalemate I was able to go on leave with my war artist friends – Comfort and Lawren Harris, the latter from the Horse Guards, a redoubtable painter and son of a famous father – to Naples. This was a rich reward for months of living in tents and bivouacs through the Adriatic winter, so different from the climate of the famous city beside the warm Tyrrhenian Sea. I can vouch for this last observation because I swam in that body of water, finding it as easy to float in as accounts of its salinity had suggested.

The Bay of Naples is embraced by a marvellous landscape stretching from the Sorrento Peninsula to Cumae of the *Sibylline Books*. It is overlooked by Vesuvius, with its plume of smoke, and washes the most historic coastline in Europe. Greeks, Romans, Goths, Lombards, Normans, Angevins, and Spaniards have left their mark on Naples and its seductive surroundings. Now the beautiful city was enduring its latest invasion, and after being grudgingly given up by the Germans, it was firmly in the hands of the U.S. Fifth Army rear echelons and cluttered with British and American troops on leave. Parenthetically, it is of interest to remember that the Fifth Army fighting troops were never less than half British, and sometimes more, although the army's commander (Mark Clark) was American, as was its administrative and logistic "tail." I was used to the careful spacing and regulated speed that distinguished the traffic control of our own and the British formations of the Eighth Army. I was thus shocked when I first saw U.S. Army convoys of massive trucks tearing along at sixty miles per hour, scattering and overturning the carts and barrows of local vendors and farmers.

This was one aspect, although I recall another to offset it. On my first visit to Naples in a jeep with my driver-batman and my sergeant-clerk, all three of us on leave, we came to a halt on the high ground above the city near the Capodimonte Palace to see the blackout below and the brightly lit harbour (too busy to afford the luxury of concealment) being bombed by the enemy from the air. Night had fallen and we did not dare descend into Naples with its notoriously trigger-happy American sentries. Fortunately, by the roadside there was an entrance to a U.S. DUKW unit. The DUKW was a wonderful vehicle, roadworthy like all American vehicles but also amphibious, designed for beach landings. Here was a whole park of them, promising shelter from the pouring rain and safe postponement of our descent into Naples. I approached the sentry and after the usual formalities a top sergeant appeared. He welcomed us warmly and suggested that we bivouac underneath one of his DUKWs and then repair to his mess tent where "chow" would be ready for us. I remember that meal vividly: pork chops (unheard of in our part of the field), fruit salad in jelly ladled out of a large tin can (never before encountered), and fragrant coffee (our staple was tea). When we left next morning, having slept the sleep of the prudent if not the just, we had traded our battledress blouses for the U.S. Army's smart gabardine, felt-lined windbreakers and our tea ration for large tins of coffee and many rare and half-forgotten foodstuffs that contributed to our comfort on our return to the Adriatic winter.

Naples, of course, has two faces, the elegance of its seafront and the buildings framing the Via Toledo (now the Via Roma) in hideous contrast with the slums of its east end, often described as the worst in Europe. The plight of the children was the saddest to see, most naked, always hungry, and murderously greedy for money, cigarettes and the distributors of trucks and jeeps. Especially because of the latter, they were at once a source of pity and a security concern, military vehicles having to be parked in areas defended by sandbags and barbed wire.

The Germans had done their usual efficient job of seizing the best wines; they had a fixation for champagne but not for the sweet sparkling *spumante* of the south. The looting of Naples with the Fifth Army on their heels had been difficult. Much was left for soldiers on leave to purchase in the shape of goods not generally manufactured by serious practitioners of war. Silk stockings, perfumes, ladies' gloves (for which Naples was famous), and many articles made of aluminum were readily available. In Naples and its surroundings there was such a glut of historical monuments that I mourned the absence of my *Baedecker's Guide to Southern Italy*, then in storage in Toronto and unobtainable in England because of the Control of Maps Order.

Although Naples itself was largely untouched by the devastation caused by gunfire and German demolitions, I was impressed by one oddity in Pompeii. In recent years "New Excavations" – Nuovi Scavi – had altered and expanded the familiar shape of this wonderful relic of Roman times. These now presented a sorry picture, having been smashed – one hopes not irretrievably – by Fifth Army gunners to discourage the Germans from using this quarter for a sustained defence. This new destruction of these ancient buildings, once lovingly recovered from Vesuvius's ash and lava, was doubly pitiful because the Germans had no intention of being trapped in Naples as they back-pedalled to the Winter Line. It may have been this bit of unconscious barbarity that led the Allied Armies' headquarters in Italy to produce a manual for commanders listing various Italian monuments to be spared at all costs. I once had a copy of this document and at the very head of the list, with a five-star rating, was the Abbey of Monte Cassino.

During these winter months of 1944 I made at least two trips to Naples and the Volturno River valley, one with Charles Comfort and the other with Lawren Harris. During the former I had bought Helen some gloves and some silk stockings. We left Naples in bad weather and somewhere in the hilly country the road we were following dissolved in mud and we were forced to take the Humber staff car off the road in spite of its four-wheel drive. We unloaded the car and pitched a bivouac tent to shelter our two men from the downpour, and then set out to explore the neighbouring hilltop town barely visible in the storm. We made our way on foot into a field posted with signs warning that it had not been swept for mines, fell in with a helpful tank-transporter troop of the Elgin Regiment, whose commander gave us sustenance, and finally started the laborious climb to the village perched high above us. This was of course to be reached by the serpentine roadway ascending at a gradient reasonable for men and horses, but we soon tired of the slow progress imposed upon us and decided to go up the steep and pathless but shorter rear approach. Before long we were in difficulty, mired in a spongy and apparently bottomless substance which, as we painfully ascended higher, turned fresher and revealed itself to be of unmistakable origin. The low wall at the back of the town had obviously been long in use and the fastidious war artist and myself were up to our armpits in human ordure. Every door was shut as we eventually clambered over the wall and we at last found shelter from the cold, driving rain in a small church. There we slept exhausted on the stone floor without cushion or covering. Next morning we went down the road, steered well clear of by all other travellers, and returned to our car in bright sunshine to find that our driver and batman had spent a reasonably comfortable night.

During the rest of the winter and in the early spring of 1944 the military historian will find nothing extraordinary about what transpired on the Adriatic front, finally taken over by the headquarters of the First Canadian Corps, now commanded by Lieutenant-General H.D.G. Crerar, brought to Italy to gain experience of command in the field before elevation to command of an army. Nevertheless, quite a lot was happening. Every day there was an exchange of fire; every night patrols went out to test the enemy's positions and attempt to bring in prisoners; and every hour men were killed or wounded. As for prisoners, two Germans ran into problems when they claimed to be from a unit which our intelligence officers were certain was not in Italy. They had in fact deserted in Russia, made the dangerous journey to northern Italy, followed the railway line down the Adriatic coast, sheltering in the numerous tunnels between Pescara and Ortona, and happily surrendered to a corporal cook well within Canadian lines.

Unusual things were happening to the historical officer of the First Division. With Lieutenant-General Crerar had come Major

W.E.C. Harrison, a gifted writer now commanding 1 Field Historical Section located at corps headquarters and a threat to the self-
sufficiency and independence of the divisional incumbent. It will
be seen later that this threat was material only once. Eric Harrison
was a senior member of the Department of History at Queen's
University (he was later to be head of it) and a man of great charm
and ability, authoritarian to his fingertips. He would later follow
the fortunes of General Crerar, write his dispatches as commander
First Canadian Army, and be promoted to the rank of lieutenant-
colonel. He was also to offer me a position in the history department at Queen's after the war, and after I had become committed
to the practice of law, a gratifying offer nonetheless.

Then Stacey, now lieutenant-colonel, paid us a visit of ceremony,
bringing in tow Colonel A. Fortescue Duguid, official historian of
the Canadian Expeditionary Force since the end of the first war
and nominally, at least, Stacey's chief. Duguid was a professional
soldier, a gunner officer with a good war record from the first war.
He had produced only one volume of the official history, ending
in 1915, frustrated by his respectful practice of circulating draft
chapters among senior officers and obsessed with his true love,
heraldry. I was able to get him and Stacey close enough to German
shell-fire of a routine nature to satisfy their martial instincts.

This was a period when the Germans were developing considerable accuracy in the use of their 88-mm anti-aircraft gun as a field
gun, first tried with great success in the western desert and later
in the turret of the otherwise unsatisfactory Tiger tank. Since the
conclusion of the battle for Ortona, main headquarters was really
only vulnerable to air attack, which was infrequent. However, one
sunny spring afternoon the enemy got the range with at least one
88-mm gun and killed one of our soldiers in the camp area.
Attention was then paid to bringing slit trenches up to standard,
and some new ones discreetly appeared. As far as I know, this attack
was never repeated. Following this, but not necessarily as a result
of it, our own heavy anti-aircraft 17-pounder guns were used in a
similar ground role and, like the 88, were adapted for our Sherman
tanks. On one or two occasions I found myself between one of
these and its target, and the vicious crack of its discharge was
almost all that my ears could handle. In point of fact, the anti-
aircraft artillery in Italy was seldom used in its appointed role, since
German aircraft activity was much reduced. Indeed, the 2nd Light

Anti-Aircraft Regiment was converted to bolster the infantry component of our Fifth Armoured Division. I can remember only three occasions on this front when German aircraft were in evidence and observed by me. One day I watched a twin-engined Messerschmidt chasing one of our artillery Tiger Cub light observation aircraft down the narrow Moro River valley, overshoot its agile target, and bury itself in the muddy bank. On another occasion Eric Harrison and I were talking to General Vokes in his caravan and our conversation was interrupted by screaming engines and the thump of the out-distanced Bofors. And once I asked George Renison to look at the "rcd stuff" on the leading edge of the wings of a visiting plane, the "red stuff" being the flash of machine-gun fire. Feeling foolish, I joined George under a neighbouring truck.

Before I leave this scene of reminiscence, I should record the transfer of John Tweedsmuir, whom I had last seen as my host at dinner in the mess of the Hastings and Prince Edward Regiment in the muddy hilltop town of Castropignano. Pale from a long sojourn in an African hospital, he was seated among the weather-beaten sons of Hastings and Prince Edward Counties, restored to his command of that regiment, serene, and, in my fancy, still wearing the laurels of Assoro, very much in command. The night march he had led around the rear of that high place had established his battalion, as dawn broke, behind the German positions. Supported in the ensuing day by the 48th and the RCR, his battalion had captured the town and routed the enemy in a daring operation of war worthy of James Wolfe. Insufficient recognition was given to this remarkable exploit. At a time when decorations were freely given, none that I know of were conferred on the heroes of Assoro, if one can except the Order of the British Empire tardily bestowed on their leader. Perhaps it was John's being a British peer that restrained timorous functionaries from conferring a DSO upon him as suitable recognition for his much-tried troops. Whatever the reason, the omission left an enduring disappointment in the ranks of those engaged.

I do not intend in this short memoir to do more than give glimpses of the operations of Canadian soldiers in Italy during the period when I was there. I have already referred to *From Pachino to Ortona*.

Stacey's preliminary volume, *The Canadian Army: 1939–1945*
(1948), gives a masterly introduction to the official history proper
and includes an account of the Italian campaign. He entrusted the
volume of the full history dealing with Sicily and Italy to his deputy
director, Lieutenant-Colonel G.W.L. Nicholson, an officer who was
not in the theatre during wartime but who would visit the various
battlefields thereafter. In 1956 Nicholson would complete his magnificent account from which all subsequent commentaries must
necessarily stem. I have in my possession inscribed copies of both
these volumes, written long after I had left the army and for which
my admiration is complete and unqualified. Let it suffice that
almost to the day that the Eleventh Brigade launched its unfortunate attack across the Arielli River, the Fifth Army attempted to
cross a swollen Garigliano River and then achieved complete surprise with an amphibious attack at Anzio, later brought to a standstill by weather and indecision. The Fifth Army's first operation was
costly, the crossings being overlooked by the enemy high on Monte
Cassino. To ensure the capture of Rome, establishment of the
bridgehead at Anzio had to be followed by thrust through the Liri
Valley, and the Eighth Army was called upon to add its weight to
the Fifth Army's efforts. Once more a demonstration in force cost
the First Infantry Brigade unwelcome casualties in the area west of
Ortona. Then the thinning out began. The First Canadian Corps,
with First Infantry Division and Fifth Armoured Division under
command, moved southwesterly by stages and occupied a rest-and-
training area in the valley of the Volturno River. Here Lawren
Harris and I were able to visit the Horse Guards on the eve of their
first real battle.

The mouth of the Liri Valley, traversed by Route 6, the more
northerly of the two main roads linking Rome and the Neapolitan
Campania (Via Latina of the Romans), was still commanded by the
hill on which the Abbey of Monte Cassino was perched, although
that ancient structure had been virtually destroyed by Allied aircraft
in the unsuccessful assaults of February. My recollection of the
approach to this historic spot and the ruined town of Cassino
beneath it was of a long night of slowly moving trucks in the first
week of May 1944, a hot but mercifully dry journey. The night
convoys continued and by day vehicles were hidden and camouflaged
in the close countryside of vines and olive groves; meanwhile, the
battle at the Garigliano River crossing thundered up ahead. Two

fortified lines were the targets of our frontal assault, designed to force through the Liri Valley a juncture with the British and American soldiers breaking out of the Anzio bridgehead. I was not conscious of the trials of 13 British Corps in crossing the turbulent river and breaking the heavily fortified Gustav Line. With the help of our First Canadian Armoured Brigade (formerly Army Tank Brigade), the work was done by British and Indian troops in fine style, while the Polish Corps and New Zealand troops scaled the long-invincible Cassino position. The role of the Canadian Corps was to relieve 13 Corps and pursue the enemy to the next fortified line in the Liri Valley, known as the Adolf Hitler Line at least to our troops, although never, it would appear, to the Germans. By May 15, after four days of fighting, the turn of the Canadian Corps had come.

The First Division, after a week's hard fighting over difficult country and with tank support from the North Irish Horse, had closed in on the Hitler Line, its main headquarters well within enemy mortar range. The Hitler Line occupied a formidable position across the Liri Valley, the dominant feature of its defences being the line of concrete emplacements crowned by Panther tank turrets carrying 75-mm guns. The division's task was to break into this position and clear a path for the Fifth Division's armoured brigade to drive through, with its tanks and motorized infantry, to clear the valley and open the road to Rome.

I retain vivid images of this situation. Amid the unnerving noise of bombardment I remember a farmer with a tank strapped to his back, spraying his olive trees and saying a quiet "Permesso?" as he threaded his way through and around the military impedimenta. He had the age-old confidence of peasantry that all plagues would pass and all destruction be repaired. We dug a very deep slit trench for each of our little party and slept well below ground level in the stifling heat, slept in spite of a visit from the Luftwaffe and woke to find not a leaf upon the lovingly sprayed olive trees. Smoke and dust and hellish noise are my abiding impressions of this forty-eight-hour period before the infantry, armed with tommy guns, grenades, and PIAT anti-tank bomb launchers and heralded by the crash of eight hundred guns, moved through the wire and engaged the enemy. The Third Brigade soon secured the objective on the left shoulder of the planned break-out gap, but the Second Brigade, overlooked by the town of Aquino, still in German hands after an unsuccessful attack by 13 Corps, had more difficulty, suffering heavy casualties. All three battalions were pinned to the ground by the guns of the Hitler Line emplacements and artillery directed from Aquino while their tank support withered away. General Vokes, one might think wisely, reinforced the Third Brigade's thrust and, with pressure from the First Brigade's fierce fighting for Pontecorvo on the left flank and the capture of Aquino by British troops on the right, helped secure the gap in the Hitler Line on May 24 through which the Fifth Armoured Brigade began to move. The Fifth Division was commanded by Major-General B.M. Hoffmeister, formerly CO of the Seaforth Highlanders of Canada, and the Fifth Armoured Brigade and its armoured component by Brigadier Desmond Smith, a professional soldier and one-time officer of the Royal Canadian Dragoons. Smith found the exploitation phase unexpectedly hampered by traffic and our own derelict tanks strewn across the battlefield. "Exploitation towards Ceprano" was not the dashing tank action that had been envisaged, and it was brought to a halt at the Melfa River, the next river crossing, secured mainly by the infantry component of the Fifth Division, with the help of a troop of the Horse Guards under Bob Rutherford, later to be my colleague. In due course, the First Division was on the move again, but the Germans had gone from the valley save only the last-ditch defenders entombed in their turreted emplacements, the living and the dead.

Our losses were heavy, as one might expect from a head-on assault on a carefully prepared defensive position; among them, and several days before the final attack, was George Renison while reconnoitring start lines and a position for headquarters of the First Division. His jeep hit a mine, killing his driver, and he suffered such severe wounds that his life was despaired of for many days. He had become chief of staff of the division (GSO 1) and was fortunately spared to continue his brilliant military career as commander of the Hasty P's.

The pursuit, if such a word can accurately describe the forward motion of two corps fighting for space to move forward on one main road, continued against diminishing resistance until Rome was entered rather diplomatically by the Special Service Force, conceived originally for airborne operations, which had a Canadian component, although it was predominantly American. Thus, faces were saved; and in any event the Germans made no attempt to defend the city, unscarred as it was except for a little bomb damage around the central railway station. Although the forward troops had reached Anogni, for practical purposes the First Division was halted at Frosinone and with the rest of the Canadian Corps would be withdrawn into Eighth Army reserve. But there for a day or two we sat looking northward to a road comparatively empty by June 4, the day that the Allied forces entered the Eternal City. Rumours circulated that orders were on the way to prohibit any further movement towards it, and I decided to act for the sake of history.

At an early hour, with Route 6 invitingly empty before us, Sergeant Taylor, my clerk, and I headed for Rome, with Ron Ellis driving. I do not now remember any details of the journey, but our arrival was electrifying. Crowds in holiday mood, intoxicated by the sense of liberation, cheered our little jeep as if we were the vanguard of a new army. Fruit and flowers were thrown into it from all sides and many kisses bestowed. When we broke through this ecstatic welcome, we found a city that would startle its present inhabitants – there was no traffic. In the brilliant sunshine we sped past scenes familiar since childhood in pictures. We crossed the Ponte di San Angelo, and contemplating the magnificent reality of Hadrian's Tomb, I was transported by triumph.

Our explorations included a visit to a bar, and like all the bars in Rome, it was serving free drinks to the Allied soldiery. An attempt to pay was roughly interrupted by a Scottish soldier of the First British Division, which had spent many miserable weeks in the Anzio bridgehead. Across the Tiber – the Trastevere – U.S. Army trucks bore their freight to the brothels. In this grey suburb there were no grapes or flowers, and we sped away across the river to be welcomed by a group of young men who took us to a comfortable house on the Aventine Hill. This house had belonged to a fugitive Fascist minister, and our hosts saw themselves as liberators – they certainly had an impressive collection of weapons. After spending the night, we hastened back next morning to our frustrated fellows at divisional headquarters to meet a sobering problem for the historical officer.

The Canadian Corps, now thoroughly exhausted after hard fighting and cruel losses, when withdrawn into army reserve were once more to inhabit the pleasant and fertile valley of the Volturno River, part

of the aptly named Terra di Lavoro. The incident I will now relate
began before the First Division started its move and ended once
the move was completed. Eric Harrison descended on me with the
news that Brigadier Smith, who had led the Fifth Armoured Brigade
through the Hitler Line and across the Melfa River, had become
brigadier General Staff, at corps headquarters and had expressed
dissatisfaction with the performance of the Second Infantry Brigade in the attack on the Hitler Line fortifications. He had called
in Harrison and ordered him to investigate. Predictably, the burden
of the investigation fell upon me. I hastened to the brigade HQ
where Brigadier Graham Gibson received me in the most friendly
manner. I was careful to emphasize the historical aspect of my
inquiries and was assured of the cooperation of all ranks in recalling and reporting every move of the two battalions, the Seaforths
and the Edmontons, principally involved. The collection and organization of the material furnished to me was laborious but enjoyable. With our limited resources, Sergeant Taylor and I managed
to construct a useful-looking report, illustrated with maps and
plastic overlays to show the positions and movements of our own
and enemy troops, with a detailed account of the fighting. After
this had been triumphantly taken up to corps headquarters and
delivered to Harrison, I was upset to be told by him that Smith was
not satisfied and that further inquiries must be made.

The essence of the brigadier's discontent was that my report was
merely a narrative without a conclusion, and it then dawned on
me that he had a bone to pick with Graham Gibson. Certainly the
thrust of the Fifth Armoured Brigade had been neither as swift nor
as far-reaching as planned, but I felt that I was neither equipped
nor required to express an opinion on the performance of the
fighting troops. I could not for the life of me return to the helpful
people at the Second Brigade with more questions, giving them
the impression that what was vouchsafed for the historical record
was to be used against them by higher authority. As I saw it, I had
finished my inquiries. So I took heroic action: I went to see my
general. Chris Vokes listened to my story with mounting irritation
and at the end said, with accompanying expletives, "Leave this to
me." I heard no more of the matter and was quite pleased with
myself. But on reflection, it now seems to me that whatever the
motive behind this initiative of the brigadier General Staff, it was

an intelligent use of an historical section in the field. Even though we had become used to having our role misunderstood, we had often contemplated a closer association with operations as they occurred. Though Brigadier Smith's use of me might be more suggestive of the German General Staff than of our own, it was recognition of a kind that we could not deny having sought.

Now it became apparent that my time in Italy was drawing to an end, but before I went back to England to start writing I visited the headquarters of AAI, now moved from Casarta to Rome, to look at its records and get an idea of the "big picture" in this part of the Mediterranean theatre of war. I was fortunate beyond measure to have this time in the great city in spite of the appalling summer heat from which even the pope takes refuge in the Alban Hills.

I managed once to escape to the outskirts of Florence to drive a friend back to the Three Rivers Regiment, which, as usual with units of the Army Tank Brigade, was supporting British infantry. We bowled along the highway from Arezzo towards the other famous city which all my life I have only seen at a distance. As we approached, we suddenly noticed soldiers, with foliage in their helmets, crouched in the ditches alongside the road, some of them looking at us in astonishment. A very sharp explosion accompanied by clouds of dirt brought us to a halt, and we left the jeep in order to look at the valley below. We saw broken bridges but the Ponte Vecchio was erect and apparently untouched. I did not then know of the devastation created by the Germans, who had spared the bridge but blown down the approaches to it and destroyed virtually all that was left of Dante's Florence.

I returned to Rome and met on separate occasions John Brown, one-time captain of the Balliol Boat Club, an Etonian with a gruff exterior and a home in Dublin, now a major in the Royal Artillery. I also contacted Louise Jamieson, Helen's lifelong friend and a Canadian nursing sister who had transferred to the South African Defence Force to fill the desperate need for nurses at the beginning of the war. She had arrived with a field hospital to sustain the Sixth South African Armoured Division, which had passed through us to maintain the pursuit of the enemy northward from Rome, a race the Germans were bound to win because they knew where they were going and had no intention of stopping south of the Pisa-Rimini line. In northern Italy before the end of the campaign, she was to suffer what might have been a permanent injury from an exploding spirit lamp, and I did not see her again till my return to Canada.

When the time came in August to return to England, I determined to go by sea so as not to be separated from my kit, the fate of so many air travellers, and drove to Naples to await transportation. This time I travelled by the Appian Way along the coast, and saw the Pontine marshes, so dramatically drained and colonized by Mussolini's government, newly flooded by the Germans with only the rooftops of modern farmhouses showing above the waters. After a refreshing sea voyage, I arrived back in England, passing through many hands, transit camps, and the ingenuities of Movement Control, to a joyous reunion with Helen, who had booked us into Duff Cooper's suite at the top of the Dorchester Hotel. From our room, we were able to see the strange, pilotless-V.1's, the enemy's flying bombs, rumbling over London, and would hold our breath, waiting for the silence which preceded touchdown and shattering blast. I could understand why this fashionable hotel was practically uninhabited. The bombardment of these weapons, which had succeeded that of the Luftwaffe, finally discouraged even the stoutest hearts, leaving nerves very much on edge.

Now there was to appear a weapon whose arrival had been foreshadowed even before I left for the Mediterranean, foreshadowed indeed by my old Trinity friend Bob Wodehouse of Ottawa. Bob had been involved in the photo reconnaissance work which had detected enemy activity on the island of Peenemünde, the birthplace of the V-2. This weapon was the first of the rocket missiles and had been intended to be first in the field, but because of the devastating raid by the Royal Air Force (RAF) on Peenemünde their development had been stalled and the V-1 had been perfected ahead of it. But when the V-2 came, it was unnerving. With no premonitory rumbling or trailing of fire, travelling at many times the speed of sound, it was a fearful explosion in our midst. One day I remember six fell in the centre of London, one of which almost uprooted our war artists in Lincoln's Inn Fields. More frightening because of its sudden and unpredictable appearance, the V-2 was in fact less damaging than the V-1, digging a deep hole for itself and causing an explosion more localized and less destructive than that of the V-1, which landed relatively softly and with a deadly lateral blast, causing much damage to life and property. And then there came the day when these missiles, which might have made life unendurable in London, suddenly stopped coming, their launching sites overrun by our armies. The last winter of the war settled into quiet nights and the knowledge that if victory was postponed it was inevitable in the new year.

CHAPTER TEN

The Way Back

Helen was working at the Red Cross canteen in British Columbia House on Lower Regent Street, and I returned to the Historical Section at headquarters with a mandate to write; my task was in accordance with Stacey's plan and it would prevent me from leaving England for the duration of the war and some time thereafter. We found a pleasant small flat in a large apartment house on Sloane Avenue called, of all things, Nell Gwynn House. At British Columbia House was the Agent-General William MacAdam, a delightful Scottish Canadian, who with his wife took an avuncular interest in the girls of the Canadian Red Cross detachment in his building. These women worked hard feeding and providing a haven for soldiers of all armies, and most of them had husbands or fiancés on active service. Casualties in the Canadian forces had become serious, particularly in the army and the RCAF, and many of the young women laboured with a heavy heart. Because I had been in Italy, I had escaped the cold of England's winter of 1943–44, unrelieved by insufficient fire and food, not to mention the mini-blitz of February 1944 when the Germans had sent fast fighter bombers on hit-and-run raids to London. The Canadian Red Cross Corps had had their hands full on this occasion and had done their share of rooftop air-raid watch in an area inflicted with much damage. When in the spring of 1945 our friends the MacAdams asked us to spend a forty-eight-hour leave at their cottage in Surrey, the rest, fine weather, and sense of security had a tonic effect, and

Helen achieved the pregnancy which had eluded us before. This was a very happy time and we made many friends.

In the meantime I had become a major and was writing drafts for the official history of the Italian campaign. I have already referred to the book *From Pachino to Ortona*, which Stacey and I completed in six weeks but which was not released from Ottawa until almost two years thereafter. Its writing was an enjoyable experience, and upon its completion Stacey embarked with his wonderful energy upon two more such narratives, one entitled *The Canadians in Britain, 1939–44* and the other *Canada's Battle in Normandy*. These three productions, beautifully illustrated and produced by the King's Printer, however tardily, were the first official accounts of operations vouchsafed to a hungry public at home.

London, which Winston Churchill was to describe as a great rhinoceros in celebration of its ability to "take it," was sadly worn down by over five years of food rationing, restrictions on recreation, fuel rationing, and bombardment; and the gaps where familiar buildings had stood in the once tidy, even elegant, city were constant reminders of deprivation and bereavement. In the City, once the proud heart of a great commercial empire, a huge area eastward of St Paul's Cathedral was a featureless desert. The cathedral itself had suffered damage, and many of the delicate Wren churches were in ruins. In the Temple, dear to the servants of the common law throughout the world, among much defacement the Temple church was roofless and the master's house a pile of rubble. Only the steady success of our armies relieved the despondency which might, had it been prolonged into another winter, been a disaster only a little less terrible than the revenge wreaked upon Germany by the avenging Allies. Upon this forbidding prospect the huge release of VE-Day shed warmth and brilliant light.

Yet there were no yells of triumph. From a window high above the Haymarket I watched a great silent river of people moving slowly down to Trafalgar Square and Whitehall, the lucky ones to hear Winston Churchill pour out his heart from the roof of a taxi and to get close to the gates of Buckingham Palace. Solemnity was the order of this unforgettable day.

The end of the war in Europe created its own emergencies. For me personally there were two, Helen's future as a mother and my own, immediately as a military historian and ultimately as a lawyer.

For the first and most pressing, we decided that our progeny should be born in Canada and that immediate steps should be taken for repatriation of its mother. Indeed "repatriation" was now all the rage. I had written a pamphlet for the army with the lacklustre title of "After Victory – What?" "First in, first out" was the golden rule, but the wives of servicemen had especial priority, and inevitably most of those seeking passage to Canada were British born. The ever-efficient Ministry of Food supplied Helen with richly encreamed milk, a luxury to which rarities such as whisky and wine took a back seat and which, after her departure, continued to appear for some days for consumption by me and by an occasional deserving friend, like Ev Broderick, recently sprung from Stalag Luft 3. Alas! On the day the legitimate object of this benefaction left by train for Liverpool, I could only find for her sustenance a nectarine nestled into a plush box like a precious jewel, which I believe it turned out to be before its owner reached the refreshment stands at Crewe in a famished condition.

With the retirement of Colonel Duguid, Stacey, now with the rank of full colonel, presided not only over the work in London but over the source of its authority in Ottawa. George Stanley left England to return to Ottawa as assistant director of the Historical Section with the rank of lieutenant-colonel. Subsequently, after VE-Day and after Helen had departed, I was offered the same promotion to manage the postwar section in London. The temptation to accept was very great. Stacey said that it would be a shame if Sir Sam Hughes's grandson were to be less than a lieutenant-colonel; yet I well knew that the law firm in Welland, and especially its head, was anxious for me to return, to qualify and join it. Stacey prevailed and in due course the management of the Historical Section's business overseas fell to me, bringing my writing on the mainland campaign in Italy to a halt somewhat short of Campobasso.

Many decisions had to be made, not only in the writing program but in such things as the supervision of the collection of enemy weapons for the National War Museum in Ottawa. We commissioned two officers with the desired piratical instincts: Captain Kenneth A. Cottam, an accomplished German-speaking intelligence officer of the British army, a large and genial Yorkshireman who had been with the First Division in Italy; and Captain Farley Mowat, to whom I have referred. They toured northwest Europe a jump ahead of their British and American competitors, commandeering weapons, vehicles, and even a miniature submarine for our collection, and sleeping in the middle of sandbagged positions at night, well wired in against predators. Through my quartermaster and Movement Control friends I was able to secure a ship to transport these acquisitions to Ottawa, where I regret to say they rusted for several years in Plouffe Park before the War Museum could look after them. The denouement of this enterprise was the appearance of a brigadier from Canada with a face to match his scarlet tabs. This individual informed me of the displeasure of National Defence Headquarters and told me that I owed the Government of Canada something in the order of $350,000. It is not easy to indulge in respectful laughter but I tried. In the end all was for the best.

Stacey, now wearing the ribbon of the Order of the British Empire and having succeeded in getting one for both Stanley and Harrison, tried to get one for me but failed when the sinister bulk of my file was disclosed to authority. His generosity and good offices in all his dealings with me were of the first order, and during this period we became close friends. He was an avid moving picture-goer and I think we must have seen, when off duty, nearly every cinematic production in the metropolitan area. Yet he was a frugal man and excess in any other direction was sternly repressed.

In these months after my return from Italy I enjoyed the companionship and the support of richly endowed colleagues who would become famous as historians: Jim Conacher, who later adorned the history department at Toronto; Mac Hitsman, who battled chronic ill health to be a mainstay of the Historical Section at Ottawa until he died; John Porter, who later graced Carleton University; and John Spurr, custodian of much arcane lore culled from the *Almanach de Gotha*, who became librarian at the Royal Military College in Kingston. John Porter credited me with teaching him how to write narrative history, a compliment he also extended, and more deservedly, to Stacey. I remember all these men with affection and regard but I especially remember Gerald Graham.

Gerry came to us from the navy, where he had been a lieutenant-commander in one of its special branches (I think Education). On transfer to the army he became a major and to me a stimulating companion and close friend. A relentless pipe and cigar smoker (he pinned cigar bands to his correspondence with friends in Canada), he was a profound scholar who hid a great deal of light under his bushel. His conversation, always on the verge of laughter, was a treat, and his engaging personality completely without pomposity or affectation. Those who found him frivolous – and Stacey was one – had never lunched with him at the United Services Institution, the senior officers' club once confronting the Athenaeum in Hamilton Place, and observed the regard – even deference – paid to him by admirals, whose profession had been illuminated and extolled by his profound scholarship. Stacey never liked Gerry, mentioning his name without comment in his autobiography. He may have felt that Gerry had used his friendship with General Stuart to secure his transfer from the navy to the Historical Section in order to prolong his stay in England. It is true that Gerry wanted to be in England. He and his wife had long been estranged and his heart was now in the hands of a gifted Canadian member of the British intelligence community, whom he later married.

Now, for obvious reasons, he did not wish to return to Queen's or Kingston and had decided to seek academic employment in England. I was privy to many agonizing confidences about his situation and was delighted when my Balliol tutor, Humphrey Sumner, about to leave his post as professor of history at the University of Edinburgh to become warden of All Souls College at Oxford, offered the Edinburgh professorship to Gerry. I thought that this was recognition with a vengeance and expected him to accept at once, but I had not taken into account the depth of his devotion to one who could not be released from her intelligence work in London. He declined the position, but was later offered the Rhodes Professorship of Imperial History in the University of London and began a career where he was emotionally at peace and intellectually supreme. When he died many years later, leading journals in many lands and many tongues celebrated his scholarship and influence.

The dilemma that had confronted me with gathering intensity – not should I leave the army but when – was dispelled in January 1946 when, after a bewildering bout of what appeared to be influenza, I was driven in a military staff car to No. 23 General Hospital at Bramshott with an acute attack of jaundice. My kit was offloaded and deposited in the entrance hall and I, feeling miserable, looked around for some help. In short order I was confronted by a magisterial-looking matron who said, "Pick that up and follow me." Almost at once I felt better. I got a room for myself and slept for many hours. A month or so later, after my blood had responded to a low-fat diet, I was advised to go on convalescent leave. I was able to remain in the hospital for my convalescence and enjoy the abundant rations and the abundance of books supplied by the Red Cross. When I returned to London, I found that Stacey had yielded with good grace to representations made for my discharge from the army.

I left England in glorious spring weather, embowered it seemed in flowers and greenery, and on April 17, 1946, I gingerly stepped off the ss *Lady Nelson* into the heavy fog of Halifax. Next morning I woke in the sleeping car of the train to Toronto in dazzling sunlight and deep snow. I asked the porter where we were and he said, "Oxford Junction." We had travelled about halfway to Truro in the course of a night of heavy snowfall that had paralysed the divisional signals. The following day or perhaps the day after I was reunited with Helen in the Coliseum at Exhibition Park in Toronto. Then, in the lovely surroundings of her father's house, Spencerwood, high above the valley of Twelve Mile Creek, I was introduced to the daughter I had not yet seen, born just before Christmas in the previous year, Lynn.

CHAPTER ELEVEN

Return to the Law

When declining the second of two opportunities to enter the diplomatic service, the first having been offered on my return from Oxford, I had said airily that my one ambition was to practise law in a small town in Ontario. Now I was to be put to the test, but first a final year of study and examination was required. As predicted, the benchers of the Law Society of Upper Canada had awarded me my second year, which had been prematurely concluded by my going on active service in 1941. I had at my disposal my gratuity and an allowance of ninety-eight dollars a month from the Department of Veterans' Affairs, a significant sum in days when the dollar was worth many times what it is today. I became a student in the firm of Raymond and Honsberger (the Raymond of this firm having been a brother of Colonel Raymond in Welland), and Helen, Lynn, and I found an agreeable habitation with my uncle Byron Green on Foxbar Road in Toronto.

I was once more a pupil, not the most natural role for someone aged thirty-three who had just spent five years in the army. Adjustments had to be made. I was happy as a student in Stanley Honsberger's firm with his sons John and Hugh. And it was easy to be happy in this season of promise reunited with Helen and Lynn (named after her grandfather Lynn Spencer), who laid down the law from her playpen. Once again I had the experience of being a member of a new generation of students, although a great number of those called to the bar in 1947 were veterans in two senses of the word. Among them was another lifelong friend, Eddie Goodman, destined to have a brilliant career at the bar and to make an equally brilliant contribution to political life in Canada as a member and organizer of the Progressive Conservative party. Another was John Robarts, who was to practise law in London, Ontario, then to become premier, and thereafter to practise in Toronto until the day of his death. Eddie had been an accomplished tank commander in the Fort Garry Horse and had been severely wounded in Normandy. John had been a seagoing officer in the Royal Canadian Navy, latterly serving in the Pacific against the Japanese. Most of us, I think, had seen service during the war, and we must have been a strange and perhaps intimidating group to those who were trying to teach us law. But we were eager and eminently tractable, anxious to begin its practice.

In the spring of 1947 the end of this extended pupillage finally came. Stan Honsberger spent a whole day going through the Rules of Practice with me. He felt guilty that he had not paid more attention to me as a student, but I felt only gratitude for the day-long effort on the part of this busy practitioner. One or two of my final examinations were written in a room on the top floor of the old Osgoode Hall building, its windows looking directly at the clock tower of the City Hall. Albert Shepherd, sitting ahead of me, wrote industriously and successfully (he took honours), while I could not take my eyes off the remorselessly revolving hands of the great clock and as a result had an undistinguished passing mark. Most discouraging of all was my paper in Constitutional Law, a course taught by Bora Laskin, an old friend of university days and an oarsman to boot. I had followed the lead of Lords Watson and Haldane in their interpretation of the British North America Act, which had increased the powers of the provinces at the expense of the federal government. Bora was then and all his life a federalist and he gave me a mark of 51 per cent. I was upset and went hotfoot to expostulate. While he was explaining to me how wrong I had been, we were visited by Cecil Augustus Wright (known to generations of students as "Caesar" and soon to be dean of the Law School), who was made privy to our discussion. I was pleased that Caesar reproached Bora for trying to be a crusader rather than an impartial examiner, but I did not get a better mark. When Bora became chief justice of Canada, he took a better view of my work.

And so with a host of friends I was in due course called to the Bar
of Ontario and enrolled as a solicitor of the Supreme Court. I was
thirty-four years old.

The city of Welland was actually a small industrial town owing its
lofty status to those provisions of the Ontario Municipal Act that
permitted any town with more than ten thousand inhabitants to
apply for and receive recognition as a city by the provincial government. Welland was indeed the "county town" of the industrially
important county of the same name. Welland County consisted of
all that southerly portion of the Niagara Peninsula above the
escarpment and contained the city of Niagara Falls, the town of
Fort Erie, the town of Port Colborne, and the town of Thorold as
well as the city of Welland. It was bisected by the Welland Canal
and crossed eastward and westward by three trunk railway lines, all
of them American, using what the New York Central called the
"water level route" to the Middle West. Indeed, a fourth line of the
Toronto, Hamilton and Buffalo Railway used the Welland railway
station in transit to and from the points indicated by its title, the
station and the line itself belonging to the New York Central
Railway. The new city had extensive suburbs outside its boundaries,
townships which were eyed covetously as targets for annexation.

Perhaps I will be forgiven for dwelling on the appearance of the
peninsula as it was in the fifth decade of the twentieth century.
The absurdity of regional government, a bureaucratic experiment
by the provincial Department of Municipal Affairs, has obliterated
two historic counties and many of their landmarks. Lincoln County
below the Niagara escarpment with its Lake Ontario littoral and
Welland County to the south with its wonderful beaches washed
by Lake Erie, incontinently swept away, have become the Judicial
District of Niagara North and the Judicial District of Niagara South
respectively. It would have been easy to preserve the names Lincoln
and Welland in this disposition, but it was evidently decided to
leave the bitterest of all possible tastes in the mouths of descendants of the pioneers whose efforts had called these counties into
being. The earliest arrivals had come to Lincoln County, the Loyalists who during and after the American Revolution had settled

on its fertile soil. A generation later the stubborn clay of Welland County had been broken up and tilled by largely Pennsylvania Dutch settlers. Both these communities had developed a basic political loyalty: Lincoln County had become a favourite hunting ground for Tories and Welland County one for Reformers, as the Liberals of the day were then called. I speak with feeling about the latter because, as I shall relate, I would later cast my bread upon the political waters of Welland County without avail. I do not suggest that the pioneer families of these two counties still dominated the scene, but I am sure that a tradition of political adherence based on heredity in the first place had for many years dictated the result in dominion and provincial elections.

The influence of the American border on the whole Niagara frontier was palpable but much more so in its Welland County portion from Niagara Falls to Fort Erie than on the peaceful parks and vineyards below the great gorge of the Niagara River. Before the war Welland County had been *terra incognita* to Toronto and barely more familiar to Hamilton. Buffalo was the big city and its prosperous citizens had almost pre-empted the beaches to which I have referred by building impressive summer houses and cottages all the way west to the Haldimand County line. Over the years American industrialists had established branch plants in Canada so that they might enjoy relief from the Canadian tariffs and the imperial preference. They had been cautious about doing more than stray across the border, and the Niagara frontier, with its abundance of hydro-electric power, its portage position between two great lakes, and its convenient railway connections with the industrial east of the United States, was a magnet for heavy industry. The future of the frontier had of course been clouded by the gridding of electrical power for which Sir Adam Beck had acquired a great reputation, which diminished the industrial attractions of the peninsula by providing cheap power far and wide around Ontario. Beck's crusade had been fiercely resisted in consequence and by none more cogently than L.B. Spencer of Welland.

Local law firms in Welland County with any pretensions to expertise in corporation law had many clients in Buffalo and Niagara Falls, New York, not the least of which were American law firms that had developed connections with their Canadian counterparts. Into this busy and resourceful environment I stepped – fully qualified if not fully fledged – in the spring of 1947 and became an associate of Raymond, Spencer, Law and MacInnes, barristers and solicitors of Welland.

This firm, the oldest in the county, had its origins in the village of Chippawa, where Lorenzo Raymond had begun to practise law in 1835. He had subsequently moved to Welland and was succeeded by his son, our senior partner Colonel L.C. Raymond. Of L.B. Spencer I have already spoken. Robert Brown Law, whose father had been a professor at Knox College in the University of Toronto, had come with his family to Canada from Scotland and first practised law in Red Deer, Alberta. Like so many veterans of the first great war, he never returned to the West but joined the short-lived Board of Commerce in Ottawa as a civil service solicitor when he left the army. From there he moved with his friend C. Fraser Elliot to the Income Tax Branch, which had been called into being by the Income War Tax Act of 1917. Elliot went on to be deputy minister of national revenue, taxation, while Law became L.B. Spencer's partner and moved with his family to Welland. Somewhat uneasy as an advocate, Law was deeply versed in the accountant's art and the principles and practice of taxation. I give one example of how his reputation grew in his later years in Welland. One of our largest Buffalo clients was concerned with a tax problem affecting its Canadian subsidiary in Kitchener. Although the Buffalo management were loyal to their Welland solicitors, they felt that this matter was of such complexity that it might better be handled by a big Toronto firm. They therefore advised their Kitchener counterparts to get the best advice available in the province. No names were mentioned, but the Canadian company was given a free hand. In due course, its thus-instructed officers arrived in Welland to consult Mr Law.

Stewart Sawle MacInnes was a short and stocky flying wing on a famous Queen's University football team of the twenties, an able and industrious lawyer, not much given to speculation. At the time of my arrival he was handling most of the litigation of the firm. He was the fourth partner in order of seniority and had been just too old for active service in the late war, but had served in the militia battalion of the Lincoln and Welland Regiment. He was shortly to become the third partner because Colonel Raymond was soon to retire from practice.

In effect, L.B. Spencer had been the senior partner and director of the firm's affairs for several years. During the war and in consequence of a substantial increase in business, he had persuaded his nephew Theodore Grenfell Spencer to leave his practice in Delhi and join the firm as an associate. Ted Spencer's cheerful disposition and charm soon established him as one of the busiest conveyancers in the county. Around this galaxy I slowly began to revolve and learn my trade. And a year later, on June 16, 1948, Samuel Garnet Spencer Hughes was born.

Almost at once this event prompted me to become an expert in a field of considerable activity but few prospects. These were the rental regulations which were devised by the Wartime Prices and Trade Board of Ottawa, but on the cessation of hostilities had devolved upon the provinces. Since my father-in-law and his wife had moved to "Spencerwood," his house on Merritt Street in Welland had been given to Helen and remodelled to provide two apartments, both of which were occupied. One set of tenants were old friends and we were ready to extend their tenure, but we hoped to obtain the other apartment for ourselves. This was resisted by its occupants, who relied upon the regulations to protect their tenancy from termination. Accordingly, I set about learning these regulations and taking proceedings to compel the not unnaturally recalcitrant occupants to vacate upon proper notice. Shortly I found myself consulted, not only from various points in the county but also from a wider neighbourhood, by people with similar problems for whom I appeared before the rental tribunals. I eventually succeeded on our own behalf and enjoyed fair success on behalf of others in loosening the regulatory grip which was keeping many returned servicemen and women out of their property. Eventually the regulations were repealed and my peculiar source of business dried up.

As almost always happens, the neophyte in any law firm cuts his teeth in court, an exercise I enjoyed. My experience as a schoolmaster and my campaigning for Leslie Frost before the war had given me a readiness of address that served me well, and I soon learned to mix my didactic offerings with the necessary deference which judges required and indeed were entitled to. The local bar was fortunate in its county judge, Harold Fuller, before his appointment a practitioner in Sarnia; clear-headed, incisive, and prompt, he did not suffer fools gladly. As a result he was an excellent teacher.

I had two old and contemporary friends at the Welland County Bar, David Cromarty, a Trinity classmate who was with the rival firm of German, Brooks and Cowper in Welland, and Franklin Griffiths of Zeta Psi, who had commanded the Highland Light Infantry of Canada in France and practised with his father's firm in Niagara Falls. He in his turn was to become county court judge in Welland. I made many more friends in the course of practice and indeed we were a companionable lot. Where lawyers in Toronto would make motions, serve papers, and strike attitudes at the drop of a hat, we found it easy to argue and settle matters over cups of coffee and through clouds of tobacco smoke. Heavens, how we smoked in those days! My father had taught me how to smoke a pipe at the age of fifteen in order to defend me against cigarettes, but the defence was only partially successful. During the war, tobacco companies seduced a whole generation by selling three hundred cigarettes for a dollar to those of us overseas. These we would readily buy on the rare occasions when we were not getting masses of them as presents from our relatives and friends in Canada. But on the whole I have been loyal to the pipe until recent years.

My first steps in the practice of law were matched by a renewed interest in politics. War service had halted my political activity in the Conservative party, and in the interval much had happened in Ontario. The Liberal party's hold on power in the province, paramount while Mitchell Hepburn was its leader, was broken in 1943 by George Drew. Against strong CCF opposition provided by E.B. Joliffe, a friend of mine in university days, Drew led his minority government to a complete victory in the election of 1945. He was tall, handsome, and eloquent, his erect carriage and imposing front habitual because of a shoulder shattered in the First World War. His political enemies, unknowing or uncaring, would mock him as a "stuffed shirt," but among his supporters and friends he inspired devotion. After five years of a successful premiership he would go to Ottawa and become leader of the Progressive Conservative Party of Canada, inheriting the post from John Bracken, formerly Liberal Progressive premier of Manitoba, and begin almost a decade of brilliant performance in the House of Commons without the mastery which he sought. I was a delegate at the convention in Ottawa which chose him as leader by a substantial majority over a rising parliamentarian from Saskatchewan, John George Diefenbaker. Helen and I went down to Ottawa on the train, and at the convention I made a speech containing a large proportion of French which was carefully rehearsed and carefully extemporized.

Having got my foot in the door as it were, I was encouraged by friends in Welland to campaign for the Progressive Conservative nomination to contest the general election of 1949. Louis St Laurent was the new prime minister of Canada confronted by George Drew, the new leader of the Opposition. Welland County had been represented by Liberals in Ottawa since 1935, and Tory prospects were not encouraging. But for a newcomer with nothing to lose, except, as my colleagues pointed out, the prospect of a successful law practice, and with the vigorous support of a ginger group in the city of Welland led by my friend Harry Holcomb, success seemed within my reach. I was given strong support and encouragement by W.S. Martin in Niagara Falls, head of the largest law firm in that city, deep-voiced and eloquent and a friend of the family. My father-in-law, who had made sacrifices to establish me in practice, was justifiably dubious about another divergence from the professional path but in the end allowed his affection to overcome his doubts. The way was clear, and after being nominated at the convention by Bill Martin in ringing terms, I won without difficulty.

For many weeks I had been attending small party meetings around the large riding in towns and villages and country school-houses and had become a familiar if untried figure. The association in Niagara Falls, always more conspicuous in political activity than those in other parts of the county, held a dinner at the General Brock Hotel at which I shared the spotlight with the attorney general of Ontario, the Honourable Leslie Blackwell. Blackwell, a native of Lindsay, had practised law successfully in Toronto and had been attorney general since George Drew's success in 1943. Drew's successor, Colonel T.L. Kennedy, in recognition of his long service and seniority had been premier of the province for a couple of years and was on the point of resignation. At this dinner my principal supporters expressed great enthusiasm for Blackwell's

declared determination to run for the leadership of the Progressive
Conservative party in the legislature and consequently to become
premier, or rather prime minister, as the leader of the provincial
government in those days was officially styled. I had heard that
Leslie Frost, who had been minister of mines and provincial treasurer in the years since 1943, was being urged to throw his hat
into the ring and I explained to Leslie Blackwell that I would be
glad to support him provided Frost was not a contender. He was
quite good-humoured about this, only pointing out that Frost, so
prominent now as a resident of Lindsay, had been born and raised
in Orillia and that he, Blackwell, was Lindsay born and bred.

My reservations were justified when Les Frost called me a few
days later, announced his candidacy, and asked me to nominate
him at the forthcoming provincial convention. I felt greatly
honoured, but I pointed out that as a newly chosen federal candidate I should consult my friends who had been so overwhelmingly
attracted to the Blackwell camp. Les was good enough to agree to
this, and the following day I sought L.B. Spencer's advice. He
looked at me with a mixture of amusement and disbelief and with
a few well-chosen words scouted my scruples and sent me to the
telephone to accept the invitation of Leslie Frost, which I did with
pleasure and eventually profit.

At the leadership convention in Toronto there were four contenders – and I apologize if there were more whom I do not remember – Blackwell, Frost, Dana Porter, and Kelso Roberts. Porter, a
polished Toronto lawyer and my senior at Balliol by a decade, had
been minister of planning and development. Although not a front
runner, he was a figure of consequence in the party, as was Roberts,
the fourth candidate, on this occasion a bitter foe of Frost, the
author of the Charitable Gifts Act. Both Blackwell and Porter were
handicapped as representatives of Toronto constituencies, and
Frost, though a late starter in the race, soon marshalled behind
him the great rural strength of the party, particularly in the Midland
and eastern districts of Ontario, that would maintain it in office for
forty years. The handicap is well illustrated by George Drew's defeat
in the Parkdale riding of Toronto in 1945 in spite of leading his
party to a commanding majority in the legislature.

Looking back, I think that Frost was in no danger of defeat, but
my role as nominator was considered of great importance and the

text of my speech was carefully scrutinized by the Conservative hierarchs, particularly F.G. Gardiner and A.D. McKenzie. Frost's victory and assumption of the premiership was well received throughout the province, and in 1951 he won a decisive victory for his government at the polls. Leslie Blackwell, who, like Frost, had a solid record from the 1914 war and carried an artificial leg as a result with increasing difficulty, retired from public life to practise law successfully for the few remaining years of his life; Dana Porter, who had run a distant third in the convention, went on to be attorney general and provincial treasurer and finally chief justice of Ontario. Kelso Roberts redeemed himself and became attorney general in due season.

My modest performance in this critical episode in Ontario's political history opened many doors to a junior lawyer in a part of Ontario so often overlooked politically and economically by Toronto. My friendship with Eddie Goodman and his friendship with Alec McKenzie made this period of my political activity a memorable experience. McKenzie, the inspired and all powerful president of the Ontario Progressive Conservative Association, had been a gold medallist at Osgoode Hall in the year when David Goodman, Eddie's father, had won the silver medal, and his liking for the father was even exceeded by his liking for the son, who was his friend and confidant for many years.

The dominion general election now impended. The Liberal party put up Humphrey Mitchell, a leading trade unionist and a former mayor of Hamilton, as their candidate for the Welland riding, already its MP since the by-election of 1942 to replace the late A.B. Damude. Mitchell was minister of labour at Ottawa, and any handicap he suffered as a carpet-bagger was offset by the advantage for the local Liberals of having a cabinet minister representing the riding. The socialist CCF candidate was my friend Armour McCrae, a popular alderman in the city of Welland, a natural orator of astonishing powers who would later command impressive fees for speaking at conventions and other functions in the United States.

The Progressive Conservative party was not rich after nearly fifteen years of opposition, and I received very little financial support from headquarters but generous support from local sources. Since this was George Drew's first general election as leader, he was much in demand as a speaker across Canada, and the best thing I could have done was to grace the platform of his large meeting at Hamilton. Instead of this I wrote to John Diefenbaker, whom I barely knew, but who in response to my request came to Welland and made an impressive speech in the hockey arena. I was surprised that he could come so readily, but he told me that he was not being used by party headquarters and was only speaking for people who had written to him and for other friends across Canada. The party erred, I think, in not using Diefenbaker. Diefenbaker was not a team player and always resented George Drew's success, but he was beginning to be accepted as a man of excellent parliamentary talents and a force on the Prairies, which had been sadly underrepresented in the Conservative party for many years.

On polling day Humphrey Mitchell was not to be denied and I ran a respectable second. My campaign manager had been George Inglis, a First World War veteran of great popularity in Niagara Falls, where he had been mayor for many years, and my official agent and manager of all my financial and legal affairs had been Stewart MacInnes, who had loyally cast aside his disapproval of my candidacy (I was, after all, only a fledgling lawyer) and worked his hardest for my election. As it turned out, that candidacy helped my usefulness as a junior in the firm because all of a sudden I was well known. And as the supposed favourite of the premier of Ontario, I quickly became much in demand for licences, franchises, and agencies in the gift of his government. Moreover, the death of Harry Lewis, the provincial member for the Welland riding, and the incapacity of Carl Hanniwell, provincial member for the Niagara Falls riding, in effect gave me the provincial patronage for the whole county as a defeated Progressive Conservative candidate, something which had to be handled judiciously. I am afraid I must have become a burden to my friends in Toronto and particularly to Leslie Frost.

The Welland riding consisted of all of Welland County including, as I have said, the cities of Welland and Niagara Falls and the towns of Port Colborne, Thorold, and Fort Erie as well as some heavily urbanized townships like Stamford, Crowland, and Humberstone. It had some seventy-five polling stations, all of which had to be furnished with inside and outside scrutineers on election day. I do not now recall the exact number of people entitled to vote, but in this respect it was one of the largest constituencies in Canada. It was therefore a shock when barely a year after the strenuous general election of 1949 Humphrey Mitchell died, and in view of the sweeping victory of the Liberal party under Louis St Laurent the year before, nobody was anxious to fight a by-election in an obviously losing cause. But I could not resist the urgent exhortations of George Drew, particularly when he assured me that the party would pay all the expenses of a by-election up to $25,000, which in those days was a great sum. Accordingly, my candidacy was endorsed by acclamation and I found myself facing a popular physician who had been mayor of Thorold, Dr W.H. MacMillan, as the Liberal candidate.

This time the level of activity in the riding was much higher and the atmosphere very different. The by-election was the first test of a St Laurent government and thus almost every Opposition frontbencher and several cabinet ministers descended on the riding and campaigned with intensity. Eddie Goodman and Rod MacAlpine were with me almost full time. Charles Dubin took time out from his busy practice in Toronto to visit the Canadian Furnace Company in Port Colborne and solicit the support of the Mine, Mill Workers Union (he was the hero of the great legal battle which had saved it from extinction). George Hees, an old friend of Zeta Psi days, Ellen Fairclough, later to be the first woman cabinet minister in Canada, Leon Balcer from Trois Rivières, and Michael Starr from Oshawa all came, the last two to visit the French and Ukrainian Canadian communities in the city of Welland and its environs. George Drew called and said that he would crawl on his hands and knees along East Main Street if it would help but he had been advised not to enter the riding for fear of bringing in the then immensely popular St Laurent and provoking a head-on confrontation. I respected this decision, although I now think it was a mistake, and a few years later such a confrontation would have been a master stroke. But Leslie Frost, still untested as prime minister of Ontario at the provincial polls, took a different view about entering the fray; he came in and made an important speech specifically about the completion of a road on the west side of the Welland Canal which I had advocated, and generally in support of my campaign. I felt enormous gratitude at this demonstration then and I feel it now.

It was all to no avail. On polling day there was initially great excitement when the first results showed that I had won the polls on the west side of Port Colborne where my friend Joe Harris, afterward to be sheriff of the county, had given me great support and had arranged one of my successful meetings. But after that, except in the village of Crystal Beach, the results ran strongly in favour of my Liberal opponent, Bill MacMillan. One unexpected development gave our battle-weary supporters great comfort. Compared with the general election results, both the Liberal and CCF vote had declined while ours had remained almost exactly the same. This was commented upon far and wide, particularly in view of the fact that the government had sent in the redoubtable C.D. Howe to intimidate local factory owners and businessmen, as well as the minister of labour, Milton Gregg, and the minister of veterans' affairs, Ian MacKenzie. Mr Howe was not popular in our domestic circle. He had persuaded the president of Atlas Steels to dismiss L.B. Spencer as general counsel because of Spencer's activity on behalf of an independent Liberal candidate when Humphrey Mitchell was first elected in the 1942 by-election. This was small gratitude for the man who had negotiated all the wartime contracts for high-grade specialty steel upon which the company's fortunes had risen to a dizzying height. Howe's many useful qualities did not include magnanimity, and he went so far as to visit various industrialists and warn them of the dangers of giving me any financial support. One of them, my next-door neighbour Desmond Weir, head of Canada Foundries and Forging, a lifelong Liberal, showed the minister the door and immediately doubled his contribution to my campaign funds, a testimonial of a friendship which endured till his untimely death.

One of my difficulties in the by-election was that the *Niagara Falls Review*, a local newspaper which circulated in the eastern part of the riding, would not report any of my activities, although they had no scruples about taking my money for advertisements. The reason for this was not a credit to journalism. I had conducted a libel suit against the *Review*, which had misrepresented the facts when reporting a robbery and had damaged the reputation of a working man, causing him economic loss. At that time, the Libel and Slander Act (not then replaced by the Defamation Act) provided that any action against a newspaper must be commenced by the delivery of a notice setting out the nature of the complaint, so that the newspaper could print an apology and in effect bring the action to an end without having to pay any forfeit. This was no doubt a wise provision when newspapers were small, with slender resources, and at the mercy of powerful institutions and wealthy individuals. With respect to my client, the provision was a sad anachronism, but we were fortunate in having an opponent who was determined to fight and was represented by senior counsel bent on not taking us seriously. To this day a libel action retains many of the formalities of earlier days. Pleadings are important and familiarity with the forms of questions to be put to witnesses is of the greatest help. When the jury found for my client and awarded him modest damages, these with the important adjunct of costs, it made all the midnight oil expended worthwhile. My father-in-law was delighted and said I had become a lawyer and not just a politician. I had certainly made many friends in the course of two elections and had acquired a considerable amount of litigation as a result of my political labours.

Ontario's first step towards compulsory automobile insurance in the postwar period was fashioned by amendments to the Highway Traffic Act giving relief to those who suffered damage and loss from accidents with uninsured motorists. The necessity of government intervention in this area had been long foreseen but was brought to the front by the refusal of insurance companies to insure motorists who had an accident record. The insurance companies, however, under pressure, agreed to what was known as the "assigned risk plan," whereby they combined to assume the risk with provincial government assistance. To a limited extent, for the protection of members of the public who were in the unfortunate situation of being unable to recover what the courts had awarded them, an unsatisfied judgment fund was available. I do not suggest that this is a faultless description of the arrangements made, but let it suffice for an introduction to their impact upon myself and other members of the bar who were designated by the provincial authorities to defend actions brought against the minister of highways, substituted for the defaulting driver. These actions were a wonderful training ground for a fledgling advocate, for in those days the highways department did not settle cases out of court and the defence fought to the bitter end. I was briefed in every Welland County case and appeared before many judges whose idiosyncracies were a constant source of interest and repaid study.

Then one day the shoe was on the other foot. Travelling to Toronto in our much-admired Sunbeam Talbot, I collided with a van whose owner sued me. I counterclaimed, and when the venue was set for Welland my antagonist disappeared and I had to join the minister in my action. H.E. Harris from St Catharines was briefed for the defence and at the hearing cross-examined me expertly and at length. The following exchange took place:

"Now Mr Hughes, how much time elapsed between the point where you realized that an accident was inevitable and the collision that is the subject of this action?"

I replied, "I have done my best, Mr Harris, in the course of your searching cross-examination to answer every question but in the case of this one I cannot oblige you. I certainly did not look at my watch."

Counsel said sharply, "I am sure that you yourself have asked this question on many occasions."

I agreed and promised never to do it again. In due course, I had my judgment and costs, but for over a year I was substantially in debt for the repairs to my Sunbeam Talbot, the frame of which had been bent and which never was quite the same thereafter.

An aspect of the law in which I found myself engaged, mainly as a junior to Stewart MacInnes, concerned resistance to the then fashionable plans of cities and towns to annex the urban areas of neighbouring municipalities on the pretext that the latter were organized for rural administration and should yield what amounted to their most valuable assessment to the annexationist municipality. This was a policy encouraged by the Department of Municipal Affairs in

Toronto, and since our firm represented most of the threatened townships, particularly Thorold and Crowland, appearance before the Ontario Municipal Board was frequently required. The board was really an admirable body and almost as independent as one could wish from ministerial direction. Its jurisdiction embraced a great variety of activities not wholly within the municipal enclosure. Buses, trucks, street railways, and other activities were consigned to its regulatory care. Boards and commissions of this type, the most powerful and impressive of which was the Interstate Commerce Commission in the United States, were an outgrowth of the disinclination of elected representatives to do the work, often unpopular, of committees of their legislatures previously constituted to do so. But even the Ontario Municipal Board, respected as it was perhaps above all others, was ultimately an instrument of policy, and its decisions could be reviewed by the cabinet. My experience was that, unless there was a definite public outcry against annexation supported by mass meetings, the board could be expected to approve in whole or in part an annexation proposal.

Yet there was hope for the hapless townships. The decision of the board to annex and the details of the annexed territory had to be embodied in a private bill and the bill brought before the Private Bills Committee of the legislature, whose approval of it was in practice necessary for it to pass the legislature itself and become law. Here I could make a contribution to the work of the senior members of my firm, and I sought help from the numerous members of the committee whom I knew as friends and political associates. On at least one occasion my endeavours succeeded against the minister of municipal affairs himself, who liked to look in at the committee's proceedings and indicate by a nod or a gesture how he would like the matter decided. In fact, in the early fifties we were successful in defending our municipal clients from the rapacity of their larger urban neighbours, who always dangled the bait of benefits that would accrue from their large industrial assessment and consequential lower taxation. In my experience, none of these promised benefits were ever realized; taxes would remain or go higher and services would deteriorate. Later on, as a resident of the village of Forest Hill, I heard the same specious arguments used by the City of Toronto when the large metropolitan municipality was created; in the end the city was appeased by having Forest

Hill and Swansea delivered to it bound hand and foot. In both cases taxes went up and the quality of services declined.

I must not give the impression that these forays were typical of the general practice which from day to day controlled my activities as a junior. Most of my time was spent searching titles, drawing deeds and wills, arranging mortgages and the conveyancing attached to them, and being wonderfully schooled by my seniors in the complexities and ethics of legal business. And of course there was an increasing pressure to appear for hotel keepers, trucking companies, and other applicants for licences and franchises dispensed by the provincial government.

Naturally I was not considered to be an effective intermediary at Ottawa, although in one pleasant experience I happened to be instructed by firebrick manufacturers – as it turned out all of those active in Canada – in a matter involving the customs tariff. The rate of the duty on firebrick imported into Canada was satisfactory, but over the years drawbacks had been allowed to the point where domestic manufacturers had almost no protection at all. This, coupled with the steady elimination of railway steam engines, which used firebrick for lining their boilers, in favour of diesel electric locomotives, had produced a crisis for the industry. I set out the problem in a letter to the minister of finance, the Honourable Walter Harris, and received a polite letter back suggesting that I come to Ottawa to discuss the matter with him and his advisers. I showed this letter to Mr Spencer, who was astonished at its agreeable tone. In his experience, letters from ministers, if written at all, were intentionally discouraging.

I met my clients in the Chateau Laurier and called my erstwhile political opponent, Dr MacMillan, as suggested by him. The next morning he conducted us into the presence of the minister, who was flanked by two senior civil servants, and we were given a cordial reception. I explained the problem, and after due deliberation on the part of our host we were given some relief, certainly enough to justify, in the opinion of my clients, their journey to the capital and the expenses entailed. I was particularly grateful to Bill Mac-Millan and we became firm friends. He was a busy surgeon and was eventually succeeded by another busy surgeon, also a Liberal, Victor Railton. Both of these men were excellent members of the

House of Commons and could have been creditable ministers of the Crown.

My criminal work was limited, as one might expect from a junior member of a firm predominantly practising in civil matters, but I record one exceptional case. Two young men, half-brothers, the elder already a petty criminal and the younger easily led, hired a taxicab to drive them to a false address in the village of Port Robinson. On a lonely road the younger brother stabbed the driver in the neck with an ice pick, and when the driver managed to stagger away from the car, the ringleader chased him and beat him to death. The taxi was later discovered abandoned and no money was found on the dead man's person, although the police were told by his associates in Welland that he regularly carried a large sum with him. Two years passed without a lead or clue for the police. Then, in Niagara Falls, New York, a young man talked to a young woman in a bar and boasted of how a perfect murder could be committed, giving so much detail that her suspicions were aroused and she later mentioned the matter to her father, a local policeman. The young man was arrested and in due course delivered into the hands of the Ontario Provincial Police. He turned out to be the younger brother and he implicated the dominant partner, who by this time had settled in Nova Scotia.

These were the days before legal aid, but many lawyers, and particularly the more successful advocates, did a good deal of free work. In Welland County a list of volunteers for free work in court was maintained by the local bar. No fees were charged but the Department of the Attorney General took care of the necessary disbursements. The accused in this case, having a Niagara Falls background, naturally picked W.S. Martin, QC, who paid me the high compliment of asking me to be his junior.

In the meantime the police had arrested our client's brother. The Crown attorney, T.F. Forestell, QC, had decided to try the older brother at the same assizes, although separately, planning to call our client as a witness against the brother whom he had already implicated; but the man whose vanity and folly had exposed a crime that might have gone undetected now showed unexpected firmness of purpose at the risk of almost certain conviction and death. At his brother's trial he stood mute, refusing to testify, in

spite of the evidence of his own statement to the police, which was
read to the jury. Counsel for the defence had little difficulty in
securing an acquittal upon such tenuous evidence, and his client,
whom we felt to be the chief instigator and perpetrator of the
murder, was a free man. In spite of Bill Martin's exertions on his
behalf, and not surprisingly, our client was convicted in his turn
and sentenced to death. All of a sudden he was transformed from
a regular prisoner in the cells of the Welland County jail into a
barely living specimen of humanity in a cage, watched twenty-four
hours a day lest he manage to end his forfeited life before being
claimed by the executioner.

Not many now alive will have participated in murder trials in
which the life of the prisoner at the bar was at stake, and even fewer
will have had daily dealings with that prisoner after condemnation.
There were no light touches in court, no little jokes between counsel, nothing to relieve the unbearable tension of a proceeding likely
to end with the terrible words of the death sentence: "Prisoner at
the bar, you have been found guilty of wilful murder. You will be
taken to a place of execution and there hanged by the neck until
you are dead and may the Lord have mercy on your soul."

During the days that followed and while the carpenters were busy
erecting the gallows behind the high wall of the Welland jail, with
hammering and sawing audible to inmates and passers-by alike, Bill
Martin and I considered the next move. Arthur Maloney, peerless
advocate and opponent of the death penalty, volunteered to take
the case to the Court of Appeal and if necessary to the Supreme
Court of Canada. Both courts in succession rejected the appeal,
and Bill decided that we must go to Ottawa and see the minister
of justice. We had at our disposal two arguments of an extra-curial
kind. At the conclusion of the trial Martin had wisely exercised his
right to have the jury polled after the collective verdict of guilty
had been given. Each juror had then risen in turn and said,
"Guilty," except one who said, "May I say something?" Mr Justice
Treleven had responded, "Only guilty or not guilty." The juror had
then grudgingly complied with the word "guilty" and had sat down.
After the trial I had sought him out in his habitation and he had
told me he did not think the evidence was satisfactory. I had asked
him if there were other members of the jury who felt the same way,

and on his assenting to this, I had suggested that he might see them and have those who agreed with him prepare a simple petition for clemency to the Governor General in Council. This he did, obtaining the signatures of seven out of the twelve jurors, unprecedented as I thought at the time and still do.

Armed with this and convinced of an inherent injustice in having the dominated partner die and the prime mover go free, we went to Ottawa at Bill Martin's expense, stayed in the Chateau Laurier (I can still hear his deep and sonorous voice on the telephone ordering two breakfasts and two *Globe and Mails*, and appeared in the office of the minister, then Stuart Garson, formerly premier of Manitoba in succession to John Bracken. Bill left to me an important part of our argument. When the minister said that he and his colleagues had sworn their oaths as privy councillors and in view of the decisions of the appellate courts they could do nothing to vary the sentence, I told him, with as much force as I could decently employ, that clemency had nothing to do with the appellate courts and that through him we had come to the foot of the throne, asking for mercy under these unusual circumstances.

Garson, who was flanked by a knowledgable official, expressed astonishment that the jury had not recommended mercy to the court. I said that it was no part of the judge's duty to tell jurors that they had the right to recommend mercy and that this was seldom if ever done. The official, who was head of the remission service, then advised the minister that this was so. This particular case may well have been a factor in subsequent amendments to the Criminal Code in which the duty to explain this part of the jurors' prerogatives was imposed upon the judge at trial.

We were successful, and only half an hour before our client was due to walk to his death, the sheriff was advised of his reprieve. He owed his life to Bill Martin's tenacity of purpose and generous expenditure of mind and money. Nor did this devoted lawyer's efforts end here. Over the long years of our client's imprisonment before parole, Bill corresponded with him and, after the latter's release, he helped him to change his identity and be rehabilitated. All of this was far and away beyond any duty owed or generally vouchsafed. Like the renowned lawyer Arthur Maloney, Bill Martin was a devout Catholic and no doubt shared Maloney's aversion to capital punishment, but I venture to say that what he did for this easily led, insignificant human being was an example of nobility of mind and spirit.

Like most law firms in the country we relied on our Toronto agents, Raymond and Honsberger, to do our routine work in the Court of Appeal and Weekly Court. Occasionally eminent Toronto counsel would be instructed, and in my time Stewart MacInnes had become a formidable counsel. I only once went to the Court of Appeal and probably because in the case in question no one else would have found my clients in any sense appetizing. I had appeared at trial for a Czech couple living on a farm near Welland who were being sued by the wife's father, a coal miner from West Virginia. The father had given his daughter money in exchange for her under-taking, so it was alleged, to look after him on the couple's farm in his declining years. He was a difficult boarder and after many disputes my clients put him out. The case was tried by Mr Justice Wilfred Judson, one of our most distinguished High Court judges. Judson was a silent judge, but he could not entirely conceal his distaste at the end of the trial when he reserved judgment. In due time, his judgment was handed down, concluding with the words: "I greatly regret that I am not able to find against these unconscion-able defendants."

Of course, my opponent headed in a hurry for the Court of Appeal and I had a very difficult time with the justices Laidlaw, Roach, and Aylesworth. Whenever I opened my mouth to make submissions on the law, I would be interrupted, and Mr Justice Laidlaw went so far as to say, "Mr Hughes, that argument won't help your clients to keep this old man's money." In the midst of my ordeal, which had almost reduced me to silence, I felt a tug at my gown. Looking down, I saw one of the giants of the bar, John Arnup. He whispered, "Stay on your feet, Sam. They can't go on forever." Thus encouraged in a manner I shall always remember, I completed my argument, and to my pleased surprise, judgment was reserved instead of being given against me from the bench. Some months later judgment was delivered by a simple endorse-ment on the record, dismissing the appeal without reasons and without costs. This was hardly gracious, but I was satisfied and always felt the credit really belonged to Wilf Judson. He had refused to allow his feelings to affect his interpretation of the law and had stated his interpretation in a way that the Court of Appeal recognized to be right, however much they felt justified in showing me their teeth.

My solitary experience of the Supreme Court of Canada was different in almost every respect. I had become a Queen's Counsel earlier than was the custom, but many things were accelerated for the benefit of practitioners whose positions had been affected by war service. The case was *Eli Lilley and Company* v. *The Minister of National Revenue*, a taxation problem which had begun in the Exchequer Court and was tried by that court's president, Mr Justice Thorson. R.B. Law had taken the case in the Exchequer Court for our client, a well-known drug company, but the action had been dismissed. In those days there was no Federal Court of Appeal, and our appeal went straight to the Supreme Court. Our client's American parent had for convenience been in the habit of transferring substantial sums of Canadian dollars to its subsidiary for reasons which are not material even if I could now remember them. Then in 1948 the Honourable Douglas Abbott, minister of finance for Canada, had announced in a radio address that the Canadian dollar would henceforth be at par with that of the United States, which incidentally meant that the Canadian taxpayer would in effect be paying the difference between the two currencies. Our client's gain was indisputable but what was its nature?

I had done a good deal of work on the law in this situation, and Bob Law was kind enough to take me to Ottawa as his junior. Because of the collapse of two cases in front of us, on a Saturday we found ourselves called for Monday morning. We flew in a Trans-Canada Airways DC 3 in driving snow, quite low above the right of way of the main line of the CPR. The staff of the Supreme Court obligingly opened the library for us on Sunday, allowing us to assemble our authorities and polish our argument in comfort. Next morning we appeared in the handsome chamber whose atmosphere was strikingly different from the one I had encountered in the Court of Appeal. The Supreme Court was a silent court and its reputation for courtesy to counsel was high. Consequently, it was not always easy to discern the success or failure of the argument before it.

We had a five-man court presided over by the Honourable Patrick Kerwin, chief justice of Canada, and after opening the case with the facts and figures, Bob generously left me to deal with the law. Our position was that the company had enjoyed a windfall by the adventitious intervention of the minister of finance, not a profit made in the course of business as the Department of National Revenue contended. The court reserved judgment, and after the judges had withdrawn, an usher accosted us and said that the chief justice would like to see us. We repaired to his chambers and found tea ready, presided over by a complimentary chief who of course knew Bob Law well from the days when the former had practised law in Guelph. The whole experience was pleasant, but we lost the case in spite of having Mr Justice Locke and Mr Justice Cartwright with us, the judgment of the majority being given by Mr Justice Estey. John Cartwright would become chief justice after the resignation of Chief Justice Taschereau. Mr Justice Estey's son, bearing the same name so that he was inevitably known as "Bud," became chief justice of Ontario and then was appointed to his father's court. He also became a friend.

The practice of law, absorbing as it is, needs an occasional change of pace for the mental comfort of its practitioners. Two were provided me in the 1950s. In the first year of the decade the "Learned Societies" (as they were known), including the Canadian Historical Association, met at Kingston in the historic precincts of the Royal Military College. George Stanley, then professor of history at the college, wrote suggesting that I might read a paper on some aspect of my grandfather's life. I jumped at the chance and decided to make my theme his lifelong conviction that practical imperialism was to be found in a closely knit British Empire where all inhabitants of the empire had the same opportunity of finding careers in the imperial service and particularly in the armed forces of the Crown. My grandfather's problem was that after he became a wartime minister in Canada, force of circumstances transformed him into a Canadian nationalist. I spent some days of my holidays in August in the famous library of the Royal Canadian Military Institute in Toronto doing what research I could in a short period and writing the paper that I would read to the association in September.

It was entitled "Sir Sam Hughes and the Problem of Imperialism." It appears in the published proceedings of the Canadian Historical Association for 1950 and was well received, although when I mounted the platform to deliver it, there were some barely audible academic sneers about "tales of a grandfather." My paper was the last of three dealing with military history, and Charles Stacey, who led the discussion, was obviously delighted that the three authors were or had been members of the Historical Section. A.R.M. Lower said that I had revealed a real distinction between Toryism and imperialism, and observed that Tories took a nostalgic view of the past while imperialists were people "whom the current scene never satisfies." Stacey hoped that the paper would be expanded into a fully documented book. Alas, indolence and a feeling of inadequacy have prevented this to this day, and I feel that Sir Sam Hughes deserved better of his grandson as he had certainly deserved better of his compatriots.

The success of my paper was gratifying. Mainly as a result of it Eric Harrison shortly offered me the appointment at Queen's University to which I have referred, and I had regretfully to decline on the grounds that I had gone too far in another direction and had made too many commitments to those who had helped and nourished my first steps in the law. I cannot leave the occasion without remembering the dinner on the last day of the proceedings, held at the National Defence College in Fort Frontenac (as the Tête du Pont barracks was now being called). The commandant was General Guy Simonds, not yet chief of the General Staff as he was soon to become. There Donald Creighton gave a masterly paper on Sir John A. Macdonald and Kingston with his usual fervour and eloquence; the paper was obviously a forerunner of the two great volumes of the life of that statesman, an important landmark in Canadian historical writing. After this distinguished and warmly received contribution, the chairman thanked various contributors to the success of the annual proceedings, and then turned to Simonds, who, with his summer uniform ablaze with medals and his striking good looks, presented a commanding figure. The applause had been warm during the chairman's first round of compliments, but when he complimented the general, a strange silence descended, almost as if Simonds had overawed the assembly and disdained applause. He was our host and had wined us and dined us well, but not for the first time had our most accomplished soldier made a distinguished company aware of his high condescension.

Not long after the by-election, and during a period when my political activities might well have been curtailed, I had a pleasant surprise in my home town. A large number of my friends and acquaintances urged me to run for the city council. In those days there was no system of representation by wards; we all were candidates-at-large and on my first try I almost headed the polls. It was as if those who had not voted for me in the two elections already described wanted to give me a consolation prize, and I was grateful. Moreover, the work was fascinating and instructive for anyone interested in municipal law. The city of Welland and its adjacent townships were inhabited by a rich variety of people. Overlying the early German settlers were English, Scottish, Irish, French Canadian, Italian, and Hungarian, to name the principal strains; there was even a Croatian Hall in the township of Crowland. The French Canadians were early on the scene, having come to work in the factories before the first war, and in both Welland and Port Colborne there was a highly visible French-speaking community, known as "Frenchtown" in both places. Italians were well represented in all the cities and towns of the county; their forebears had worked on various editions of the Welland Canal. We had an excellent mayor in Welland, Armour McCrea, whom I have referred to above as my former CCF opponent and a brilliant natural orator.

It may be remembered that when the coronation of Queen Elizabeth II took place in 1953, all the mayors in Canada were invited to Westminster Abbey. Many could not afford to go, but in the small city of Welland my fellow alderman Joseph Lemelin, who represented our citizens of French Canadian origin, at once moved to send the mayor to England, a motion unanimously adopted. In his absence I was in charge of the coronation celebrations. These involved a parade to the park marshalled by Lieutenant-Colonel James F. Swayze, DSO, who had commanded the Lincoln and Welland Regiment in some desperate actions in Belgium. Plenty of patriotic songs and speeches ensued. I thought that on this occasion it would be acceptable to fly the Canadian Ensign, not long before approved as the official Canadian flag, and I requisitioned a handsome nylon flag for the purpose, nylon flags being then a novelty. When it fluttered bravely from the flagpole in the park, many heads were shaken and many eyes regarded it doubtfully. The Union Jack was still the Canadian flag in that community of many origins. The Ensign had at one time been the Canadian flag, but after Sir Wilfrid Laurier's return from the Imperial Conference in 1897, it was ousted in favour of the Union Jack; now it had been cautiously reintroduced, by Mackenzie King, as the emblem to be flown from Canadian government buildings. It would have barely fifteen years to enjoy this limited recognition.

During this period we were confronted by an order from the provincial government to cease from disposing raw sewage in the Welland River and to establish a sewage treatment plant for the municipality. Present-day readers may not understand the significance of this pronouncement, nor may it be realized that municipalities in Ontario all around the Great Lakes and their tributary streams had all been polluting the waters in much the same way. Hamilton was the largest offender, and our neighbours in St Catharines used the regatta course of the Royal Canadian Henley in like manner. The provincial Department of Health now made a heroic effort to impose new standards; it took a decade to achieve compliance in the face of the inability of the municipalities to exceed the borrowing limits imposed by the Department of Municipal Affairs. In the event, limits were relaxed and loans of many millions provided at rates of no more than 3 percent were made on very reasonable terms for repayment.

Our problem in Welland was aggravated by the fact that the great Welland Canal was originally carried across the Welland River by an aqueduct but that later the sluggish river was carried by syphon under a much deeper canal. The city was in fact divided into four parts by the conjunction of the east-west flowing river and the north-south passage of the canal, and the new sanitary sewers had to surmount or be submerged by the waterways to reach the disposal facilities. In the middle of all this, the International Joint Commission made threatening noises about polluting the boundary waters of the Niagara River. The Welland River, otherwise known as Chippawa Creek, had in early times flowed into the Niagara River above the cataract at Niagara Falls but for many years past had been completely diverted into the Chippawa Power Canal and delivered into the gorge below the falls through the penstocks of the Hydro Commission's plant. The Joint Commission was neither mollified nor amused when I advanced the argument that this sewage must be the best treated in North America.

In those days municipal elections occurred annually, and I was elected three times as an alderman in Welland. As the days passed, I became busier in my profession and Helen continued to be my right hand in all senses of the word, most conspicuously in my political endeavours. The children throve in the city's public schools. Then there was an unforeseen and painful change. Helen's father and stepmother had returned from a cruise, he, usually so energetic and robust, in uncharacteristic poor health. He was found to have a shadow on one lung and a biopsy performed in Toronto revealed a malignancy. He was advised about the required surgical operation to remove the affected lung and decided not to have it. I visited him in the Toronto General Hospital and heard him discuss the situation with his surgeon calmly and precisely. His decision was respected and considered acceptable in the case of a man over seventy, an age then felt to be more advanced than it would be today. We also talked about a new situation that had confronted me.

A client in the furniture-moving business in Fort Erie had suffered a deadly blow because one of his drivers had been charged and convicted on driving one of his employer's vehicles while drunk. At once his insurers cancelled the policies under which all his vehicles were insured and thus imperilled the public vehicle licence under which my client operated. We travelled forthwith to Toronto to secure protection under the assigned risk plan, and after the necessary business had been done, I called on A.D. McKenzie before returning to Welland. He told me that the bus and truck licensing jurisdiction of the Ontario Municipal Board was about to be transferred to a new body called the Ontario Highway Transport Board. A vice-chairman had been appointed.

The chairman's position had been intended for a retiring cabinet minister who now found it impossible to accept. Was I interested? I said I would certainly consider it, since the salary was in excess of my current income. Not long after my return to Welland, the Honourable W.A. Goodfellow, minister of municipal affairs and member of the Legislative Assembly for Northumberland County, telephoned and offered me the appointment. I sought time to think the matter over and to discuss it with my family and particularly with the head of my firm, to whom I owed so much and whose opinion would in effect be decisive.

To my surprise my father-in-law thought Bill Goodfellow's offer should be accepted. He was kind enough to say that perhaps the time had come when governments needed good men as administrators, but I am sure he had doubts about the future of the firm in Welland and my position in it after his death, which he knew was inevitable. Had he shown any resistance or disappointment I would have declined the appointment. I did not for a moment think that he doubted my capacity to practise law successfully, but he would have been justified in thinking that I was too easily diverted from that sphere by my political activities and association with such organizations as the Greater Welland Chamber of Commerce, of which I had become president. I shall never know, but I took away from this sad encounter an abiding impression of far-sighted judgment and his usual affectionate concern. In any case, I called the minister and accepted the appointment as chairman of the Ontario Highway Transport Board, to take effect after a reasonable interval to allow me to settle my affairs in Welland.

CHAPTER TWELVE

Public Necessity and Convenience

I have often in fancy transposed my life into the previous century on the assumption that I was born in 1813, the year when the great tyrant of his day, Napoleon, was first brought to book at the battle of Leipzig. Now, upon our move back to Toronto, I had reached the time of the fierce and futile war in the Crimea, and as I write today, the wholly unjustifiable Spanish-American war is about to begin. But in comparison with the fifties of the nineteenth century those of the twentieth were full of hope. Nevertheless, personal sorrow cast its shadow. Of the two men who had in large measure taken the place of my father, Cyril Douglas Hughes MacAlpine died in 1952 of cancer and Lynn Bristol Spencer was also about to be claimed by this same fell disease. His decline in physical health, although scarcely in mental vigour, was to end in the bereavement of his daughter and son-in-law, having now to make their own way in the world without the precious parental refuge which had hitherto sustained them. But I must confess that there was a lightening of spirit for me at least, though as yet unperceived, in leaving the hazards and daily anxiety of the practice of law and taking a position where the one overriding concern was the success of an administrative task.

The separation of the regulatory authority for buses and trucks (conferred by the Ontario statutes known as the Public Vehicles

Act and the Public Commercial Vehicles Act respectively) from the multifarious jurisdiction of the Ontario Municipal Board was caused not only by laxity in the latter's administration in dealing mainly with the burgeoning trucking industry, but also by the rapid increase in the growth of motor vehicle transport across Canada. This in part was owing to the stimulus provided by the railway strike of 1951, when in a suicidal withdrawal of service the railway unions had flung open the door to what had hitherto been a jealously preserved monopoly of the Canadian National Railways and the Canadian Pacific Railway. This monopoly had been established at a time when there were no other means of transporting goods across the continent, except by the laborious if economical passage by sea. There now ensued a period when roads were made available, but those wishing to reach western Canada by links through the United States had to seek the approval of licensing authorities in midwestern states and latterly of the great Inter-State Commerce Commission. This body, laying its hands on American transportation by rail, road, and air, had no counterpart in Canada, where each province had its peculiar arrangements for motor transport. Commercial transport by rail and air was firmly under the jurisdiction of the federal government.

This anomaly, largely expressive of lack of the means to develop interprovincial transport and still unaddressed by public law, was removed at least in theory by the case of *SMT* v. *Winner,* finally decided by the judicial committee of the Privy Council in London in favour of the proposition that interprovincial motor transport was the regulatory responsibility of Ottawa. Ottawa somewhat reluctantly assumed this responsibility, and I say reluctantly because no sooner had its position been established by the highest court in the British Commonwealth than the government of Canada divested itself of the administrative responsibility thus acquired by delegating it to the relevant administrative tribunals of the provinces under the provision of the Motor Vehicle Transport Act of 1954. This enactment, of some half a dozen lines in length, was said to have been drawn in at least tentative form by the deputy attorney general of Canada and the deputy attorney general of Ontario in the course of a train journey from Ottawa to Toronto. Thus, on the eve both of the constitution of the Ontario Highway Transport Board and of my assumption of office, a great and

attractive opportunity for provincial cooperation in the exercise of
federal power was suddenly opened up.

I shall return to this development but first I must introduce my
colleagues and the work we accomplished at the outset of our
association in 1955. The vice-chairman already in place was Edward
James Shoniker. With his brothers, he had operated bus lines in
Scarborough Township before the business was expropriated, as it
were, when the Toronto Transportation Commission became the
sole operator in the new Metropolitan Municipality of Greater
Toronto. Shoniker had acquired experience of applications for
licensing under the statutes I have mentioned, operating licences
on prescribed routes, in the months when he had been a member
of the Municipal Board. A short man, he was a well-remembered
quarterback at Malvern Collegiate Institute in the east end of
Toronto, where he had many friends and connections. He was a
personal friend and trusted agent of the Roman Catholic archbishop of Toronto, the redoubtable Cardinal James Charles
McGuigan, and was himself an indefatigable and devout Catholic
and a thorough-going Conservative. In those last months of 1955
the two of us became close and lasting friends, working long hours
to establish the Highway Transport Board with all the necessary
civil service linkages, staff, and pay, leaving policy largely to be
formulated as we acquired knowledge from the evidence to be
given at the public hearings before the board. We were under
extreme pressure to begin these hearings right away, just as soon
as the Ontario Highway Transport Board Act was enacted, much
less proclaimed in force, since the Municipal Board had ceased to
hold hearings in anticipation of losing the jurisdiction.

Of special interest and importance was the appointment of a
third member of our board. I was determined to have three-
member panels at all hearings if possible, and we were fortunate
to find a veteran member of the Municipal Board willing to assist
us. This was Howard Yeats, QC, who had served in the Royal Naval
Air Service in the first war and was a popular lawyer in Hamilton.
His habitual good nature and friendliness had often made Draco-
nian decisions of the Municipal Board palatable, and he continued
to be an ambassador of goodwill throughout the years of activity
remaining to him before retirement. Always at our side and deeply
versed in civil service procedures was George Marrs, a native of

Brockville recommended to us by Bill Goodfellow and later, before his untimely death, to be chairman of the board. We were a happy group of friends as well as colleagues and often worked long hours late at night fascinated by the problem of creating something new, something better, as we hoped, than what had gone before.

At the outset of the hearings to consider applications for public vehicle (bus) and public commercial vehicle (trucks) licences, the challenge of our mandate was clear. The two industries we were concerned with had long been subject to government regulation beginning in the United Kingdom and the United States. Canada had kept pace in varying measure with its historical exemplar and powerful neighbour. But as I have said, the provinces had hitherto made their own arrangements with respect to the operations of their own commercial traffic on their highways, as distinct from operations inside municipalities and confined thereto.

The test which was applied to every applicant for admission into a controlled environment was "public necessity and convenience," the regulatory authorities being concerned that all sections of the community should be served and that unrestricted competition should not result in concentration by operators on the most profitable areas and sources of business to the detriment of the public welfare. Therefore, access to the markets and establishments of industry and commerce by the operators of motor vehicle transport was to be controlled so that the public should be served methodically and efficiently rather than be left to the devices of those who had forced the weakest operators to the wall in their own rather than in the public interest. Nor were governments and their tribunals entirely opposed to a type of regulation that not only preserved the public from the effects of the chaos of unrestricted competition but also provided security of an important kind to lawful operators in the jealously guarded districts and routes authorized by their operating licences.

Present-day readers, and particularly exponents of privatization and market economies, may regard with aversion, and perhaps contempt, a system which apparently gave artificial protection to the "haves" against the aspirations of the "have-nots." In a rapidly expanding economy, however, particularly such as prevailed in the years after the Second World War, the test of public necessity and convenience as a means of controlling expansion had its advantages, and it may well find its place again after the frenzy of deregulation has subsided. Certainly the ethos of the motor vehicle transport community was one of implacable resistance to the entry of new operators into the carefully controlled and cultivated environment where great fortunes were being made.

I hope to save time and verbiage by describing in an unidentifiable form a typical hearing before the Ontario Highway Transport Board in 1955 or 1956. This hearing takes place in a long room that was once a ward in the Sick Children's Hospital but is now furnished with chairs and benches for the public and their representatives, and a dais, desk, and chairs for the three commissioners, above whose heads are mounted the arms of the province of Ontario. The case for an applicant for a certificate of public necessity and convenience is opened by counsel (very seldom is an applicant present unsupported by counsel), who describes and dwells upon the need of the public for an additional operator in a particular part of the province and for a particular purpose. Ranged against him are counsel – experienced, instructed, and expensive – representing the already licensed operators, who are asserting that the public is sufficiently well served by them without the intrusion of a novice. Counsel for the applicant calls witnesses drawn from the persons and bodies who say that the existing services are inadequate and that they need what the applicant is offering. These witnesses are then cross-examined by a number of the counsel for the respondents, sometimes by the secretary of the powerful association which embraces in its membership virtually all of the already-licensed operators. Re-examination might take place, and then the respondents and their supporters are called in their turn by counsel for the respondents, several of whom may have long left the courts unattended, preferring to reap the rewards provided by their transportation clients. Arguments range from the piteous to the passionate, and in most cases of consequence the board reserves its decision and proceeds to the next case.

In due course, a decision is handed down, either dismissing the application or granting a certificate of public necessity and convenience addressed to the minister responsible, who without further ado issues an operating licence in the terms of the certificate.

The Municipal Board had been remarkably loath to grant applications of this type, and some rumours reflecting discreditably on the members engaged in hearing them had long been afloat. I was determined that a reasonable amount of competition should be allowed, and convinced that the health of the industry and the interests of the public would benefit from a judicious increase in the number of licensed operators. The licences issued and exercised were of great variety, including the majestic highway transportation of less than truckload lots, the carriage of goods or products of one particular concern between specified points, and transportation by tank transporter, by automobile carrier, and down to the ubiquitous dump truck, essential to the construction industry. Cattle truckers, humbler but nonetheless important to agriculture and food processing, located throughout the farmlands of Ontario, were separately licensed. In its infinite variety the trucking industry portrayed the complexity and vigour of the postwar economic life of Canada's richest and most populous province.

I quickly came to the conclusion that neither the Department of Municipal Affairs nor the Department of Highways, however legitimate their interest in certain aspects of the trucking industry might have been, was sufficiently organized and equipped to formulate an administrative policy in this area on behalf of the government. I therefore wrote a memorandum to Premier Frost setting out proposals for the creation of a new department, which I suggested might be called the Department of Highway Transportation. The premier found my suggestions useful, and in time the department was created, although to my regret it was named the Department of Transport, creating some confusion with the functions of the federal department of the same name. The department's first minister was an influential member of the legislature from Dunnville, James N. Allan, with whom I had been friendly in the days of my practice in Welland. His deputy minister was Donald Collins, hitherto Mr Frost's trusted personal assistant. No protest, as I recall, was made by the Department of Municipal Affairs, which had for so long been responsible for our peculiar function, dating from the days when its board was called the Ontario Municipal and Railway Board, its jurisdiction, although faithfully discharged, having become an anomaly. On personal grounds I would not have relinquished the connection with my friend Bill Goodfellow, to whose sure-footed judgment we owed much, but he had become minister of agriculture before the changes I have described were made, and had left the portfolio of municipal affairs.

For me, Collins was the source of new light on Leslie Frost's work as an administrator and conduct in cabinet, where the former regularly accompanied his chief. Frost's image in the province was that of a benevolent and frequently humorous leader who liked to invoke the image of "Old Man Ontario," a character frequently portrayed in newspaper cartoons of an earlier date. It was in the guise of Old Man Ontario that the affable, easygoing premier appeared in all parts of the province, rarely referring to his opponents and almost never responding to their accusations. In council, on the other hand, he was a subtle authoritarian chief who scrutinized the work of his ministers and was quick to discard those whom he considered unfriendly or incompetent. In this he was the complete opposite to George Drew, who allowed his ministers great latitude and independence in conducting the affairs of their departments and who in his public activities dealt faithfully and pugnaciously with his opponents at every opportunity.

The truth was that Old Man Ontario, whimsical and accommodating in his many public acts and appearances, was at heart an autocrat – but in a way that could not be more palatable, as I had found in the days of my practice. I had had the temerity to appeal to the cabinet after the Liquor Licence Board's refusal to allow wines and spirits to be sold in the Cherry Hill Golf Club, a club mainly patronized by Buffalonians for whom Prohibition was a nightmare of the past. Under the provisions of local option the Township of Bertie was dry, and I had failed to convince Judge Walter Robb that this was an exceptional case that would do no harm. Premier Frost had said, "No, Sam, they will simply have to do what we do in Lindsay – keep a bottle in our lockers." So it was settled, but the frequently favourable countenance of the chairman of the Liquor Licence Board did not smile upon me for a season.

I thought that Ontario, being the busiest trucker of all the provinces and therefore the hungriest for good order in regulation, should take the lead in seeking consensus in exercising the jurisdiction so incontinently delegated by Ottawa, and much of 1956 was devoted to this end. I visited my opposite numbers in the provinces (except for Newfoundland, which in those days had no interprovincial trucking problems), travelling mostly by train to get the kind of feel for the country that going from airport to office and back can never provide. On my western trip I was accompanied by M.L. Rapoport, a Toronto lawyer with an extensive knowledge of trucking problems in Canada and the United States.

Nothing can be more wonderful for Canadians than the first sight of their country unfolding before their eyes from rail or road. In those days the railroads had, for all practical purposes, this enchantment exclusively in their gift. The Canadian Pacific Railway, in particular, with its luxurious trains, the *Canadian* and the *Dominion*, now, alas, defunct, provided a never to be forgotten experience of travel in the West, and the Canadian National Railways with somewhat less spectacular trains opened vistas of its own just as historic and exciting. Of course, I was familiar with Quebec, New Brunswick, Nova Scotia, and Prince Edward Island from my honeymoon and other journeys, but the West, as I had not travelled westward from Winnipeg, was a revelation which abides with me in old age. I must have inherited my grandfather's love of railway travel as well as my father's vast knowledge of all railway lines and systems from his railway location days. I have never lost this passion and in conversation still enjoy the capacious railway knowledge of my friends and colleagues Brendan O'Brien and Meredith Fleming.

On this occasion in 1956 I was able for the first time to return to my birthplace, the small house at 1009 Chamberlain Street in Victoria, derelict and untenanted as it was. Everywhere I went, I preached the gospel of provincial cooperation as a substitute for federal indifference towards an activity that might well threaten the cherished railroads. And I invited my many hosts, the provincial regulators of motor transport, to a conference in Toronto in the fall.

This conference, which was held in the Royal York Hotel, culminated in a plenary session at which ministers from across Canada appeared to endorse the work of their permanent officials. Following the conference, many loose ends were gathered up and tied together, and provincially issued extra-provincial licences were recognized by provinces to which operators were authorized to enter by an issuing province. In due time and long after I had left the scene, the federal government constituted its own motor vehicle regulatory authority, but until then all our affairs proceeded harmoniously.

Quebec as usual asserted its individuality. When apprehended by the Quebec Provincial Police, unlicensed operators were often compelled to offload their trucks into the nearest ditch or have the vehicle chained from its steering column to the nearest tree to await disposal by the authorities. These were the days of Maurice Duplessis, then head of Quebec's Union Nationale government. Duplessis had appointed Colonel Joe Harold, MC, head of the Regie des Transports. Harold lived in the largely English-speaking town of Hampstead in Montreal, where the offices of this authority were situated. Eddie Shoniker had met and liked Joe Harold, as did I in my turn, and a fruitful and cordial relationship developed, not uncharacteristic of the many bonds which had sprung up between Ontario and Quebec officialdom owing to various differences of opinion with Ottawa. Harold was trusted by the all powerful "Chef" and Quebec truckers alike. I well remember the occasion of perhaps his last speech to the latter after the removal of a malignant larynx and the installation of a "voice box"; his courageous and exhausting effort was greeted with a tumult of applause.

As one might expect, there was a price to pay for a cordial relationship with Quebec authority: for every operator licensed to proceed over the border from Ontario, there had to be one received into Ontario from Quebec. Lack of punctilio could mean trouble, and I recall the difficulty that arose from our board's refusal to certify a Quebec applicant from Matane, well down the St Lawrence where even the descendants of Wolfe's Fraser Highlanders had long lost the use of the English tongue, when it transpired that he and his drivers spoke and read only French. My explanation that in Ontario roadside signs and other instructive material appeared only in English was not well received, particularly as in those far-off days one-sidedness of this kind was not as evident in Quebec. I forget now how the matter was resolved but I am sure that an extra deployment of liaison with Joe Harold was necessary, replete with gossip about the army.

Slowly but surely the Ontario Highway Transport Board was established as a forum where public necessity and convenience were treated seriously and political influence could not be exercised with impunity against public policy. Needless to say, a great many counsel appearing before us were influential supporters of the Progressive Conservative party and some did not hesitate to remind us of how influential they were. It was not unusual for a distinguished advocate, closeted in my office, to ask if he might use my telephone to talk to "Les." The telephone would be offered with alacrity but the ritual resulted in little except a smile later shared with my colleagues. Having the confidence and support of the premier, and in Eddie Shoniker's case, an additional spiritual and secular benison from his great patron, we could pursue our policy unperturbed.

The personnel of the Transport Board did not increase notably during my time. We added George Stoddart and were fortunate in obtaining the services of Nicol Kingsmill as permanent counsel for the board. This position, which Kingsmill filled with distinction, had among other things the salutory effect of raising the board higher in the quasi-judicial scale, above the fierce contentions of counsel for applicants and respondents, including such formidable figures as C.P. McTague, E.A. Goodman, Roland Michener, and D.J. Walker. The board travelled and I began to accumulate an intimate knowledge of Ontario, constantly refreshed over the years in different employments. And incidentally I became familiar with the practical aspects of the licences for which we were responsible. I soon developed an unusual and sometimes embarrassing ability to spot errant vehicles and showed excessive zeal, I now admit, for enforcement. There had been precious little of it in the days before the board was constituted.

Every now and again an unexpected anomaly would be revealed by our activities. The industries of Sault Ste Marie, for instance, notably the Algoma Steel Company, sought to break the stranglehold exerted by the Canadian Pacific Railway, which was without competitors between Sudbury and the Soo. Algoma encouraged many truck operators to apply for authority to carry its goods and those of others along that section of the Trans-Canada Highway hitherto unserved. All the bridges along this route were conspicuously marked with load limits very much lower than the weight of the great tractor trailers that the applicants proposed to use. When I pointed this out at the hearings in the Soo, the result was consternation. Then it was found, on reference to the Department of Highways in Toronto, that the signs prescribing load limits at bridges were not supported by any legislative authority, but were only cautionary observations by the department's engineers, admittedly out of date and unrealistic. The operating authorities that were granted at this time conferred no lasting benefit upon the eager applicants, and the railway fell back upon what its highway competitors regarded as an inequitous expedient known as the "agreed charge." The shipper who surrendered all his traffic to the railway enjoyed rates frequently less than half of the standard charges. It was not long before the industrialists of Sault Ste Marie were once more enslaved, seduced by their first experience of the agreed charge, and the CPR triumphed. This was no isolated example of the railways' fighting back to recover transcontinental traffic temporarily lost as the result of a ruinous railway strike. Their most effective stroke was the piggy-back, or "trailer on flatcar," which allowed intra-urban truckers to load their trailers on railway flatcars to be off-loaded in some city hundreds of miles away, thus avoiding the expense and responsibility borne by the highway carriers subject to provincial regulation. This expedient certainly breathed new life into the long-distance freight traffic of the railways. But the writing was on the wall for their passenger traffic, although we did not discern it then.

Passenger traffic by road, or the inter-urban bus business, was the concern of the Highway Transport Board under the Public Vehicles Act and subject to the same standards as prevailed for the trucking industry; applications for entry and approval of transfer of operating authorities also applied to it. But here one encountered a very different atmosphere. The passenger vehicle operators were, generally speaking, large, rich, and few in number, and their humbler brethren in the school bus business shared their stability if not their wealth. Gray Coach, Colonial Coach Lines (later Voyageur), Canada Coach, and Eastern Canadian Greyhound dominated the field. Now the railways, anxious to cut costs by discontinuing branch lines and generally unprofitable routes, sought entry into this field for their own buses on routes formerly served by passenger trains. Naturally there was fierce resistance from the entrenched operators, and I confess that I sympathized with their position. It seemed to me that they were well able to provide the service the railways had chosen to relinquish. At the board we had some searching discussions with representatives of the CNR and CPR, and particularly the latter, which got me involved with Canadian Pacific's chairman, N.R. Crump (widely known as "Buck"), its only chief who had risen from footplate to boardroom.

As it turned out, the authorized operations sought were in selected areas where the existing operators could not or would not assume the burden, but it was my impression that the railways were more interested in buying up freight carriers than in developing a bus service. In any event, I can remember Mr Crump citing to me the many money-losing operations of his great company. I had said, "But at least you have the *Canadian*," and had been astonished to be told that the great train had also been unprofitable from the beginning.

Throughout my tenure of office as chairman of the Ontario Highway Transport Board I tried to make it a place where lawyers would feel at home, as they often did not before the Municipal Board or the Labour Relations Board and similar tribunals. As for the Labour Relations Board, I recall appearing before it to resist an application by the United Electrical Workers to organize dairy workers in the Niagara Peninsula. The chairman, Professor Jacob Finkleman, after unloading a lot of technicalities about charges and so forth on my uninstructed head, asked me why I was so upset at the prospect of the union succeeding. I said, "I don't think it's an appropriate bargaining agent for dairy workers." "Oh," said the chairman, "I don't suppose you think that the present government at Ottawa is appropriate for Canada." "You read my innermost thoughts, Mr Chairman," I replied, adopting his mood, but of course Jake Finkleman had been a young lecturer in the law department when I was an undergraduate at Toronto. We were on friendly terms but even this sort of badinage failed to establish the appropriate atmosphere; nor did the stereotyped procedure with which only aficionados before these boards were familiar. Many applicants, represented by counsel or not, would retire from the contest disconcerted and remain bitter as a result. I determined this would not be the case in hearings before the Highway Transport Board and decided that adherence to procedure in court would be observed, including application of the rules of evidence. I was accused of being legalistic, but my withers were unwrung. Only later did I realize that I was giving vent to a not-long-repressed desire to be presiding in a court of law.

As I have said, Eddie Shoniker and I became firm friends. Helen and I were frequently at his house, much more frequently than he and his wife Rita were at ours because, although Eddie was a lavish host, he was a difficult man to coax outside his comfortable home in Moore Park, a neighbourhood he called the "little Vatican." Rita was his second wife, his first having died tragically years earlier. Rita was charming and well educated. She came from Kitchener, where her sister had married a doctor, the eldest of the Shoniker brothers, and where her brother, John Wintermeyer, practised law and won a seat in the legislature in 1955. I liked John and some years later played a small part with some mutual friends in persuading him to run for the leadership of the Liberal party in Ontario after his re-election in 1959. He succeeded a long line of rather ineffectual leaders of that party and did good work for it, although he was unable to stem the strong tide of Conservative dominance that was only halfway through its hold on the voters of Ontario, lasting over forty years. Rita and Eddie had two small sons, Peter and Paul, and Eddie was a most indulgent father. In the course of our work together and recreation in each other's company, we often spoke of the future. He was aware of my feelings about the bench and nursed an understandable ambition to succeed me as chairman.

The creation of Metropolitan Toronto, as I have explained, put money in the hands of bus operators, and they were in easy circumstances, but another aspect of this consolidation of Toronto and satellite municipalities had benefited one of Eddie Shoniker's greatest friends, Harold Adamson. As deputy chief of police in Scarborough Township, he became a staff inspector in the metropolitan municipality and was clearly marked out for advancement by the incumbent, Chief James Mackie. Adamson, of impressive size and great sagacity, was to become a formidable chief of the Metropolitan Toronto Police from 1970 until his retirement, always retaining the confidence of his force and of the general public. He became a friend. Now in his mid-seventies, he is indefatigable in volunteer work and still within a few pounds of his service weight.

Although none were nor could be closer to him than Harry Adamson, Eddie had many other friends among the police. He was also well known in the fire department, a regular attendant at the more important fires, of which he had miraculously early knowledge.

I had kept in touch with my friends in Welland, who had on two occasions celebrated my appointment to the board: the Welland

County Bar Association had presented me with one of Charlie Comfort's watercolours at a farewell dinner, and my lay friends from Welland and Crowland had a party for me at a well-known hotel on South Main Street in the latter municipality and presented me with a liquor cabinet. Both of these gifts, representing as they do two important interests in my life, are to this day prominently displayed in my house. At the Crowland party, my friend Ellis Morningstar, MPP for Welland, proposed a toast and I replied, both of us, good friends that we were, in high good humour. Ellis, of Loyalist German stock, born on the farm, had been a member of the township council since virtual boyhood, reeve of the township, and warden of the county, and in 1951 had wrested the Welland seat, being the western half of the federal constituency, from the Liberals, sitting for at least twenty years thereafter, never defeated. He typified the character of his constituency in many ways. Although of farming stock, he was a superviser in Page Hersey Tubes, one of the many great plants lining the Welland Canal. A tall, powerful, somewhat corpulent figure, he radiated benevolence and was a great favourite with all the elements of our polyglot community, learning by heart a few words of Hungarian, French, and Italian for use on public occasions. We saw him often in Toronto, where he was a general favourite in the legislature and was naturally upset when a newspaper photographer took a picture of him asleep on one of the back benches. Considering that he rose before dawn, laid out the work in his section of the plant in Welland for the day, and took a 7:00 a.m. train to Toronto every day of his long political life, one can sympathize with his irritation with this example of media spite. Nonetheless, he was indefatigable in the interests of his constituents and they knew it.

The year 1956 was a critical one in Canadian politics. George Drew entered hospital in Ottawa and resigned the leadership of the Opposition in the House of Commons. He had long been an effective and sparkling opponent of the much-respected but staid Louis St Laurent. My friend Bill MacMillan used to tell me that his constituents from Welland County would come to Ottawa and ask to be introduced to George Drew, seldom to the prime minister. I had often thought that George's lack of success in the general elections of 1949 and 1953 convinced him that the party should not suffer a third defeat under his leadership, though the popular vote in his favour had been steadily rising, especially in Quebec. Perhaps he had not the toughness that R.L. Borden had displayed in similar contests with his great opponent before the First World War. Fortunately, Drew's illness, if illness it was, did not persist. The door was now open; the Prairie populist John Diefenbaker had no difficulty in fending off his principal rivals, Donald Fleming and Davie Fulton, and easily captured the convention and the leadership of the party on the first ballot. Great changes now impended.

I had spoken to many friends and well-wishers about my interest in being appointed a judge of the Supreme Court of Ontario. Interest, of course, is too mild a word, and as time passed, the prospect of a secure and rewarding career in the law until terminated by death or resignation became a ruling ambition. The discreet agitation which ensued even reached the ears of the prime minister, who made what could only be considered a favourable commitment. Then, on June 10, 1957, we all hailed – I with mixed feelings – St Laurent's defeat at the polls by John Diefenbaker and the installation of the first Conservative government of Canada in twenty-two years.

The mystique of judicial appointment has spasmodically provoked chiding from press and podium alike. Why should judges be plucked out of the legal profession apparently at the whim of executive authority without consultation or debate? The answer is that under the British system – "example" is perhaps the better word – the judges are Crown officers and always have been, at least since the Norman Conquest. For reasons which are historic, they were (and remain) creatures of the Crown and in an earlier day were liable to be removed at the pleasure of the sovereign. The practice of royal appointment and removal was, like so many other practices, acceptable until abused by King James II. Subsequently, by William and Mary's Act of Settlement, although royal appointment was retained, judges were given security of tenure as long as they behaved themselves (*dum bene gesserint*). This meant that they were for practical purposes secure for life unless assailed by madness or corruption, in which case dismissal could only be effected on the advice of Parliament through impeachment.

To this day, dismissal of high court or superior court judges in jurisdictions where the British example prevails can only be achieved by this means. Yet there are other ways of terminating tenure. The most humane and characteristic is the one that was followed in England in my time and probably still is. When a judge showed signs of feeble-mindedness, or of otherwise running out of steam, the Lord Chancellor would summon him to his chambers, express his sympathy, thank him for past services, and issue a recommendation for rest, whereupon the judge would be expected to, and generally did, resign. This practice has succeeded in more recent times with some exceptions; no Lord Chancellor could be expected to succeed in the cases of such judicial heroes as Lord Goddard and Lord Denning, the one Lord Chief Justice of England, the other Master of the Rolls, neither of whom was likely to have played the game. But judges of lower rank and more sensibility usually did.

In the United States, where the British example is still strong, other important exceptions have been made. In colonial days judges were more than usually unpopular because they were appointed by Westminster and thus were symbolic of a system in which the colonist played no part. Furthermore, they were often of poor quality. The solution appeared to be one of "representation" – "democratic" being an unacceptable word in those days – and after the revolution several states introduced choice of judges by election, although the federal government of the day did not favour the expedient. Nor could this new system be said to have achieved impressive results. At first glance, a second innovation was more rational: federal judges were to be examined publicly before their nomination took effect by a committee of Congress empowered to give or withhold confirmation of their nomination. Whatever the faults of this process, they did not become glaring until the age of television. Now it appears that such trivialities as the unwitting employment of an illegal immigrant can serve to destroy a reputation and ruin a career.

In the fierce currents of public opinion, real or media-manufactured, many words have lost their original meaning or have had pejorative versions thrown to the surface. I think that the word "gay," in its use as a euphemism for homosexuality, is not a good example of this process, being an atrocity in a class by itself. "Discrimination" in its various forms is a better example. This word is used as if it were ordinarily followed by the word "against." Who now talks about a discriminating taste in wine? The word "patronage" has suffered a similar change in emphasis. It once described the benevolent act of a patron and in the eighteenth century became associated with public offices, benefices in the Church of England, and the support of artists and the literati. It now serves almost exclusively as an insult to politicians who have the effrontery to appoint their friends instead of their enemies. Nevertheless, the appointment of judges is still firmly in the hands of the executive, testified to by documents bearing the great seal of Canada, and issued in the name of Her Majesty the Queen.

The Supreme Court of Ontario consisted of the Court of Appeal and the High Court of Justice, the latter known familiarly as the Trial Division. The late Liberal government, confident of office in perpetuity, had left many vacancies in the courts across Canada. The new government quickly filled three vacancies in the Court of Appeal, Dana Porter as chief justice and Kenneth Morden and George McGillivray as puisne judges, bringing the number up to nine. The elevation from the High Court to the Supreme Court of Canada of Mr Justice Wilfred Judson left a vacancy on the High Court bench which I now aspired to fill. Needless to say, there were other aspirants, particularly among members of the Progressive Conservative party whose hopes for appointment to the bench had been frustrated over twenty-two years of Liberal government in Ottawa.

But I was fortunately situated in many respects. Eddie Goodman, fresh from the victorious campaign of 1957 in which he had been the principal organizer of Diefenbaker's victory in Ontario, wrote a letter on my behalf to Davie Fulton, the minister of justice. I have a copy of that letter, and when occasionally I feel depressed in old age, I take it out and read it with tonic results. Then there was Eddie Shoniker, busy reweaving the spell which had favourably disposed Mr St Laurent in 1956. One day Alec McKenzie returned from Ottawa and said of Davie Fulton, "He's going to appoint you, but not just yet." Fulton's practice was to make informal inquiries among members of the provincial bar about the suitability of candidates. Whether he did or not in this case I cannot say, but finally, in June 1958, the minister called me and asked whether I would accept an appointment to the High Court. I answered that I certainly would. This, I felt, was the response he was expecting. Later that day I said to Helen, "We are set for life." And so it appeared, judicial appointments being then for life as I have pointed out. Lynn had just finished her first year at Branksome Hall and Sam was still thriving at Whitney Public Shool. In that long, tranquil summer evening, we looked forward to the placid procession of the years from our early forties to old age, secure and uneventful. We were indeed quite young.

CHAPTER THIRTEEN

The High Court

Because I was appointed in the last week of June, there was no
work for me to do at Osgoode Hall of an organized nature until
after the long summer vacation and I was not actually sworn in
until the first week in October, when Stanley N. Schatz and I were
sworn in together. The custom in those days was for the judge
taking the oaths of office to receive with thanks but no comment
the agreeable address of welcome given in court by the treasurer
of the Law Society. In this case the address was given by John J.
Robinette, QC, and it was very agreeable indeed. During the
summer and while waiting for this ceremony, from which my functions and receipt of pay necessarily began, I had attached myself
to the Weekly Court conducted for urgent matters only, as was the
case in those days. Here I found Dalton Wells, who gave me some
good tips and the pleasure of his company and conversation. On
my first day in the venerable building I ran into Ken Morden, and
he introduced me to everyone in sight and took me to lunch. My
welcome was warm and included a letter sent from the Canadian
embassy in Madrid by the chief justice of my court, James C.
McRuer, couched in terms of which few members of the bar would
have believed him capable.

The judges' chambers were of uneven quality, some floridly late
Victorian, others of an earlier date, spare and well proportioned.
I was fortunate in falling heir to one of the latter and furnished it
carefully with good copies by Rawlinson. My list for the sittings in

1958–59, picked from the two remaining after all the judges senior to me had made their choice, proved to be exciting enough. It took me first of all to the Welland assizes where, in spite of dire warnings not to return so soon to my origins, I knew that my inexperience would be softened by the friendly support of the sheriff, the local registrar, down to the most junior constable. So it turned out.

At the assizes, criminal work takes precedence until exhausted, and here it should be said that Chief Justice McRuer had long since arranged with the attorney general that High Court judges should only try cases of murder, manslaughter, rape, and criminal negligence causing death. This arrangement did not please Harold Fuller, our able and energetic county court judge, who thought that a superior court judge operating under a commission of general gaol delivery should deliver the gaols and not leave much of the criminal work and the accused associated with it to await the General Sessions of the Peace.

I was fortunate in having the two accused in my first criminal case defended separately by Joseph Sedgwick, QC, and G. Arthur Martin, QC, both at the height of their distinguished careers at the bar. It will be appreciated that my charge to the jury was as careful and balanced as I could make it and on the whole acceptable to these formidable advocates.

During the course of the next nine months I sat in more county and district towns than I would later on in many years, and I did a good deal more work than would be now considered possible in these days of judicial timidity and the dragging of forensic feet. For example, in this period I tried four men accused of raping the same girl in Sault Ste Marie, even with all the unavoidable delays, although admittedly the four accused were defended by the same able counsel. When the case went into its fourth day, I telephoned the chief justice and explained to him why the trial was taking so long to complete, but was able to assure him that it would end that evening. Now I suspect a similar trial might well take three weeks. A good deal of the superior dispatch of business was due to the judge's practice of settling procedural difficulties as they arose, listening to the briefest of arguments, and disposing of the matter from the bench without arguments at length or equally lengthy adjournments to consider a decision. Needless to say, the cooperation of counsel was essential if time and money were to be saved the parties in this manner. Now, indeed, judge and counsel have gone down the same dreary road together and cases get longer and more expensive as a result. But in the fifties the handwriting was not yet on the wall.

My friend Wilfred Judson was a great admirer of the court which I had recently joined and which he had adorned since 1951. Before leaving to take his seat on the Supreme Court of Canada in Ottawa, he left me robes which I wore for years in the High Court and books that I read with pleasure and profit. Oddly enough, it fell to him to deal a mortal blow to my pride and joy that first year on the bench. At issue was a case involving an apparent conflict between provincial securities legislation and a section of the Criminal Code dealing with false statements in a company prospectus. I held that, on a proper interpretation of section 91 of the British North America Act, the federal power occupied the field, but before releasing my reasons for judgment, I wrote a tailpiece validating the provincial legislation and sent the reasons and the two alternative solutions to my friend Professor Bora Laskin, then still a senior professor in the Department of Law at the University of Toronto (John Cartwright, later chief justice of Canada, used to refer humorously to Bora as "the court of last resort"). Bora selected my federalist solution, which I had originally determined to hand down. Unfortunately, the clean lines of contrast between federal and provincial jurisdiction under the Constitution had been blurred by members of the Supreme Court of Canada and in particular by Judson in a case called *O'Grady* v. *Sparling*, which held that apparently competing jurisdictions could coexist and overlap in cases of this kind. Thus, my judgment was overruled, together with one of Chief Justice McRuer's, but the thrill of being engaged in such a stately controversy quickly overcame any lingering sense of disappointment at the result, particularly since Messrs Justices Locke, Cartwright, and Ritchie agreed with me (and incidentally with Bora!). Looking back, I feel that we should have been more concerned with what then appeared only as a straw in the wind, and not as it has proven, a substantial obstacle in the way of clear-cut constitutional interpretation. Some two years later I had a talk with John Cartwright in the Rideau Club in Ottawa, and he was good enough to say that he felt our view was right.

I began finding my feet at the beginning of 1959, sitting in Windsor and Sudbury and coming south again to Kitchener. However, in the solid comfort of Kitchener's Walper House, I encountered disquiet. A telephone call from David Walker, parliamentary assistant to the minister of justice and a familiar of the prime minister's, advised me that I was wanted for the chairmanship of the Civil Service Commission of Canada. Thenceforward I had no peace. First of all, the hero of the hour, leader of the largest majority in the history of the House of Commons, wielding his mandate as prime minister like a flaming sword, sent in the skirmishers. I had calls from all sides. On one occasion I had a "conference call," three ministers in Ottawa, Davie Fulton, Howard Green, and J.W. Monteith, converging on me in Toronto. I said I would serve as chairman of the commission for a limited time, but I would not resign as a judge. I did not think it was proper to resign from the bench in good health and furthermore I liked being on it. This was the stumbling block, and in a fateful hour I went to Ottawa to preside in the non-jury sittings of the court. Every morning, either at the Chateau Laurier or at the courthouse, I would receive a call from the Prime Minister's Office and be asked to see Diefenbaker before going into court. Day by day for a week I visited the East Block; day by day the prime minister laid out the landscape like Lucifer. I would be the greatest employer in Canada. I would retain the title "Honourable" after resigning from the bench. When the time came to leave the commission, I would be appointed to a higher court. His door would always be open and he would welcome any suggestions I had to make on any subject. I returned to Toronto badly shaken. Pressure from prime ministers must be felt to be believed.

Many considerations militated against yielding: uprooting the family in the middle of the children's education, exchanging security for life for security for ten years (the term the civil service commissioners enjoyed), love of the law and preference for it over any contemplated interest in personnel administration, and, above all, the casting aside of judicial office so long sought and so briefly enjoyed. I disliked also the faintly improper quality of casting aside that office in what would undoubtedly be construed as seduction by the substantially higher salary attached to the chairmanship. Helen was staunch in whatever was decided.

Of the people I consulted, Eddie Goodman was my closest adviser, an intimate of the prime minister's but, convinced as he was of the importance of the offered appointment, nonetheless anxious that I be protected. We agreed that if I were to resign I should be guaranteed reappointment to the bench if and when I decided to return. One evening Goodman, Charles Dubin, and I repaired to the house of John Bassett, publisher of the *Telegram* and my grandfather's godson. Although not taking my devotion to the bench as seriously as did my two friends, Bassett was equally determined to see that reappointment down the road should be a condition of my accepting the chairmanship. In our presence he telephoned Diefenbaker and after receiving his assurance said, "That is an undertaking given to me," and so it was. Thus fortified, I agreed to go, but I said to Goodman, "Suppose he is unable to deliver when the time comes?" He looked at me with wonder. "We're in power for ten years, aren't we?" he said. I had to agree. How could the great majority of March 1958 be shorn away in less than two parliaments? All of this did not impress Alec McKenzie. "Tell him," he said to Goodman, "to turn it down as flat as piss on a plate."

CHAPTER FOURTEEN

Ottawa, 1959–1963

An announcement of the appointment was not made immediately, and the melancholy business of resigning from the court was briefly postponed. Nevertheless, the rumour mill was busy. Articles appeared in the Ottawa and Toronto press anticipating that the vacancy left by Arnold Heeney's return to Washington as ambassador would be filled by me. Diefenbaker was incensed at this breach of security and complained about it to Eddie Goodman. On investigating, the latter found that the press was relying on inspired leaks from the Prime Minister's Office itself and no more was heard from that quarter. When in due course the rumours were confirmed, we journeyed to Ottawa, as I recollect, on Dominion Day, 1959. The next day the *Ottawa Citizen* said that my appointment was the greatest single act of patronage in recent times. Little did the writer know how forlorn I felt, having abandoned a cherished vocation for a future which, in spite of all assurances, instinct told me was uncertain and laborious. Habitation was a problem, but Alec Perley-Robertson, a friend and an Ottawa real estate agent, found us a cottage at Larrimac on the Gatineau River in Quebec. There we spent a pleasant summer and in September moved into the Heeneys' house in Rockcliffe Park as tenants.

Arnold Heeney had long been a familiar figure in the corridors of power. A Rhodes scholar from Manitoba, he had practised law with distinction in Montreal and had served as principal secretary to Mackenzie King, clerk of the Privy Council, under-secretary of state for external affairs, and ambassador in Washington. In 1957 St Laurent had appointed him chairman of the Civil Service Commission of Canada, but scarcely two years later, at John Diefenbaker's earnest request, he resumed the post of Canadian ambassador to the United States. He was a man of great charm and great good looks; few people in the public service were as knowledgable and as influential as he. To Helen and me, he and his wife were unfailingly helpful and hospitable.

As chairman of the Civil Service Commission, Arnold Heeney had been given the task of shaping a new Civil Service Act. He and his colleagues Ruth Addison and Paul Pelletier, with the staff of the commission (equal to that of a medium-sized government department), produced what was widely known colloquially as the Heeney Report. This document had been justly extolled by those who had read it and had acquired vast prestige among those who had not. Since the operative portions of it appeared to take the form of a draft bill, it was frequently understood to be just that. In discussions with my colleagues, I began to make critical comments about the draftsmanship in various places, and it then occurred to me that it was not a draft bill at all that was thus set out in the report, but a statement of recommendations designed to achieve the optimum result, never before submitted to the Department of Justice or parliamentary counsel. My colleagues somewhat hesitantly agreed when I suggested that this was the case. Since I had been asked by the government to express my view of the report, I was able to begin to consider it with this important disclosure in mind.

There was no doubt that the Civil Service Act of 1918 had put an end to many irregularities in the recruitment and promotion of members of the civil service. There was also no doubt that it had inaugurated the so-called merit system and was a monument to the sagacity and disinterestedness of Sir Robert Borden's government in laying the foundation for a service which, in my respectful view, was highly professional and ready to serve whatever party triumphed at the polls, loyally and without partiality. This opinion I formed not long after I took office and maintained until I relinquished it, but I am bound to say that it was not shared by the Progressive Conservative rank and file members of the House of Commons, and particularly the influential members of the party from the prime minister down, at least until later. I had the mandate – scarcely ever expressed – to turn the service back from what was perceived to be a bias in favour of the Liberals, not too surprising considering their twenty-two years of uninterrupted power.

The one spectacular exception to the almost universal trust that soon developed between the new ministers and their senior professional advisers was supplied by Gordon Churchill, the new minister of trade and commerce, and his deputy minister, Mitchell Sharp. Churchill professed to find the influence of his predecessor, C.D. Howe, oppressively pervasive in his department and the condescending mandarin at his elbow unacceptable. Generally speaking, the transition had been smooth, but it was to be overshadowed by an internal crisis that confronted me almost at once.

I must set down as briefly as possible the origins of the crisis and its impact upon the commission. Since the end of the war, the conviction had been growing among government functionaries that the central problem for the service concerned employer-employee relationships, which in practice meant pay determination and, to a lesser extent, conditions of employment. The growing militancy of the staff associations, which were scarcely disguised trade unions and which by the mid-fifties had a good deal to be militant about in the area of pay, was a factor not previously experienced in Ottawa. Two of the ablest of the functionaries, Arnold Heeney, already referred to, and R.B. Bryce, a friend of mine in university days, had by 1956 reached agreement on the need for the Civil Service Commission to act as an independent arbiter between the staff associations and the government (that is, the Treasury Board). Both men were of unchallenged ability and experience; both had occupied great offices of state, Heeney's roots being in External Affairs and Bryce's in Finance.

I have often speculated on the part Bryce may have played in advising St Laurent to persuade Heeney to leave the prestigious and congenial position of Canadian ambassador in Washington to take the chairmanship of the commission in early 1957. When in the summer of that year the minority Conservative government took office, Heeney obtained from Diefenbaker a confirmation of his mandate to complete his report on what should be embodied in a new Civil Service Act. He was, however, disappointed in the coolness with which his proposals for a new system of collective bargaining were received by the prime minister and his minister of finance, Donald Fleming.

For many years it had been the accepted function of the commission to make wage and salary recommendations which the government could accept or reject *in toto*. There was no obligation on either party to reveal the nature of the recommendation, nor were the staff associations consulted. Three new developments had now to be taken into account: the increasing militancy of the staff associations; the emergence of the Treasury Board (in practice, the cabinet) as a contender for the Civil Service Commission's long-exercised prerogative of personnel management; and the recent creation of the Pay Research Bureau as part of the Civil Service Commission. The bureau gathered information about rates of pay and conditions of work in the private sector so that service pay could keep pace with commercial concerns as a matter of fairness and even more as a way to protect the government's position as a competitor in the labour market and a source of rewarding careers. All parties to the pay process initially hailed the Pay Research Bureau as an improvement of the first order. It was aided by an advisory committee on which the commission, the staff associations, and the Treasury Board were represented and to which the findings of the bureau were disclosed as a matter of course. Thus, the former conditions of secrecy and staff association obsequiousness ceased to prevail; yet what had been hailed as a master stroke had simply set the stage for strife.

However this might be, Arnold Heeney and his two colleagues, with all the resources of an experienced and sophisticated staff, pressed on with the completion of the report on the reorganization of the service to be expressed in a new Civil Service Act. During this period the commissioners made no recommendation to increase service pay and in fact recommended against it. The report was presented to the government, although not immediately released, at the end of 1958, after which Heeney was persuaded by the prime minister to resign as chairman of the commission and return to Washington as ambassador. I must say that when I first met Heeney he did not seem despondent at this development. The commission, however, was left six months without a chairman, and under the leadership of Ruth Addison and Paul Pelletier, the task of completing a pay recommendation for 1959 was accomplished without one. The recommendation, when it came, was a shock to the government, since it not only upset their financial calculations but required a matching increase in military service pay and a matching deposit in the Consolidated Fund. There was a polite exchange of letters and the recommendation was rejected. The reaction in the staff associations, the Civil Service Federation, the Civil Service Association of Canada, and the Professional Institute of the Public Service was predictable. The Heeney Report's nicely balanced recommendation for consultative collective bargaining and pay determination was discredited. The associations' leaders henceforth looked for and welcomed the prospect of confrontation with the Treasury Board alone.

The Civil Service Commission was nevertheless a majestic body, regardless of what way straws in the wind were blowing. It exercised exclusive jurisdiction over the recruitment and staffing of the federal service apart from casual and contract employees, the classification of positions, the control of appointments, promotions, demotions, and transfers, and, as already observed, pay and conditions of service. It had no minister, the secretary of state merely answering for the commission in Parliament and submitting its estimates. Each of the three commissioners ranked as deputy ministers, or, as they were officially called, "deputy heads."

There was a potential weakness in this last arrangement, since although the chairman was obviously *primus inter pares*, there was no statutory provision for disagreement among them. I liked my colleagues and got on well with them, though there were bound to be differences of opinion, especially in the unusual, and I think unprecedented, situation where a chairman joined the other two commissioners subsequent to their own appointment. The spirit of Arnold Heeney hovered over our early deliberations, but since Addison and Pelletier had been running the show on their own for six months, its presence was not as palpable as it might have been. In any event, we all three buckled down to the task of implementing the Heeney Report. I was asked by Donald Fleming to express my views and give, as it were, a concordance of them side by side with the sections of the recommended bill for perusal by members of the government.

Aside from the report's recommendation that all members of the public service should be governed by the new act and that the veterans' preference should be abolished, I had nothing but admiration for the recommendations which Heeney, Addison, and Pelletier had presented to the government. There was, however, one difficulty which I felt had been overlooked. That was the lack of definition of the chairman's function and status. This seemed particularly problematic because a great deal of the day-to-day business of the commissioners was shared with the francophone member, who had virtually unchallenged jurisdiction over the affairs of the commission in Quebec and had in previous years run it almost as a private satrapy. I therefore saw to it that in the new bill the chairman should be styled the chief executive officer of the commission. This was a delicate matter to broach with my colleagues, but after expressing their misgivings, they ultimately conceded.

The work of implementing the report had scarcely begun before we learned that Prime Minister Diefenbaker was contemplating what he called a "Hoover-type" inquiry, referring somewhat imprecisely to the mammoth investigation in the United States conducted by ex-president Herbert Hoover. What at first was hardly more than rumour materialized all too soon in 1960 in the shape of the Royal Commission on Government Operations. Its chairman was W. Grant Glassco, already a prominent figure in the world of finance and executive head of the accounting firm of Clarkson Gordon and Company, which was familiar with the federal scene through the activity of its associated firm Woods Gordon and Company. Grant's brother Meredith had been a colleague at Ridley and I had known Grant in Zeta Psi some twenty-five years earlier. During the coming months we were to have several agreeable luncheons in the Rideau Club, sometimes with the executive director of his royal commission, Ronald Ritchie. I kept my fingers crossed but, alas, to no avail. The best account of the ensuing struggle is in Part One of the history of the Civil Service Commission of Canada (1908–67) entitled *Biography of an Institution*, sponsored by the Institute of Public Administration and published by McGill-Queen's University Press.

The royal commission skated serenely around the perimeter of government operations, picking up complaints against the Civil Service Commission from departments that not unnaturally, considering the csc's tight rein on staffing, classification, and pay, were inclined to blame their inadequacies on it. I was cast in a role

I had not expected to assume, as defender of the Civil Service Commission as it stood against the royal commission's efforts to introduce private-sector personnel management to the Ottawa scene. For the first time I questioned the single-mindedness of John Diefenbaker. What was the point of having the Glassco Commission, with its sweeping mandate to examine civil service operations and recommend changes, work contemporaneously with the CSC, which was engaged in the implementation of the Heeney Report and the drafting of the first new Civil Service Act in forty years? I am satisfied that Grant Glassco and his colleagues felt very much as I and mine. Did the prime minister really understand what he was doing in setting up this cacophony of recommendations or did he, as I now believe, simply wish to make a demonstration for the benefit of press and public and go on to some more congenial political activity? However that may have been, it was not for this that I had resigned from the Ontario High Court, even though I was being paid substantially more than I would have been paid as a judge. I was determined more than ever to procure fulfilment of his promise to send me back to judicial office.

Before leaving the subject of John Diefenbaker, I must say that the closer one stood to him the more enigmatic he became. He was magnetic but not magnanimous. The people of Canada had overwhelmingly elected a man who had successfully posed as a visionary; they had in fact installed an old-time party politician, full of the lore and love of Sir John A. Macdonald and with a talent for retaliation rather than responsibility. I only once tried to accept his invitation to give him suggestions and advice from time to time. On this occasion, in his office in the East Block, I suggested that his government review the salaries of judges. It had seemed to me that because of their traditional linkage with the sessional indemnities of members of Parliament and the necessity of having an express vote in both houses, such a review had been long delayed. He stared at me and then said, "I have no difficulty finding judges." As repartee this was no doubt effective because it silenced me for good, and the judges too, who had to wait until the Progressive Conservatives were out of office before any salary increase was vouchsafed. The amendment to the British North America Act made by the British Parliament at the instance of the Canadian government at this time had its own quality of vindictiveness. It said simply and brutally that on his or her seventy-fifth birthday a judge in office ceased to be a judge, with the result that those who had been appointed for life found themselves adrift, not, be it said, unreasonably, but with no effort to cushion the shock with "grand-father's rights." It was said, I do not know how accurately but with some point, that the prime minister had thus dismissed the whole Court of Appeal of Saskatchewan, which had of course from time to time reversed decisions he had won at trial.

Diefenbaker's treatment of Earl Rowe was also revealing. Rowe was the only cabinet minister to survive the Bennett government's dismissal from office in 1935 and to be still in the House of Commons. He had promoted Diefenbaker's career in the early days and voted for him in the leadership convention of 1948 that chose George Drew. When George became leader of the Opposition, Rowe had loyally supported him. Diefenbaker considered this betrayal, and when he became prime minister, Earl Rowe, although the senior member of his parliamentary party, was given no employment. Only at the end of six years of diminishing popularity did Diefenbaker, on the insistence of his Ontario advisers, make Rowe lieutenant-governor of that province.

A minor irritation for me concerned the title "Honourable." In conversations before my appointment, the prime minister had led me to believe that its retention would be automatic, but for many months the official lists omitted it. I finally inquired of Howard Measures, the chief of protocol, what had happened. He said that he had no knowledge of my particular problem, but if I was anxious to secure the title, the matter would have to be presented to the Palace and ordered personally by Her Majesty the Queen. This was eventually done, although it would not be necessary nowadays, the title being conferred by statute and not relinquished. If it is thought that this is a triviality, let the reader consider what such a title would mean to one who might have had to return to the practice of law because of an undertaking unfulfilled.

Having said all this, I must confess that after the first few weeks of unease I thoroughly enjoyed my great office, my colleagues and our coadjutors, and Ottawa in general. Half a dozen of the members of the cabinet were our personal friends and others were soon added to their number. Fortunately, we had many old friends from university or army days who were native or permanent residents of the capital, not there by virtue of their official functions or diplomatic appointment. Typical of these were Denis and Jean Coolican, who lived across the road from the Heeneys' house in Rockcliffe Park. I first met Denis when we were competitors at the Royal Canadian Henley Regatta of 1932; his wife, Jean, had come to Ottawa with her parents when her father, Sir Gerald Campbell, became British high commissioner. Stewart Wotherspoon had been a contemporary of mine at Trinity College and had married another contemporary, Enid Palmer, Ottawa born and bred; he became one of the capital's leading lawyers. Murray and Nancy Cleary were also indigenous and dear to us, and many more were our good friends and still are.

Then there was the diplomatic circle, very agreeable, very hospitable and only really accessible in Ottawa. I remember being at a party at Earnscliffe, the house on the Ottawa River in which Sir John Macdonald spent his last days, and hearing my host, the British high commissioner, Lord Amory, say *sotto voce* and incredulously, "He didn't resign from the bench?" – an eccentricity of which I was only too conscious.

The final stage in the implementation of the Heeney Report was the preparation of the bill that became the Civil Service Act of 1961. The drafting process was interesting. The deputy minister of justice, Elmer Driedger, called before him all the people he thought should be involved (and these of course included me) for discussions. In due time, he sent us draft sections of the bill, which bore his stamp. He was a master draftsman who subsequently, in his retirement, lectured on the subject at Queen's University. Then came the appointment of a select committee of the House of Commons before whom I appeared on several days, as did my commissioner colleagues. Representatives of the Treasury Board and of the staff associations were also called and examined by the committee under the leadership of my friend R.A. Bell, parliamentary secretary to the minister of finance, Donald Fleming. I was the first to appear before the committee following the opening statement which Fleming made to it. Much in evidence at this stage were representations made by two organizations from the province of Quebec, the Saint Jean-Baptiste Society and Le Conseil de la Vie Française, expressing a by no means novel complaint about the lack of French-speaking officers in the civil service. When tested, the deficiency amounted to the lack of French names on the list provided. I well remember the reply of the member for Hull, a Liberal and a French Canadian, to one of these complaints: "There will be no difficulty about this. We will teach these people to speak French and to be bilingual." It was amusing to see the shades of disapproval falling upon the determined features of these advocates. They were not really interested in having anglophones learn French, but wanted French blood rather than the French language to be more evident in the civil service. I must cite two further examples of this somewhat illogical sentiment.

The Board of Broadcast Governors asked for a bilingual program director. When the personnel selection branch of the Civil Service Commission referred a bilingual anglophone to the board, Dr Stewart called me in anguish and said, "But we wanted a Frenchman." Another instance of the same obsession was provided by the deputy minister of finance, Kenneth Taylor, who came to see me to secure the services of our information officer, Wilfred Trudeau. I thought I knew what was coming and tried to anticipate it. I said, "Ken, Trudeau is an excellent information officer and I don't want to stand in the way of his promotion to the position you have in mind for him, but I must tell you that he is a graduate of Carleton University, a member of the United Church of Canada, and does not speak a word of French." "It doesn't matter," said the doyen of the deputy ministers, "it's the name that counts."

The stresses of wartime administration had taken a heavy toll on constitutional propriety in the government of Canada. I discovered that the civil service was governed by a bewildering profusion of regulations that seemed to have no connection with, much less authorization by, any section of the Civil Service Act. The War Measures Act had not only superseded the operation of any statute that might have presented difficulties to the wartime administrators, but had deprived these administrators and especially their successors of an understanding of public law. When I ventured to suggest to my officers that there might be some difficulty in legalizing something adventitious they wished to practise, I was met with, "Oh, we'll get an order in council." When I explained that an order in council could not materialize out of thin air but must have precise authority from the act of Parliament to which it was subordinate legislation, I was regarded as "legalistic." A minor example of the lack of sensitivity induced by coping with an emergency such as war was the inclusion of the following question in the application for entry into the civil service: "Have you ever been *charged* with an offence?" When I insisted that the word "charged" be changed to "convicted," I observed deference rather than understanding.

The stamp of legalism was placed upon my stereotype when, sensing the hostility of the Glassco Commission and anticipating the loss of pay determination and organization and classification for the service to the Treasury Board, I endeavoured to give new direction to the Civil Service Commission. We had indeed authority from the act of 1918 to conduct appeals by civil servants aggrieved by decisions of their own department, but it was cumbersome and little resorted to until we were able to insert a section in the act of 1961 expressly enlarging the appellate jurisdiction of the commission, hoping to set it on a new course. On two occasions, indeed, I conducted investigations at the request of ministers which, while not technically hearings of appeals, illustrate the authority of the commission when invoked in the area of grievance. The first was at the request of Michael Starr, minister of labour, to enquire into the dismissal of a Winnipeg employee of the Unemployment Insurance Commission, effected, as it turned out, by entrapment. In the course of the investigation I found Stewart Garson pleading for justice for his client as I had once pleaded before him for the life of mine. This was in 1961, and in the following year I went at the request of William Hamilton, the postmaster general, to Fort St John, British Columbia, to investigate the circumstances under which the behaviour of the postmaster had induced all his staff to leave their employment. For two days in this dusty frontier town I listened to the embattled postmaster and his staff and heard arguments from representatives of management and the postal workers' staff association.

In these two cases I made a written report to the ministers concerned recommending action that was in both instances undertaken. In Winnipeg Garson's client was reinstated; and in Fort St John the postmaster was reassigned, but the employees who had withdrawn their services could not be re-employed. The latter result may appear harsh by modern standards, but in those days the idea that civil servants could strike against the Crown was unacceptable. It did not receive countenance until a Liberal party election promise was redeemed by Prime Minister Pearson some five years later. In Ontario the un-unionized civil service had to wait for almost thirty years before a similar determination was reached by a socialist government, the effects of which are causing some inconvenience as I write.

By 1962 I had visited every CSC office in the ten provinces, had twice addressed the annual meetings of the Public Personnel Association in the United States, but because of serious preoccupations with the new Civil Service Act and the forays of the Glassco Commission had been forced to ignore our considerable establishments in the United Kingdom. Around this time I received from the Department of External Affairs a routine announcement of the quinquennial plenary meeting of the International Institute of Administrative Sciences. The meeting was to be held in Vienna and representation by the commission was requested. I regret to say that I ignored this as a frill for which there was no time, but on receiving a sharp reminder from External Affairs, I decided to attend the meeting myself and combine the journey with a visit to London. At this time Lynn was at Lisgar Collegiate Institute in Ottawa, and Sam was finishing up at Rockcliffe Park Public School prior to going to Upper Canada College as a boarder. Because our children had no close relatives within easy reach other than ourselves, Helen and I had made it a practice not to fly together, and so as a matter of routine I had made most of my arrangements without telling her of my plans. To my surprise and pleasure I found that she, perhaps with some assistance from my secretary, had made her own arrangements to follow me to Vienna on a separate flight. The children were fortunately at camp in the July fortnight of our expedition, and we felt that we could safely spread our wings.

Other than an unforgettable family trip to the Pacific coast on the CPR's *Canadian* and back by the CNR's *Super Continental*, both providing a standard of luxury now no longer available, we had not had a holiday since my appointment. Vienna, rich in song and story, was a wonderful prospect, as was London. We had not been in the latter since the end of the war and we would now be able to enjoy it all the more because our old friend George Drew was there, serving as high commissioner.

Underlining these yearnings was my conviction that my work in terms of the original mandate was done. The new Civil Service Act was in place and regulations thereunder almost ready for enactment. There was no doubt about the integrity of the service, only about the wisdom of its political masters. It was therefore time for me to present the prime minister's pledge for redemption and return to Osgoode Hall.

Nevertheless, I found it strangely difficult to get the ear of the one whose door would always be open to me. He could not have been in any doubt as to what subject I wanted to broach to him because, in the intervals of complaining about my persistent attempts to speak to him either in person or on the telephone, he let it be known that he did not think my job was done. To give an edge to my frustration, a general election impended on June 18, 1962. The great majority given Diefenbaker in 1958 would certainly be reduced, but by how much? The man the people of Canada had hailed as a visionary had proved to be more like an old-style politician and a devious one at that.

When the day of the election came, Helen and I and Wilfred Judson went to Kenneth and Shirley Campbell's house to see the results on television. Ken Campbell had been secretary to the chief justice of Canada since the days of Sir Lyman Duff. He was the repository of much history and much information and had been the confidant of two generations of judges of the Supreme Court of Canada. Both Shirley and he had their roots deep in the Ottawa Valley. Our high spirits at the beginning of our evening evaporated as Liberal victories piled up in eastern Canada, particularly in the big cities. When the tide flowing from east to west reached the head of the Great Lakes, I felt that John Diefenbaker would not be able to redeem the pledge he had given me, and that although I would be secure for another seven years in the Civil Service Commission, I should contemplate a new career beginning precariously in late middle-age. Well, I thought, I have often laughed at the jibes of friends who said I could not hold a steady job and now I had better put a good face on it. But the old magic still prevailed in western Canada for the Prairie populist and at the final count he was still prime minister, although shorn of over ninety supporters in the House of Commons. Wilf and I had reason to be grateful that Helen was driving us home.

I could not help reflecting on my conversation with Eddie Goodman only three years before, when we had confidently assumed that

Diefenbaker would enjoy at least ten years of power. I flew off to
Vienna with my own future undecided, having found the leader of
a minority government no easier to pin down than I had the triumphant head of the largest parliamentary majority in Canadian
history. Helen joined me in the superb Imperial Hotel, recently
evacuated by the headquarters of the Russian occupying force. The
Russians had looted it thoroughly and shipped all its furniture and
hangings downstream to Budapest, thus ensuring a complete and
highly successful refurbishing. We were warmly received by Canadian ambassador Margaret Meagher, who entertained for us and
drove us around the famous city and its green-walled environs.
Under her auspices we met Kurt Waldheim, an agreeable function-
ary later to be chancellor of the Austrian Republic and not then
suspected of ss anti-Jewish activity in Yugoslavia. The conference
was preceded by a visit by train, at the invitation of the governor
of Lower Austria, to the village of Durnstein on the fast-flowing
Danube. High above the village loomed the forbidding castle where
the great warrior king, Richard Cœur-de-Lion, on his way back from
the Third Crusade, was held to ransom by Duke Leopold. The occasion was not to celebrate this infamy but to taste the new wine culled
from the vineyards which clothed the steep slopes above the mighty
river, a pleasant if somewhat bibulous occasion.

The conference itself was a sterile review of the work of various
local bodies in countries supporting the institute, distilled into
resolutions and translated into four languages. Each delegate was
issued a "polyglot," an instrument worn around the neck so that
the wearer could by pressing buttons listen to the proceedings in
the language of his or her choice. We were fortunate in making
early acquaintance with Roger Stanton and his wife, Françoise.
Roger was, if I remember correctly, associate deputy treasurer of
the province of Quebec and he was armed with a special *passe-
partout* from his premier Jean Lesage. We spent many agreeable
hours in the course of the week, but I felt that my diplomatic
passport had been squandered on a rigid and unproductive function only enlivened by the complaints of African delegates that the
material aid they had received from the developed countries had
not been installed by their benefactors.

In my report to the government I suggested that although
Canada had for some years been a financial supporter of the

institute, serious consideration should be given to terminating this assistance. In case I should be considered churlish after the visit to Durnstein, I hasten to say that the arrangements made by the government of Austria were generous and imaginative, ending in a superb banquet given by the chancellor in the great Hapsburg palace of Schönbrunn. We left Vienna with regret, deeply imbued with a sense of its beauty and prominence in the history of Europe, but conscious too of the current uneasiness of its population about the menacing presence of the Red Army, still so close at hand. These were the barbarians who had defaced the Schwarzenbergplatz with their monstrous war memorial crowned by a concrete carbine-carrying soldier with a gold-painted helmet.

As our aircraft climbed steeply over the Wienerwald, the ennervating charm of Vienna slipped from my shoulders like a cherished but discarded cloak. What lay ahead in England was more serious business. However, the habitat was as beguiling as it had been in Austria and the Savoy in London had long been our favourite hotel. George Drew had made a great effort on our behalf, and my conscience was troubled when I thought of my own efforts to leave the chairmanship of the commission as soon as my reappointment to the bench could be arranged. We were met at Heath Row by Graham McInnes, the senior counsellor at the High Commission, and we were whisked into Canada House for lunch with the high commissioner. We had not seen George since before the illness which had induced him to resign as leader of his party. He was a friend of both our families, although more particularly of Helen's, and the reunion could only have been improved upon by the presence of Fiorenza, unavoidably absent.

A busy week had been planned for me, divided between liaison with the British civil service commissioners and the representatives of our own government's departments in Britain, a significant part of our own civil service. The British commission was essentially an examining body, without the Canadian commission's responsibility for selection and promotion in government departments, but it had a science branch for establishing appropriate standards in that field and a pay research unit much as we had at home – for all I know, the exemplar of our own Pay Research Bureau, a point I do not remember pursuing. I was indebted to the first commissioner, Sir George Mallerby, virtually retired from a distinguished procon-sular career, for easing my path and giving me much good advice. But the real power in the British service is the Treasury and here I was helped by meeting the permanent under-secretary, Sir Norman Brook (later Lord Normanbrook) at a luncheon given in my honour by George at the Junior Carlton Club. He told an amusing story about his wife, a great "rattle" as she would have been called in the eighteenth century. Finding herself sitting at dinner beside an elderly man with piercing eyes and a somewhat aquiline profile, she asked him if he knew anything about Sicily. When he said emphatically that he did, she then asked if he knew anything about the beaches in Sicily. To this, he snapped, "My dear lady, whom do you think you're talking to?" It was Monty.

Our high commissioner had in those days at least an unspecified but traditional superintendency over our diplomatic activities in Europe, no doubt because of his accreditation to the Court of St James. The title even now remains the same, although the commis-sioner's political master has become minister for foreign affairs instead of secretary of state for external affairs as of yore. In the period I am describing, the commissioner's staff contained a number of External Affairs officers who were closely linked to the diplomatic posts on the Continent and made periodic reports in person and in conclave to the high commissioner. It was a measure of the delicate attentions paid by him to me that he asked me to attend one of these meetings. At a certain point he abandoned his chair at the head of the table, asked me to take it, and then suggested that these members of his staff make their reports to me. Although I was taken off guard by this procedure, I realized it was the highest compliment my old friend and mentor could pay me. On the last day of our visit I unburdened myself to him about my anxiousness to rejoin the Supreme Court of Ontario and my inabil-ity to get an appointment with the prime minister to discuss my resignation. George pointed to a coloured telephone (green or red, I do not remember which) and said, "Try this." I lifted the receiver and was immediately put through to the Prime Minister's Office and told that Diefenbaker would call me at the Savoy Hotel in one hour's time. I said goodbye to my distinguished host and hastened back to our room, where at the appointed time John Diefenbaker rang and said in a weary voice, "Well, if that's what you want, all right." When I later learned that not long before that call he had broken his ankle, I realized that his lack of cordiality was not solely directed at me.

With a great sense of relief we flew home the following day. Although my plane left Heath Row ahead of Helen's, hers arrived in Montreal first and she was there to welcome me when I reached our small but delightful Ottawa house on Minto Place. (We had acquired this house three years before and providentially it over-looked the immaculate lawns of the Norwegian embassy and shared a boundary with the house of our friends Murray and Nancy Cleary.) The emergency financial regulations of that summer had enlivened the pay determination issue and Donald Fleming was pleased to see me back in Ottawa. I lost no time telling him of Diefenbaker's under-taking made on the telephone. This was appropriate, since Donald would be acting prime minister in case of any absence of or mishap to the PM himself, but I could tell no one else for obvious reasons.

I had made a number of speeches on various subjects to the Institute of Public Administration of Canada, and I had written and spoken frequently in explanation of the changes made by the new Civil Service Act. A speech I delivered to the Canadian Club in Ottawa, entitled "Service of the State," attracted particularly favourable comment. All the speeches were composed by me, and all but one of the articles, the exception being an excellent "ghost" by Wilf Trudeau which I heartily endorsed, summarizing the changes made by the new act in comparison with that of 1918. I mention my habit of composing my own speeches not through any pride of authorship but because when I arrived at the commission I found an officer of ability, and in the middle ranks, who did nothing else but write the chairman's speeches. I thought this was a luxury that could be dispensed with, and I prevailed on him to go to Alberta as a senior personnel selection officer. There, con-trary to his own misgivings, he did extremely well. I had already persuaded Marion Roach, long-time secretary to the successive chairmen of the commission and the perfection of good judgment and efficiency, to leave her lofty position in the clerical grades to become an untried administrative officer. She did so well that after my departure she became secretary to the commission itself.

I made my final address as chairman to the senior class in administration at our training school in Arnprior. I chose as my subject appeals to the Civil Service Commission, and I emphasized the importance of developing this function as a means of filling the void left by our effective loss of pay determination to the Treasury Board. Then in September 1962 I travelled to Regina to take part in the annual convention of the Institute of Public Administration, where Arnold Heeney, back from Washington and now chairman of the Canadian section of the International Joint Commission, was scheduled to speak about the recently released report of the Glassco Commission. He did not for a minute reveal the disappointment he must have felt at the approaching destruction of his work, but with great dexterity and a show of sweet reason he put his finger on the weakness of the royal commission's report, its failure to fully understand the role of the Civil Service Commission as an independent and unifying force. Arnold told me that he thought the Glassco Report's statement of the problem in personnel management was admirable, but he felt that the mores of the private sector had dominated the commission's recommendations to the detriment of its work. Indeed, in his address to the institute, he said: "I am not appearing in the guise of a defender of the *status quo ante* or the Civil Service Commission or indeed of any of our existing arrangements. But here is something under our system which I do not think has been fully appreciated by these able men." The soft impeachment is all the more telling. This was the last conversation I had with my distinguished predecessor, with whom I had always been on the friendliest terms and whose work I greatly admired.

I owe it to his memory to comment on John Diefenbaker's slighting allusion to him in his memoirs. Diefenbaker mentions his own fear that Heeney, Ruth Addison, and Paul Pelletier would perpetuate the Liberal party's influence in the civil service, but says that, on closer acquaintance with Arnold, he changed his mind and appointed him ambassador to Washington out of respect for his abilities. This patronizing statement makes no reference to the fact that Heeney was not only ambassador at Washington when he was induced to become chairman of the Civil Service Commission, but had filled more of the high offices in the state than anyone else then living. The plain truth was that he was moved to Washington to make room for me, the prime minister thinking characteristically that because of my known political activities in the past I would be more pliable. No doubt he was disappointed and my name does not appear in his account, which admittedly was written over ten years after I left Ottawa. At all events, Heeney spent another three years in Washington before he was succeeded by Charles Ritchie, whose whole career had been in the diplomatic service but who enjoyed an impeccably Conservative ancestry.

Three days after my return to Ottawa I received a minute of the order in council reappointing me to the Supreme Court of Ontario. Only the Toronto *Globe and Mail* suggested that I had been dismissed because of criticism levelled at the commission in the Glassco Report. This provoked an emphatic denial from Don Fleming as acting prime minister, describing the *Globe*'s effort as a "shocking statement" and pointing out that the bench had been my first love and that my appointment to the chairmanship of the commission had always been considered temporary. The *Globe*'s alert correspondent had, however, spotted two shreds of evidence to support his interpretation: there was, in spite of what all the other journals had to say about my return to the bench, nothing in the official statement to say I had resigned; and I had evidently relinquished a salary of $22,000 a year as chairman for one of $16,900 as a judge. In fact, no formal resignation was effected until several weeks later when Bob Bryce asked me to come to the Privy Council Office to sign the necessary documents while I was sitting in the Ottawa court. If that detail was overlooked, so, I can honestly say, was the difference in salary. In the course of his vigorous and generous statement, Fleming denied that appointment to the court could be regarded as a demotion and I agreed with him. But on reflection I am not surprised that the *Globe and Mail*'s correspondent drew his bow at a venture to provoke discussion and produce information, although at the time I was heartened by Fleming's denunciation.

Notwithstanding the pressures of life at the top of the government service, Helen and I greatly enjoyed our nearly four years in Ottawa. I say "four" when three and a quarter might better reflect the span of my period of office because the Department of Justice gave me leave to use Ottawa as a base for my judicial employment until the spring of 1963. This facilitated our transfer of residence to Toronto and allowed Lynn to complete her school year at Lisgar Collegiate. The capital of Canada was a good place to live and an especially good place to bring up children. Grandeur was not among its attributes; yet it was ceremonious in a modest way. Men wore full evening dress with decorations and white kid gloves at Government House evening functions, but protocol was not stiff among those who directed the affairs of the nation, most of whom knew each other intimately and used their first names. Prime Minister Diefenbaker, indeed, went a little further than was necessary, being conveyed about in a second-hand Buick automobile by a driver disguised as a constituent from Prince Albert. When Senator Wallace McCutcheon arrived to take over the portfolio of Trade and Commerce in a chauffeur-driven Rolls Royce, it made a considerable stir.

Although I had bitterly regretted having had to resign from the bench after only one year, I took some comfort from Davie Fulton's assurance that "men of all parties" had approved of my work on the High Court. After a month or two with the Civil Service Commission I was caught up in the excitement of a task clearly of great national importance and not yet shadowed by the Glassco Commission. As I have said, I liked my colleagues and got on well with them, fully understanding that they had some reservations about me as a replacement for the much-admired Arnold Heeney. As time went on, we drew closer together, sharing the same anxieties and animated by the same purpose of preserving the commission's traditional role. By the standards of other countries, the Canadian Civil Service Commission was unique in its comprehensiveness and independence of government control, saving always the supremacy of Parliament to which it was alone responsible.

The staff of the commission was of high quality, capable of producing prompt solutions to most problems and unperturbed by the universal experience of having to supply the ministers with the information they needed to survive in the helter-skelter of the House of Commons' question period. Heeney had organized the meetings of the commission along the lines of those of the cabinet, which he knew so well, and the commissioners sat frequently, regularly furnished with papers, and heads of departments attended as required. Even when it became apparent that the pay determination recommendations of the Heeney Report, although enshrined in the Civil Service Act of 1961, would be made unworkable because of the intransigence of both the staff associations and the Treasury Board, we had high hopes right up to the time of my departure. But there was much more to be implemented and other challenges to meet. In short, I greatly enjoyed my association with the Civil Service Commission of Canada and appreciated the honour of being its chairman in those difficult years.

I suppose it falls to few people to sit on the floor of the House of Commons without being an elected member or one of its staff, such as the clerk of the House or the sergeant-at-arms. There was, however, and perhaps still is, an occasion when a minister presenting his estimates from the front row of government benches is entitled to have one or two of his officials sitting facing him to provide information and to organize papers. The first occasion when I assisted the secretary of state in this role was made more difficult because he was in no sense our minister, had no personal knowledge of the detail which he had to convey to the House, and was effectively dependent upon me and my senior officer for answers to opposition questions. I was greatly alarmed when the secretary of state, Henri Courtemanche, began his speech by introducing me to the House. He was almost immediately interrupted by Liberal member Lionel Chevrier, who rebuked him for forgetting that public officials, however eminent, are traditionally faceless and nameless in Parliament. Nevertheless, when the dust settled, George Hees leaned across his desk on the front bench, waved his hand and said, "Hi, Sam." On another occasion, when our estimates were being presented, I received rude notes, borne by pages, from my old friend Judy LaMarsh.

Life was made pleasant for us through our friendship with many of the leading figures in government, friendships which in many cases antedated my appointment in Ottawa: George Hees, Davie Fulton, Donald Fleming, Ellen Fairclough, and Jim Macdonnell, an elder statesman to whom the Progressive Conservative party owed a great deal, unacknowledged by the contemporary leadership.

Generally I lunched at the Rideau Club, that comely building on the south side of Wellington Street, opposite the Peace Tower, long since reduced to ashes. The Supreme Court contributed a regular detachment of its more sociable judges with whom I used to foregather: Wilfred Judson, Douglas Abbott, and Roland Ritchie (younger brother of Charles). Occasionally Ivan Rand, already retired from the court, would make an appearance and be companionable. Most of all I looked forward to long talks with Colonel Harold M. Daly, my grandfather's military secretary in the first war and a barrister and solicitor in Ottawa. He regaled me with many stories of the past, starting with the time that he had sat on the lap of Sir John A. Macdonald, but he spoke most of all about the years he had spent with my grandfather, to whom and to whose memory he was devoted. These conversations stimulated his memory to produce a steady flow of memoranda, preserving for me the fruit of his recollections.

All honour to Denis Coolican, who during his presidency successfully relocated the Rideau Club in its present situation atop the Metropolitan Life building, the décor cunningly suggestive of the old club, but of course without its grand staircase bifurcating halfway up and creating two ascents. At one of these my grandfather used to take his stand at lunchtime to shake hands with members and their guests during his years of power. On the day of his resignation all but a very few went up the other side to avoid this greeting.

Because of the old association, the hall porter at the Rideau Club, Archie Lacaille, always called me "Colonel" and showed me marks of favour for old times' sake, which gave me great pleasure. Ken Campbell told me how Chief Justice Sir Lyman Duff used to ask him what the time was, and on being told would always say, "Better call Archie at the club" for confirmation. Ken would say from time to time, "But Sir Lyman, all you have to do is look over your left shoulder and there's the Peace Tower clock." "Call Archie anyway," the chief would reply without looking. Archie had served the Rideau Club since boyhood and was unique in his knowledge of the members and his capacity to help them in any emergency great or small. "All, all are gone, the old familiar faces."

Helen, as she always has, took the second uprooting in her stride. Like me, she thought Ottawa a fine place to live and rewarding for the children. The importance of the capital city was only a small consideration in assessing its attractions. Its environs are nothing short of spectacular: the swift and noble river thundering over the Chaudière Falls and sweeping past the great promontory supporting

Parliament Hill; the distant prospect of the Laurentian hills fronted by the closer King Mountain; the vivid scarlet and gold vestments of its autumnal glory; even the sharp, often bitter winters, made hospitable by the season's recreations, including the ski slopes of Mount Fortune, a bare half hour's drive into Gatineau country – a wonderful tapestry to frame the transactions of a nation great and small. Helen made many friends for herself and me. Having been an enthusiastic worker for the National Ballet in Toronto, she headed the Ottawa committee that paved the way for the company's first appearance in Ottawa, held at the Capital Theatre on Bank Street. In the days before the National Centre for the Performing Arts had risen across Confederation Square, this moving-picture theatre provided the only suitable stage in the still culturally nascent capital of Canada. We shared a box with the Vaniers and the Simonds, Guy being then president of the National Ballet, and the performance was a success.

Helen was also responsible for an event which I take pleasure in recording. She said to me one day: "Do you realize that your children have never met the prime minister?" I said, "I suppose not." "Your father," she said, "would have seen to it." Remembering how I had been taken as a boy of seven to be presented to Arthur Meighen when he was prime minister and even introduced to Winston Churchill when he was in Canada in 1929, I could not disagree. Not many days later I had a call from the East Block to say that if my children were present in the prime minister's office at eight in the morning, he would be glad to see them. So on a wintry morning we rose betimes and, freshly scrubbed and dressed to the nines, repaired to Parliament Hill and mounted the East Block steps. The PM had already been in his office for an hour and had disposed of his mail for the day. He radiated cheerfulness and enthusiasm, amply justifying his reputation for interest in young people, with whom I think he was at his best. He took us into the cabinet room and showed Lynn and Sam the chair in which he believed their great-grandfather had sat half a century before. He must have spent almost an hour with us, talking volubly with the starry-eyed youngsters before signifying dismissal with the most charming apologies. All together he seemed transformed by this simple exercise. I said some bitter things about John Diefenbaker in the previous chapter, but I shall never forget this occasion and the care he took to make

it memorable. Helen, of course, had triumphed over my indifference as might be expected of a life member of the Imperial Order
of the Daughters of the Empire (IODE).

Wilfred Judson bought our house in Rockcliffe Park and I think
ended his days there, certainly after a brilliant career on the
nation's highest court. Born in Yorkshire, trained in medieval
history in the University of Manchester, a teacher of Latin at
Parkdale Collegiate Institute in Toronto, and a rising practitioner
at the Toronto bar before his appointment to the High Court and
subsequent elevation to the Supreme Court of Canada, he proved
what a first-class mind can do even when applied to a discipline in
circumstances far removed from early environment and training.
I returned to Toronto and rejoined my brethren on the bench in
a mood of self-justification, but I left Ottawa with more regret than
I had expected and a feeling that there is no better place to live
in Canada than the village of Rockcliffe Park.

One of the worthies of the Liberal party, George McIlraith, who
had relentlessly but, I felt, sympathetically questioned me when I
was before the Select Committee of the House of Commons on
the Civil Service Act of 1961, was clearly, in spite of the appearance
of opposition, of the same mind as mine, being greatly concerned
with the preservation of the traditional independence of the Civil
Service Commission. After serving as a cabinet minister, he was in
due course summoned to the Senate. Years later, at Dalton Wells's
funeral he said of Ottawa: "Sam, you wouldn't like it any more."

CHAPTER FIFTEEN

Return to Judgment

I returned to the High Court to a warm welcome, nobody having expected me to come back in spite of all my assurances. Chief Justice McRuer at my second swearing-in handsomely acknowledged that these had been redeemed. But my furniture had been dispersed among the unbelievers and seven judges had been appointed to the court since my departure, thus preceding me in seniority. In truth, the seniority business, seemingly so trivial, can be a nuisance; in this particular aspect it meant that the circuit lists were offered to judges in order of seniority and thus I had to yield to seven who were not members when I was first appointed. Time would be the great healer, and I could now at the age of forty-nine look forward to twenty-six years of uneventful but fascinating activity in the courts before the dread hour of dismissal would strike on my seventy-fifth birthday. Yet, as will be seen, there would be divergences as well as diversions on the way.

In my last year on the court, beginning in July 1988 and finishing in November when I had ceased to be a judge, I was interviewed intelligently and at length by Christine Kates of the Osgoode Society. Although the questioning was wide-ranging and covered parts of my life before I became a judge, it very largely concentrated on the cases that had produced written judgments by me reproduced in the law reports. The record of these interviews will not be published, if at all, until after my death, but because the questioner focused on the published reasons for my judgments, I thought I

should address some of the misconceptions about a judge's working life, at least as I knew it, from the point of view of a trial judge.
First of all, it is commonly thought, that a judge's day begins when
he ascends the bench, say at 10:00 a.m., and ends when he
descends therefrom at 4:00, 4:30, or 5:00 p.m. A second common
misconception is that a judge tries exclusively criminal cases, from
murder down. In fact, any judge of whatever court in the country
spends more time working out of court than in, considering his
judgments, reading law, and writing when he has reserve judgments and has been unable to deliver them orally. Furthermore,
at least in my day, the work and time involved in trying civil cases
far exceeded that demanded of a trial judge handling criminal
matters. Of course, this observation does not apply to the magis-
trates, who I think in the sixties became provincial court judges
and continue to be appointed by the provinces and not by the federal
government. The jurisdiction of the magistrate-cum-provincial-
court judges was almost exclusively criminal but was generally
confined to the trial of the lesser offences. In my time at least, as
I have earlier pointed out, crimes such as murder, manslaughter,
criminal negligence causing death, and rape were reserved for the
Trial Division of the Supreme Court of Ontario while it existed as
a separate court. Indeed, this was one aspect of the centralist
position of every court in which Her Majesty's judges of assize, with
the commissions of "oyer and terminer" and "general gaol delivery," discharged judicial business throughout those portions of the
globe where the royal writ ran. I make no apology for using terms
which may at first glance appear to be affectation; they among
others were used throughout my judicial life and may well have
survived the reckless iconoclasm of recent years.

We were bound by law and custom to live in Toronto or no
further therefrom than a mile from its borders, Toronto being the
centre from which the circuit, being all the county and district
towns of Ontario, was served. This system may have appeared
cumbersome or at least a target for change to the people who
destroyed it, but it had two advantages of great importance. One
was the awareness of precedent vital to the common law system of
justice and without which lawyers would have difficulty advising
their clients of the probable outcome of a trial. Then there was
the easier impartiality in the situation of a trial judge free of the

kind of local prejudice and perhaps dislike that members of a local bar might derive from a close association with a local judge. The tradition of sending out judges on circuits from the seat of government, beginning in the time when the Normans were reorganizing England, is ancient and salutary. It remains to be seen if displacing it is an improvement, for the weight of tradition is the strength of many institutions. Without tradition there can be no law, without tradition there can be no organized religion, and without these what is left of civilization?

Ignorance of law and how it has developed, of justice and how it is administered, is to be expected among laymen, but it seems to be more widespread in Canada than in most countries. Even the simplest illusions – judges and lawyers wearing wigs in court, the former wielding gavels – persist in defiance of facts which one may ascertain by simply walking into a courtroom and taking a seat. Wigs, a fashion in eighteenth-century England, were worn by lawyers and laymen alike and, like the archaic French language used in the English courts till discarded during the Cromwellian Commonwealth, have had their life in the courts of Britain and many of its colonies prolonged to the present day. But in the common law courts of this country we owe emancipation in this respect to the Loyalists who brought their fashions here after the American Revolution, wearing their own hair or lack of it in and out of court in the frontier society they created. I only dwell upon these small points to illustrate the pervasiveness of tradition, a subject about which a great deal more could be written.

Press and public are strangely incurious about procedure in the courts. This apparent indifference is matched only by the inability of the legal profession to keep them informed. The hue and cry raised against Mr Justice Kovacs for imposing a ban on the publication of proceedings at the preliminary hearing of the case against Paul Bernardo was allowed to intensify without anyone explaining that the preliminary hearings had taken the place of grand juries, whose proceedings were always secret, and a simple reference to the Criminal Code of Canada would have shown that bans of this nature are a matter of course. Many years ago an alert observer in my courtroom wrote a letter to a Toronto newspaper expressing wonder that, while the court reporter was busy making a stenographic record of what was said in the trial before me, the judge was laboriously writing it all down with an old-fashioned pen. He expressed the view that this was not only odd but wasteful. The letter was published without any editorial comment. Presumably there was no journalistic inquiry and no one explained to the industrious correspondent that trial judges have to charge juries at the conclusion of the evidence or give oral judgments, both operations being dependent upon the old-fashioned pen. The transcript prepared by the court reporter would never see the light of day unless it was ordered by a party appealing and it would then be weeks before it was furnished to the Court of Appeal. And I regret to say that among those who did not trouble to explain was the judge with the old-fashioned pen.

We soon grew tired of being shown the same half dozen houses in Rosedale by a dozen different real estate agents and in the spring of 1963 settled for a house in the village of Forest Hill, later unable to resist the annexationist predators of the city of Toronto as the village of Rockcliffe Park has resisted those of the city of Ottawa. Forest Hill Road was convenient for Sam, who could walk to Upper Canada College with ease; not so convenient for Lynn, who returned to Branksome Hall with contentment. Our friends welcomed us royally, but we had an odd and disturbing experience our first night in the new house, which had been empty with shrouded furniture for some time before we arrived. As we slept peacefully upstairs, a burglar ransacked the rooms below, having gained entry through a downstairs locked window, a means which called forth admiring comments from the police. Nothing was taken except a jacket of mine. A jacket of Helen's (mink, no less) had been negligently tossed on the floor, eliciting predictable comments from its owner (if not worth stealing, mightn't it require replacement?). The police were at a loss as to what if anything had disturbed the burglar and I was questioned closely about my cases. We were told, I felt somewhat inconsiderately, that the thief would be back but over thirty years have passed and he has not retraced his steps. My colleague Mr Justice Ferguson, a good neighbour now alas gathered to his fathers, thought he had seen a white-shirted figure at the back of our adjoining gardens but decided that his eyes were playing tricks in the late twilight of the previous day, and this may explain the solitary purloining of my dark jacket.

In 1961, while we were still in Ottawa, Leslie Frost had resigned the premiership and the leadership of the Progressive Conservative party in Ontario, loaded with honours and showered with the affectionate tributes of thousands, allies and opponents alike. He had held office in the provincial government for eighteen years, twelve of which had been spent as prime minister, as the office was then officially described. I wrote from Ottawa to express my regret that Les had decided to step down and my admiration for what he had accomplished for the province and for Canada. In his reply he concluded by saying: "I may say at the moment my mind is taken back to the time of the Convention of 1949 when you nominated me which seems to be an incredibly long time ago." He had never ceased to champion the memory of Sir Sam Hughes. When he died, almost a decade later after a busy retirement to law and commerce, the chief justice of Ontario, Bill Gale, with typically generous consideration asked me to accompany him as his sole companion to the funeral in Lindsay. There Leslie Frost was laid to rest in Riverside Cemetery, a stone's throw from the little hill bearing the monuments of the Carew family of which his wife Gertrude was a daughter, adjacent to the monument bearing the name of Hughes.

Frost was succeeded, after a strenuously fought convention, by John Parmenter Robarts of London, who prevailed over Robert William Macauley; both were friends and contemporaries of mine.

From 1962 to 1965 I was very busy on the bench and still, to adopt Otto Lang's disparaging phrase, "seeking immortality in the law reports." In August 1965 Helen and I were staying with Jack and Janet Paddon in their house on the majestic strand of Long Beach, one of the then barely frequented Lake Erie beaches beloved of Buffalonians and virtually unknown outside Welland County. On a hot afternoon I was called to the telephone, and after the intervention of a flurry of intermediaries I found myself talking to John Robarts, who had evidently been scouring the province to find me. Would I accept a royal commission to inquire into the collapse of Atlantic Acceptance Corporation? I had of course read of this company's difficulties, made public on June 6 by its default on the repayment of a loan and exacerbated by the company's issuing a worthless cheque for five million dollars to the lender. I said I was very much interested provided I could have Albert Shepherd as counsel. John said there might be some difficulty about this because of his own close association with Shepherd in Conservative party circles in London. The matter was settled at our subsequent meeting in Toronto, and I called Albert forthwith. He accepted the fascinating invitation with as much alacrity as I had.

It may well be asked why judges are, at least inwardly, generally enthusiastic about doing the often laborious work entailed in a royal commission, particularly since, when it is done for the province, no emoluments are forthcoming. No doubt a commission is a change of pace from the routine of work in court and there is the opportunity of starting something from the ground up and leaving one's stamp, not only on the proceedings, but on the result of the inquiry. I have now done three royal commissions as a sole commissioner and I much prefer, for constitutional and perhaps artistic reasons, to have my commission issued in Her Majesty's name than to proceed simply under an order in council. The result is now no doubt the same, particularly since the royal institution, as old as the Domesday Inquest and thus older than any parliament, is now hedged about by acts of legislative bodies and courts vigilant as to jurisdiction and capable of bringing its proceedings to a halt. In the sixties, however, there were fewer sanctions to be applied against a royal commission and the executive power which initiated it was concerned to see that it was equipped in its terms of reference with wide-ranging and almost unchallengeable power.

For a matter of some weeks the attorney general had maintained that the Securities Commission could sort the Atlantic Acceptance matter out, but the chairman of that body, my friend Jack Kimber, had soon decided that the finance company's collapse was too indigestible for a commission engaged in routine duties and the premier had been asked to appoint a royal commission.

There is not much that a commissioner can do in the early stages of such an investigation other than assemble his staff and then place his authority at the disposal of counsel and their investigators. The task of organizing the evidence that was to be given before the commission by a legion of accountants, company executives, and police investigators from two forces (Metropolitan Toronto and the province) was wonderfully discharged, evenly and continuously over many months, by Shepherd and his assistant counsel, Ian Cartwright (later to be a county judge for the judicial district of York), and occupied the remaining months of 1965. Central to this task was the work of John A. Orr as our financial and auditing adviser. John was a senior partner in the accounting firm of Touche Ross and Company, an old friend and like Shepherd a veteran of tank warfare. Clarkson, Gordon and Company were already involved on behalf of Montreal Trust Company but soon contributed a great deal to the work of the commission.

Special emphasis had been placed in my terms of reference on investigating the affairs of British Mortgage and Trust Company of Stratford, which had failed at the same time as Atlantic Acceptance and for related reasons. Its president, Wilfred Gregory, had been a close associate of the president of Atlantic, C. Powell Morgan. In the early weeks of this period I received a masterly opinion from Shepherd outlining what was necessary to launch an investigation of hitherto unsuspected magnitude, with ramifications in the United States, Germany, Luxembourg, and the Bahamas. In due course, we paid visits to all these countries with the exception of Luxembourg, as the operations of one Frank Kaftel, tap-dancer turned bucket-shop tout, had been moved from there to Paris; Shepherd and I interviewed him there, in the Hotel Georges Cinq.

The whole story of these companies and their numerous subsidiaries and affiliates, creditors and debtors, is contained in my report, released in 1969 after four and a half years, two of which were spent in hearing the evidence led by commission counsel – and be it said only by commission counsel. The report, over seventeen hundred pages in length, fills three volumes of text and is accompanied by a massive volume of appendices in the form of tables, graphs, and reproductions of some of the five thousand exhibits filed. Stored long since in the provincial archives, it is the record of an enterprise conducted under pressure and without waste of time or effort, suffering only the unforeseen delay attended upon having it translated into French. I cannot contemplate and will not attempt going over this ground again, but I will try to recall episodes which may recreate the atmosphere of this inquiry into the greatest commercial failure in Canada up until that time. While the loss of $135 million will scarcely make present-day financiers blink, in those days of more valuable money it was of great consequence.

One the creditors, through one of his companies, was Wallace McCutcheon. He had been summoned to the Senate in order to become minister of trade and commerce in the last Diefenbaker cabinet and had subsequently resigned in order to contest one of the Ontario seats in the House of Commons. He confronted me one day in the University Club for conversation.

"This will take you six months, Sam."

"Well, Wally, the present estimate is two years."

"You can do it in six months, Sam."

"But, Wally—"

"Six months, Sam," he repeated as he moved to the door.

Shepherd insisted that virtually every piece of paper of any consequence be produced and marked, and he would not let the accountants simply offer a nicely bound written opinion as to what had transpired. In those days we were not troubled by applications for status and it was generally agreed that all witnesses would be questioned by commission counsel and not cross-examined by counsel for interested parties. Except for supplying commission counsel with a list of questions which the interested parties would like put, counsel for interested parties had no active part to play. A great deal of time was thus saved, and the saving was augmented by the Public Inquiries Act of Ontario not having any provision for sending out notices to persons about whom the commissioner might make unfavourable observations. At this particular inquiry all parties were advised that time would be set aside at the conclusion of the evidence called by counsel to the commission for hearing evidence and representations called and made on their behalf. At the appointed time no one appeared. Had it been otherwise, as it might have been under the Inquiries Act of Canada, where such provisions were earlier introduced, it is difficult to see how the royal commission would not have gone on for at least a year longer.

For a time, while rumours were blowing about like the warning gusts of wind before an approaching storm, it was believed that the financial disaster of Atlantic Acceptance was due to the machinations of organized crime, but it soon became apparent that all the deceptions, blind alleys, false fronts, and concealments led back to Campbell Powell Morgan, the corporation's president. A chartered accountant by profession and a one-time company treasurer, he had started Atlantic as an in-house finance company to assist the former company's salesmen. Because of Morgan's uncanny head for figures (he kept few files except what could be borne by the radiator and windowsill behind his desk) and ability to inspire confidence in the hardest business head, the enterprise flourished. With one of its small loan subsidiaries, it established a conventional finance company business, providing funds for instalment purchases from retailers and acquiring respected directors, auditors, and solicitors. Below this conventional surface was a sort of loan-shark business, but notably without teeth. Loans were made without any form of prudent inquiry, and financial statements of subsidiaries were usually fraudulent, being based on the certificates of auditors as dishonest as Morgan himself. Such titans as the Ford Foundation and the Carnegie Institute were his victims, but he was paradoxically gullible before the blandishments of his least-reputable borrowers. Outwardly he showed every disposition to cooperate with the commission, even after his death sentence was delivered by a diagnosis of leukemia. His counsel, E.A. Goodman, arranged a session of the commission at his bedside, and Morgan showed great courage with everything collapsing around him. What might have been the extent of his cooperation had he lived can only be guessed at, but his papers revealed applications for visas to two countries not having extradition treaties with Canada.

At the end of two years the massive evidence was all in and safely stored by the commission's registrar, Victor Cunnington. The secretary, Lieutenant-Colonel Jack Lind, a retired professional soldier who had seen service with the truce team in Vietnam as well as in the last world war, was seconded from the provincial civil service to our infinite advantage. As I have already mentioned, in addition to visits of liaison to Washington and New York, we had been compelled to visit the Bahamas; several dubious transactions that had taken place in the colony required investigation, and its then minister of finance had threatened a Canadian chartered bank of which he was a director with reprisals if it furnished the royal commission with pertinent records. In Germany evidence was taken in Nuremburg and Hamburg. The government of the Federal Republic said with some justification that the commission would not be allowed to take evidence, and the good offices of our Department of External Affairs were sought and freely given so

that we were able to travel about our business under the auspices
of young members of the staff of the embassy in Bonn acting as
vice-consuls. Tim Beatty, president of Burns Brothers and Denton,
Toronto, and a member of the Ontario Securities Commission, was
able to arrange the attachment to the commission of one of his
firm's directors, Sylvester von Hermann. Von Hermann was able
not only to interpret for us but also to open many doors which
might otherwise have been closed or unsuspected. In the United
Kingdom Shepherd and I were able to consult officials of the Board
of Trade in conversations arranged by the Ontario agent general
James Armstrong, and I have already described a pivotal conversation in Paris.

When all this dust had settled, Albert Shepherd, whose practice
had suffered from his single-minded devotion to my commission
(not to mention the affairs of the University of Western Ontario,
where he had been deputy chairman and was about to be chairman
of the Board of Governors), bid me goodbye to return to urgent
business in London. After he left my office, I looked down from
the window towards the busy corner of Dundas Street and University Avenue, oppressed with the realization that the rest was up to
me. A report, and a very full report, containing every ascertainable
aspect of the collapse of a far-flung enterprise, undermined by
fraud and improvidence, had to be compiled and delivered to the
government of Ontario.

Of the twenty-two chapters in my report all but one, chapter
nineteen, were written by me. The nineteenth, entitled "The Effect
of the Collapse of Atlantic Acceptance Corporation upon the
Money Market," was, with the exception of some introductory
paragraphs of mine, written by John Abell, then of Wood, Gundy
and Company. John was among many other things an Oxford
cricket blue and an expert in the operations of the money market
in Canada and the United States. He accepted the commission to
prepare this chapter and made extensive inquiries across North
America. For the other twenty-one chapters the work was laborious
and prolonged by day and by night, but greatly facilitated by the
orderly way in which the evidence had been organized and produced at the public hearings. Transcripts of the evidence filled 120
volumes, and I relied on these for purposes of the narrative. As
each chapter was drafted, I sent it off to Shepherd in London, and

to my surprise and gratification each one returned to me accompanied by words of commendation and without amendments. He was particularly pleased with the one hundred or so pages at the conclusion of the report in which I summarized the three volumes of text. When all was over, he sent me the original manuscript in four volumes, beautifully bound in blue calf with a moving inscription on the flyleaf of the first which I cherish and which makes me pinch myself every time I look at it.

As the next two years passed with writing, revising, proofreading galleys and page proofs, and all the concomitant concerns of preparing the large work for the press, I was acutely aware of the impatience of politicians in particular, assailed as they were by one or two opposition members who not surprisingly made much of the report's taking longer for completion than had originally and optimistically been estimated. Throughout this period John Robarts was admirably patient, and we corresponded at some length on proposed changes to the Loan and Trust Corporations Act and the Trustee Act in particular. I took the position that the necessary amendments to the statutes should be made as soon as possible and not await completion of my report; the financial health of the province demanded it and any question of *amour propre* should not arise. Throughout the period, in a manner not frequently perceptible, I was sustained by the objective and informed scrutiny of the press, which had faithfully chronicled the public hearings.

When in the early winter of 1969 the report was ready for release, I was pleased that the government decided to mount a press conference in the Parliament Buildings of Queen's Park. I had for some time been back on the bench and was then presiding at the assizes in Windsor. The plan was for me to fly back, attend the conference to answer questions and make explanations, and return to Windsor forthwith. When the time came, nothing was flying except snow, and in the most hazardous weather I was driven in an Ontario Provincial Police car the 250-odd miles from Windsor to Toronto. At the press conference kits containing an offprint of the report's last chapter summarizing the work were made available.

The Atlantic Acceptance case was seminal in the sense that it was a landmark for overstated accounts receivable, much as the McKesson & Robbins case in the United States was a landmark for the exaggeration of inventory. While the conventional sales finance part of the company's business prospered, its assets consisting of accounts receivable (in the form of overvalued and improvident loans, in connection with which no adequate reserves had been made) and senior, subordinated, and junior subordinated notes that yielded an attractive rate to the purchaser were being manipulated by C.P. Morgan and the auditors of its subsidiary and affiliated companies. In weaving this intricate fabric of fraud, they were assisted by the then acceptable practice of the accounting profession in Canada of allowing, and virtually requiring, the auditors of a parent company to accept reports of auditors of subsidiary companies without making inquiries of their own, such as inspecting their working papers. On page 1589 I wrote:

> Two things, indeed, were essential to the success of Morgan's scheme; the auditors of the Adelaide Street subsidiaries had to be his confederates and the primary auditors kept at a safe distance. Morgan, himself a chartered accountant, reacted sharply to a suggestion by (the primary auditors) that their auditors' report should mention the names of the subsidiary companies of which they were not the auditors, refusing to consider such a proposal because it was not Canadian practice, a contention with which (the auditor) had to agree.

I made a specific recommendation (No. 4) that the primary auditors could only rely on the reports of auditors of subsidiary companies to the extent that they took responsibility for the work of the latter, "as if the relationship between them was that of principal and agent."

Fraud had been assisted by the feckless practice of "borrowing short and lending long," or borrowing short-term funds that the lenders might be expected to roll over and making long-term loans that could not be realized at short notice, thus creating a liquidity problem that afflicted both Atlantic Acceptance and British Mortgage and Trust. The situation so created was aggravated by insufficient lines of bank credit and unexpectedly by the intervention of the president of the United States. In the early months of 1965 he issued economic "guidelines" that virtually put an end to the practice of rolling over loans made to concerns in foreign countries. The borrower was then forced to scramble for short-term funds, and its default was inevitable.

Since all the obligations of Atlantic Acceptance were secured by deeds of trust to the Montreal Trust Company which provided that default on any one of them would make all the rest due and payable, the company's insolvency was immediate and irreparable.

On the whole this report, which had taken so much time and labour from the ordinary duties of a middle-aged judge, was well received. Gordon Sinclair, formerly of the *Toronto Star* and a household word through his broadcast with the radio station CFRB, telephoned in a state of generous excitement, saying that the companies involved were "like people." At the other end of the scale the *Scottish Accountant,* while commenting favourably on the report's substance, deplored its length in measured terms. I can sympathize with this criticism, but I felt that the public were entitled to all the facts and arguments in a case from which at a later day new conclusions might have to be drawn. For me the Atlantic experience was a post-graduate course in corporation finance and accounting practices. It so increased my awareness of the importance of the accountant's art that when, during this period, my son-in-law-to-be John Clappison expressed interest in entering the legal profession I urged him not to overlook that of the chartered accountants and this was his ultimate choice. I am sure, of course, that he would have made an excellent lawyer.

Of the nineteen recommendations made in the report, one of the few not in some measure implemented by either the provincial government or the professional bodies concerned was the recommendation that foreshadowed a lifelong concern for a subject dealt with thus:

> XVIII   Consideration should be given in consultation with the government of Canada with respect to necessary amendments to the Criminal Code with the Judges of the Supreme Court of Ontario with respect to necessary amendments to the Rules of Practice and with the Law Society of Upper Canada with respect to questions of professional conduct, to expediting proceedings in the Courts of the Province by limiting the number and length of adjournments obtainable on the application of any party including the Crown, or upon consent.

I do not now recall whether I first discerned the danger of easily obtained adjournments in connection with proceedings taken during the period of this inquiry, or simply confined the recommendation to questions of professional conduct for the sake of relevance. In these years there were signs that adjournments to proceedings were becoming increasingly numerous, particularly in cases where adjournments were made with the consent of all parties and without any serious inquiry by the judges granting them. It was not long before criminal proceedings and civil litigation were delayed to the point of scandal in comparison with the practice in what may be called an age of innocence in the first half of the century, where an adjournment was neither automatic nor easily come by except in cases of extreme urgency or hardship. Perhaps we should adopt the American word "postponement," which more accurately describes what these applications are really designed to achieve.

Albert Shepherd, John Orr, and Jack Lind are now gone, and I alone am left to give an adequate account of the great inquiry which fascinated us all. Albert died in 1981 at only sixty-two, and I think his absorption day and night with the intricacies of the concealment practised by Morgan and his associates sensibly shortened his life. He confided in me that he had had some sort of a seizure in our office in the early hours of one morning. His exertions, and the changes and reforms which flowed from them, were widely recognized and enhanced his reputation in the business and professional world. He became at once a director of the receiver and manager of Atlantic Acceptance Corporation, the Montreal Trust Company, which had been trustee under all the deeds securing the company's obligations. He was asked to become sub-treasurer of the Law Society of Upper Canada to give greater security to its financial transactions. He became, as I have said, chairman of the Board of Governors of the University of Western Ontario and a leading figure in many companies and charitable institutions. His untimely death, a peaceful passing as he read a book in his library at home, was a great loss to many people and, outside his young family, to none greater than to me.

CHAPTER SIXTEEN

Hobby-Horses

In 1969 I still had nineteen years on the bench to look forward to before the operation of the Diefenbaker amendment to the British North America Act would summarily remove me from office. Lest talking upon this subject should give the impression that I felt the age of seventy-five, if and when reached, was unreasonable for retirement, I should say that I did not at the time think it was, and I do not now. The latter-day development which encourages retired judges to take on laborious arbitration work and secure ample additional income thereby testifies to the fact that the mental powers of those who are fortunate enough to survive the statutory determination of their tenure are by no means impaired. The question became critical when the Liberal administration of Pierre Trudeau attempted to reduce the compulsory retirement age to seventy years, and here Bill Gale, who had risen to be chief justice of the High Court and then to chief justice of Ontario, stepped into the breach and led the judges across Canada to call a halt. As a corollary and perhaps as a forfeit, the agreement was reached that after a certain period, in my case twenty years of service, a judge could elect to become supernumerary, in which case a vacancy in his position was allowed to be filled, allowing the executive to make a fresh appointment, and he could continue to work on what was hoped to be a reduced scale of effort until the age of retirement was reached. These arrangements were a great tribute to the sagacity of Chief Justice Gale and established his reputation as a judicial statesman of the first order.

I cannot leave the sixties without referring to the rich domestic developments of which no memoir should fail to take notice. My daughter, Lynn, proceeded from Branksome Hall to Trinity College in the University of Toronto, where she spent three blissful years largely in the company of John Clappison, formerly of Upper Canada College, whom she married in 1969. John decided to become a chartered accountant in spite of having failed an accounting examination during his Commerce and Finance program in the university. It must have been of great satisfaction to him, and certainly to me, when five years later he returned there to lecture as a member of the historic firm of Price, Waterhouse & Company. He is now managing partner for the whole of Metropolitan Toronto, an accomplished golfer, and the father of two daughters upon whom two sets of grandparents continuously dote.

A year after Lynn's marriage, Sam, inveigled into playing cricket by his friend Adam Hermant, met Jane Crookenden on a tour of the West. She was visiting Vancouver from her home in England, and in due course their engagement was announced. This meant a trip to England for a wonderful wedding in Chester Cathedral, where her father, Lieutenant-General Sir Napier Crookenden, was stationed as commander-in-chief, Western Command. Jane's maternal grandmother, Lady Kindersley, had been Nancy Boyd of Toronto, and thus Jane, with this connection to a large family in that city and in Georgian Bay, would not have to rely solely on her grace and charm, which were very considerable, to make her way in the new environment. Helen had suffered a serious heart attack in 1967, but mercifully she was able to enjoy these celebrations. Her health was precarious for the next twenty years until Hugh Scully replaced all the arteries of her heart in a brilliant operation at the Toronto General Hospital, enabling us to reach together the sunlit levels of octogenarian life.

The constitution of the Divisional Court was a benefit for all the judges of the Supreme Court of Ontario, both appellate and trial. Originally it was designed to take the always burgeoning cases of judicial review, such as certiorari, mandamus, prohibition, and the like, out of the Weekly Court, where a single judge might have as many as thirty applications before him or her in the course of a day, thus being unable to do more than scant justice to the complexities of these forms of action. By having three judges of the High Court deliberate upon such applications it was felt that the Court of Appeal would be spared some business it could well afford to relinquish, and that the new court would be able to sit at major centres around the province. After a period of successful trial a great many statutes were amended to transfer appeals provided therein from the Court of Appeal to the Divisional Court. The Court of Appeal was further relieved from a mass of routine business, and the jurisdiction of the High Court became more various and consequently more interesting. As time passed and I rose in seniority, I spent more time in the Divisional Court and Weekly Court until I elected to become supernumerary in 1979, after which I was employed almost entirely in Toronto in these two courts except for the occasional long trial.

There are three ways in which judges could, and perhaps can, record their reasons for judgment. First, they can reserve judgment and write reasons for subsequent delivery. Second, they can give oral judgment at the conclusion of the argument, a method much to be preferred in the case of a trial judge. Third, they can simply endorse the record as they must, in any event, in every case endorse the result, in particular cases adding a few words of explanation. The late John Aylesworth, a down-to-earth judge of the Court of Appeal in Ontario, told me: "All we need to know is what you were thinking at the time." Not every reserved judgment delivered in writing gets reported, and the editors of these publications are generally compelled to report only those raising interesting and important questions of law. Nor should I suggest that reasons for judgment given orally at the conclusion of a trial are never reported, particularly since I have been the beneficiary of editorial acknowledgment in this respect on many occasions. In these days of prolonged and expensive litigation the immediate delivery of judgment *ex tempore* is generally much appreciated by the parties on their way to the Court of Appeal and beyond.

In this narrative I have no intention of combing the *Ontario Reports* for examples of these dissertations, although a fragment here and there may serve to illustrate controversies and concerns which are part of every judge's generally uneventful and cloudless life. In the early 1970s I sat very frequently in the Divisional Court because Dalton Wells, chief justice of the High Court, who enjoyed presiding there, felt comfortable with his old friends and associates as coadjutors; I sat less frequently when Chief Justice Estey succeeded him, since Chief Justice Estey liked to familiarize all the trial judges with the appellate atmosphere. But there is one case from the Divisional Court which I cannot resist digging up from the charnel house of old causes. It was entitled *Re Nicholson and the Haldimand-Norfolk Regional Board of Commissioners of Police*, 9 O.R.(2d)481. Because of its almost accidental beginnings and subsequent notoriety it deserves disinterment. Nicholson was a policeman of some experience in the small town of Caledonia, which, with many other municipalities in Haldimand County, had been brought by the politicians in their folly into a regional municipality. The thus-created regional police force absorbed all the local forces and made Nicholson, like many other police officers with established tenures, a probationary constable. For a variety of reasons he did not give satisfaction. The Board of Police Commissioners discharged him out of hand without any hearing or explanation as they believed they had the right to do under the Police Act.

Nicholson went to court, and his case came in the first instance to the Divisional Court of myself and my brethren Mayer Lerner and Allan Goodman. We might very well have dismissed the application but something about the general attitude of the police commission offended me, and after a brief consultation we decided to reserve judgment. I thereupon wrote my reasons for allowing the application for prohibition (a remedy by way of judicial review which if granted would have prohibited the dismissal) and passed them to my colleagues for their comments and more than likely their dissent. I had simply asked myself whether it could be lawful for a constable in Nicholson's position to be handed a notice to clean out his locker and depart without being called in and given an explanation and perhaps asked for one. I said that I did not think it could be, and buttressed my misgivings with some ancient cases about the peculiar position of constables as Crown officers. Lerner thought well of this, but Goodman, who had a good deal of experience acting for police associations in the Niagara Peninsula, was dubious. On reflection he concurred, and the police commissioners went off to the Court of Appeal and got satisfaction from a court led by John Arnup. Arnup, marshalling as he always did the statute and case law in impressive array, gave the judgment of the court allowing the appeal.

When I next saw John Arnup, I said to him ruefully that he was too good a lawyer to uphold my rather tentative reasons and he gave me his usual kindly smile in acknowledgment. But then a remarkable thing happened. Nicholson, naturally litigious, although we did not know it at the time, and faced indeed with the ending of his career in law enforcement, decided to appeal to the Supreme Court of Canada. I cannot remember whether it was before or after the hearing of his case in Ottawa that Bora Laskin, now chief justice of Canada, accosted me at a social function at Osgoode Hall. Placing both hands on my shoulders, he said, "Thank you for Nicholson." He had for some time been waiting for such a case so that he could apply his now generally established doctrine of fairness as an attempt to supplement, or perhaps displace, the complexities of the prerogative writs on which judicial review had hitherto been based. For a season Nicholson's case was famous and fashionable as the great chief justice nailed it to the mast in Ottawa.

Much as it may be deplored, there is no doubt that judges develop idiosyncrasies, especially those who sit alone as at trials or on other occasions where applications are made before a single judge. Over the years these idiosyncrasies may become more marked and, in the worst examples (rare I am happy to say), oppressive and offensive to counsel and witnesses. Even the most humane and disciplined judge may have an off day when appearing in a county town and in a short time earn the reputation of being a tyrannical judge, supplying several generations of local lawyers with horror stories, doubtless greatly exaggerated. In this respect, my experience sitting with colleagues in the Divisional Court was a great benefit. Most lawyers and many laymen are familiar with F.E. Smith's (later Lord Birkenhead) devastating use of Francis Bacon's aphorism: "A much-talking judge is like an ill-tuned cymbal." During a case in

London my friend and colleague Mr Justice W. Gibson Gray had told the court that his brother Hughes had advised him to always keep before him a slip of paper that said, "Keep quiet" or "Don't interrupt" or words to that effect. In response, the eminent advocate Earl Cherniak had risen ponderously from counsel's seat and, looking thunderstruck, had said, "Your brother *Hughes* said that?" I do not recall giving this advice to the learned judge but evidently the beam had been firmly in my own eye when it was done.

Riding a hobby horse may be idiosyncratic but is generally harmless. One of mine was born of a discussion with my father-in-law, L.B. Spencer, about the deadly delays in trials in the United States caused by the practice of cross-examining jurors before they are sworn in an attempt to discover their prejudices, preferences, and anything else that might be considered a disadvantage to the accused in a criminal trial. Certainly by the postwar years the practice of hiring psychologists and private investigators to comb the jury lists and secure prior knowledge of a juror's background had acquired a firm hold in many American jurisdictions and caused delays. Mr Spencer had indeed experimented with this technique early in his career when he was frequently in the courts. The experiment ended abruptly when Sir William Mulock came to the Welland assizes, an unusual but not in those days an unlikely activity for the chief justice of a division of the Court of Appeal. When in a murder case counsel began to question a juror as he came to the book to be sworn, the judge said, "Mr Spencer, you know better than that. Sit down." And indeed in the matter of challenging a juror for cause, the only permissible sanction for questioning a juror had been enshrined in the Criminal Code.

In the code certain categories of men, and in those days men only, were specifically excluded and could be challenged as such, but the section dealing with challenges of a juror for cause also contained the provision that one cause for challenge was that the juror "did not stand indifferent between our sovereign lady the Queen and the prisoner at the bar." It is hardly necessary to say that recent draftsmen of amendments to the section in question, with their thirst for the commonplace, have altered this picturesque phrase to "between the Queen and the accused." However that may be and in spite of the fact that a form was provided in an appendix to the code for "assignment of the cause," many lawyers, with the assistance of some judges, treated these words as authority for cross-examining jurors about their background and possible prejudices in the hope that some "non-indifference" would be disclosed and justify a successful challenge. But it was a tradition of the criminal law, upheld by authority for three hundred years, that a juror could not be cross-examined before he was sworn and that any but the most perfunctory questions of identity constituted cross-examination; the presumption of his indifference could not be rebutted except by extrinsic evidence of prejudicial conduct or utterance bearing upon the case at bar.

This for the time was my hobby horse, and I rode it at every opportunity for a number of years. In one criminal case involving homosexuals I declined to allow counsel to cross-examine jurors about their feelings towards homosexuals in support of a challenge for cause, but this failed to raise an issue because no appeal was taken. Finally in 1975 I tried a case of savage homicide in Brantford. I refused to allow counsel for the accused to question any member of the jury panel coming forward to be sworn as to their view about his client's previous detention in a hospital for the criminally insane, and after his client's conviction for murder he appealed on this and other grounds. The Court of Appeal, in what I maintain with respect was a masterly judgment, condemned the practice of indiscriminate questioning, expressing its approval only in cases where excessive publicity was found, in the discretion of the trial judge, to have affected for the worse the likelihood of a fair trial. The judgment left to that discretion the careful framing of questions to be put to the potential juror, and to be predetermined by the judge himself. A further appeal was taken to the Supreme Court of Canada after leave had been given, but was dismissed from the bench without counsel for the Crown being called upon to argue. This was the case of the *Queen* v. *Hubbert*, and thus the matter was laid to rest, at least in my time, and I trust beyond.

Of the many commercial and other cases not involving the criminal law that fell to my lot for trial, more interesting to me than many criminal cases, I will not here make mention, their being largely of professional interest only and all in a day's work. Nonetheless, the

appearance of an Evidence Code produced by the Law Reform
Commission of Canada in December 1975 produced another
hobby horse which I mounted with alacrity, and none too soon.
The minister of justice for Canada – and I must say that in those
days there was only one minister of justice and not a rash of them
from province to province – speaking to the Victoria Bar Society in
British Columbia and perhaps nettled by the general indifference
on the subject, announced that one year would be allowed for criticism and comment and implied that after that the Evidence Code
would be adopted. In July the code was published in a series of
criminal law reports, and the warning repeated. Some six months
later I was alarmed to learn that more than half of the period for
studying and commenting upon what the Law Reform Commission
had taken five years to produce had passed without any attempt on
the part of the Supreme Court of Ontario to do so. I sought out
the new chief justice of the High Court, Willard Estey, and
expressed my concern. He, following a familiar army practice,
struck a committee of the judges of his court, making me chairman.
Shortly afterwards, when he had became chief justice of Ontario in
succession to Bill Gale, he added judges of the Court of Appeal to
the committee; I tried to escape in favour of one of these, feeling
that the joint committee might benefit from the leadership of a
judge of a senior court, but he confirmed my chairmanship.

There followed a number of meetings of this committee, and in
due course I prepared a report which the committee unanimously
approved. On June 10, 1977, the report was adopted by a meeting
of all the judges of the Supreme Court of Ontario, the Court of
Appeal and High Court alike. Bert McKinnon, the first associate
chief justice of Ontario and a leader of the Ontario bar previously,
said to me, "You've destroyed it [the Evidence Code]," brandishing
a copy of the report. At least we heard no more of it.

To be fair it must be recorded that the Law Reform Commission
had done a great deal of work and in the end stimulated much
interest in and knowledge of the law of evidence by arousing stiff
opposition to its recommended Evidence Code. In the first place
they had explicitly dismissed the common law and all its precedents
and had offered a code in the style of the civil law (of Roman
origin and in place in Quebec), eschewing precedent and the
Evidence Act then in place federally. The following paragraph on

the first page of the commission's report was bound to produce an unfavourable impression:

> But if the public find trials and trial tactics splendid fare as drama, those who are involved with them in real life are somewhat less enthused by it all. Probably no part of law is less attractive to them, unless perhaps it is the language of the law (about which we will have more to say later). They are confronted with technical, and what seems to them sometimes arbitrary, rules when they seek to tell the truth as they know it. Evidence commonly accepted by reasonable men in determining facts is rejected as hearsay, or because it is thought prejudicial to a party, or for other cause. And the litigant is sometimes appalled by the consequent delay – and the expense. As George Herbert put it: "lawsuits consume time and money, and rest and friends."

With the approval of my colleagues I had observed as to this:

> Nobody will quarrel with the first sentence of this paragraph. In the third and fourth sentences the Rules of Evidence against the reception of hearsay, or what is thought prejudicial to a party are suddenly and without explanation described as unacceptable to reasonable men. The fifth sentence, equally without justification, seems to attribute delays and the expense of trials to the existence of these rules. The last is a literary flourish referring generally to litigation but without any visible connection with the Rules of Evidence.
>
> The authors of the Introduction then go on to explain, and very fairly, why Rules of Evidence are necessary and then ask the question, "Must evidence be so complicated?" They make no attempt to distinguish between the volume of the law and its complexity, cheerfully confusing both by referring to Wigmore's eleven volumes and Phipson's seven thousand precedents. They proceed: "How then is a judge in the heat of a trial expected to cope with fine points regarding the admissibility of evidence which may be raised at the time? And how can he be expected, other than on the spur of the moment, to assess numerous conflicting or narrowly distinguishable precedents cited by opposing counsel? The simple fact is: He can't." To this we would have to answer from our combined experience over many years that he can and does. Very few criminal cases and even fewer civil cases are decided on questions involving interpretation of the Law of Evidence. A further

statement in the same paragraph apparently sacrifices truth for the sake of epigram: "The Law of Evidence functions because it is often ignored." This is followed by the phrase, "Surely this is not good enough" and indeed it is not. It may serve to stir a somnolent classroom but as a contribution to serious discussion it is sadly wanting.

We went on of course to consider the code clause by clause, and the experience was rewarding. Apart from the repudiation of the common law, the commissioners had adopted two expedients that seriously impaired their work. When they ran into a difficulty in framing rules for the acceptance of evidence at a trial, they expressly consigned it to the discretion of the trial judge. If it were not something requiring a ruling of the judge, they would use the word "reasonable," the very questionable drafting device of which they were certainly not the first, and regrettably not the last, to make use. Although judicial discretion must be exercised judiciously and consistently with authority according to the common law, there was no such sanction contained in the code, and wide variances among judges exercising it, explicitly freed from the discipline of precedent, might very well have been expected. Furthermore, what is reasonable as a test can seldom be precise. What is reasonable to one man or woman may not be reasonable to another, or it may be partly reasonable or partly unreasonable as the case may be. It is only necessary to consider the position of counsel advising their clients as to their chances of success in a lawsuit. Counsel, I suggest, would be compelled to say that their clients' chance of success depended, not upon rules or indeed precedents, but on the purely subjective view of a judge or judges as to what was reasonable. To put it another way, rules should be precise and not capable of misinterpretation. The threat to sanctity of settlements or contracts by reliance on the word "reasonable" is not, in my respectful view, diminished at all by a phrase which has recently found favour at high levels of judicial contemplation, to wit, "reasonable under the circumstances." So I have another hobby horse to ride, although the horseman is now paling.

On the very day that the report of the judges was adopted and forwarded to the Department of Justice in Ottawa, a great meeting of representatives of the judges, practising lawyers, and professors of law took place at Osgoode Hall. The assemblage expressed emphatic disagreement with the principle of the draft Evidence Code and sent to Ottawa a resolution in favour of statutory amendments and a process of consultation across the country after the first reading of an amending bill. In due course, a new approach to the development of the law of evidence emerged from the Uniform Law Conference of Canada, and a federal-provincial task force on Uniform Rules of Evidence produced a draft Uniform Evidence Act in 1982. (I have often wondered how the title "Task Force," a purely technical term for the detachment of specially designated units of the United States Navy, should have become almost universally a substitute for the terms "committee" and "subcommittee." But there it is, and when it is used, one can almost hear the fluttering of flags.) When this draft document, accompanied by an exceptionally useful exegesis, full of learning and useful illustration, reached Osgoode Hall, I was again appointed by the chief justice of Ontario to be chairman of a joint committee of the two courts of the Supreme Court to report to the Council of Judges on the proposed bill, a Uniform Evidence Act for use federally and provincially. This time our task was greatly simplified by the instructions given to the task force by the Uniform Law Conference specially addressing what we considered to be the defects of the draft Evidence Code. The following gave me great pleasure and a sense of relief:

> Although legislative statement can assist in making the Law of Evidence more understandable and more certain, provisions which create wide discretions in the trial judge, especially with respect to admissibility, can reduce, rather than increase, the very certainty and uniformity that are rationales of legislating. For example, broad exclusionary rules regulating an individual trial judge to decide what an "abuse of process" is, or what "brings the administration of justice into disrepute," without further legislative guidelines, may create more uncertainty and lack of uniformity than is desirable. The Task Force should therefore strive to avoid submitting model sections creating wide unfettered judicial discretion.

This passage made the labours of 1977 seem worthwhile. We did not have to meet a philosophy which we felt was alien, and indeed hostile, to the common law. Two members of my committee in particular, Bert McKinnon and my friend since university days, the great criminal lawyer and judge Arthur Martin, gave me invaluable help. We made, I believe, useful criticisms and comparisons dealing with the proposed act section by section as need arose. At the end of the day, however, we warned against the rigidity to be expected in a statute which fully stated the existing law at the time of enactment. Our report was submitted to a special meeting of the Council of Judges in the afternoon of October 1, 1982, a copy of the minutes of which are before me. I was invited by Chief Justice Howland to explain the report already in the hands of judges of both courts. The minutes drawn by the council's secretary, Boris Krivy, faithfully record what I had to say, which included the following:

> There had been some internal criticism by some members of the committee with respect to the mild tone of the Report. However, the Report as drafted by Mr. Justice Hughes has received the unanimous approval of the Committee. In it he had attempted not to be patronizing and not to hector the Department of Justice or whoever was the moving spirit behind the Act. He said he hoped that the tone of the Report was restrained so that it might be regarded as useful rather than merely hostile.

I then moved the adoption of the report, seconded by Arthur Martin, and the motion was carried unanimously. Bill Howland was complimentary with his usual felicity of phrase, and my involvement with the law of evidence was henceforth confined to the courts. I am glad that I had the opportunity at this meeting to express special thanks to Bert McKinnon, who had not missed a meeting of our committee and was soon to lose his life to an untimely heart attack, a tragic loss to the law, his family, and his friends.

CHAPTER SEVENTEEN

Ten Years to Go

In 1971 John Robarts resigned and retired from public life. He was not a wealthy man and felt that he must provide for his family from the private practice of law. He had gone from strength to strength and was winning golden opinions for his initiatives in the field of constitutional development and discussion on a national scale. In the private sector he made a brilliant start, but a crippling stroke snuffed out his hopes, and his life ended tragically thereafter. He was succeeded as premier by William G. Davis, the last of the four paladins of the Progressive Conservative party who for forty years produced and presided over the golden age of Ontario in the twentieth century.

If Davis was the last he was by no means the least, commanding a rare mixture of affection and respect. Like Robarts he had established his right to the succession in the portfolio of Education at a time when open-handedness and a certain degree of profusion had not come amiss. And Bill Davis had encountered electoral vicissitudes which his predecessors had not. He enjoyed a majority in the legislature at first, lost it for the precariousness of minority government, and then triumphantly recaptured the majority which he enjoyed to the end of his time as premier. Withal, he was a pleasing and effective speaker, and the wit which suffused his eloquence was always good-humoured and on a special occasion and among friends could arouse an audience to a high pitch of laughter and applause. He was to show the same highly informed interest in Canada's constitutional problems as John Robarts had done, and in 1981, in a season of bitter confrontation, he had by a single act of statesmanship combined with Pierre Trudeau and saved the new constitution, with Quebec *non obstante*. The best account of this hectic period is to be found in Eddie Goodman's sparkling memoirs entitled *Life of the Party*.

Less than a month before polling day in the provincial election in Ontario, May 12, 1977, the *Globe and Mail* of Toronto, to use the words of the first page of the report which I subsequently wrote,

> disclosed a contribution of $35,000 made to the Progressive Conserva-
> tive party of Ontario by Disposal Services Ltd., a company engaged in
> the collection of industrial waste and its disposal by a process known as
> land-fill. The newspaper account was circumstantial, describing the
> donor company as a wholly-owned subsidiary of Waste Management Inc.
> of Oak Brook, Illinois in the United States. It named, as president of
> Disposal Services, Norman C. Goodhead, former reeve of the township
> (now city) of North York, the second largest constituent of the Munic-
> ipality of Metropolitan Toronto, describing him as "a volunteer campaign-
> funds collector for the Ontario Tories." The article was furnished with
> a picture of Mr. Goodhead standing at the edge of an exhausted gravel
> pit near Maple, Ontario for which his company had made an applica-
> tion to the government for a land-fill permit in 1973, and which it was
> suggested had been granted in August, 1974, following the $35,000
> contribution in the previous month.

This *Globe* item was derived from a story in the *Wall Street Journal*, which had derived it from an examination of correspondence in the Securities and Exchange Commission of the United States pursuant to the Freedom of Information Act dealing with Disposal Services' parent company, Waste Management Inc. Over twenty years ago the sum of $35,000 was of greater consequence in terms of real value than it is today, and indeed the Electoral Financial Reform Act of 1975 made donations of such a size unlawful. In spite of its authorship of this reform, the government felt that the implication in the *Globe*'s article was deadly enough in the middle of an election campaign, and moved to put the whole matter in the hands of a judicial inquiry. The premier asked me to undertake this inquiry, charging me to

> inquire into any wrongdoing or impropriety or any improper influence being brought to bear on members of the Ontario Government, or the public service on the part of officials of Waste Management Inc., Disposal Services Ltd., and affiliated Companies, or of any other individual or individuals, in respect of applications for land fill sites by the said Companies or affiliates, or any agency, thereof since 1971, to the Ministry of the Environment or the Department of the Environment or the Department of Energy and Resources Management and to report thereon and to make such recommendations to the Lieutenant Governor in Council as the Commissioner may deem fit.

In those days, it will be observed, there was no hint that the commissioner in a situation such as this could not draw conclusions hurtful to a person's reputation, and in this case I was specifically directed to do so if the circumstances warranted it. In fact it was the main issue.

I was lucky to find Barry Pepper available to act as counsel. He was a bencher of the Law Society, counsel to the firm of Fraser and Beatty, and a polished, not to say elegant, leader of the Toronto bar with an Oxford background. He brought with him as his junior Paul Lamek, of the same background (and Balliol to boot) and subsequently treasurer of the Law Society. John Orr once again shouldered the accounting burden, and Leslie Hiscoke, retired from eminence in the court reporter's art, became secretary to the commission, in which role he had already acquired experience. Our first public meeting took place on June 3, a scant week before polling day, and produced a wealth of documents from the Ministry of the Environment and the cheque for $35,000 made payable to the Royal Trust account where donations to the Progressive Conservative party were held. I confidently adjourned the proceedings to September to allow counsel and our police investigators time to marshal the evidence for early presentation.

I do not propose to distort these memoirs with details of the investigation, which involved the examination of a mountain of files, including those of the Securities and Exchange Commission in Washington and of Waste Management Inc. in Illinois. Search warrants were freely employed without any protest from those companies and the accounting firms subjected to them. Three ministers of the environment in office during the period of Disposal Services' transactions in the towns of Vaughan and Whitchurch-Stouffville gave evidence of their involvement with these companies and of their complete lack of knowledge of the $35,000 donation until reading about it in the *Globe and Mail* three years later. There was also the voluntary attendance of officers of Waste Management Inc., who could easily have defied any summons directed to them from the royal commission, as well as visits by counsel and me to the landfill sites where Disposal Services and its subsidiary companies were dumping industrial waste under provisional approval certificates or no certificates at all.

The scale of this inquiry was not comparable with that of Atlantic Acceptance, and my report of somewhat more than one hundred pages was delivered to the Lieutenant-Governor-in-Council on March 30, 1978. My counsel had been imaginative as well as diligent in calling as witnesses the principal fund-raisers of the Liberal and New Democratic parties. He questioned them about their operations in raising money from corporate donors for purposes of comparison with the evidence of Mr Kelly, the Progressive Conservative treasurer, and to show that all major political parties had the same problems and applied similar solutions. Above all, light had been shed upon the problems of the Ministry of the Environment, which from its birth had been plagued by a bewildering variety of legislation and the truncated tenure of a number of ministers passing through to more important portfolios. Its staff, finding itself deployed as a peacekeeping force between the environmentalists and the crass exploiters of natural resources, had little time to develop plans or policies for the future.

Moreover, the ministry had an astonishing internal problem. Certificates of approval of the landfill projects, sympathetically called industrial garbage dumps, were not granted by the minister, or even by the deputy minister or any assistant deputy minister, but by a relatively obscure civil servant – I hasten to say in this case a very able one – called the director of approvals. The occupant of this position could not only grant or refuse applications at his sole discretion, but could refer them to the Environmental Assessment

Board for an opinion with which he did not have to comply. An obvious recommendation to correct this extraordinary situation (which seemed to have escaped the attention of parliamentary counsel in the drafting process) was to make the minister who had to answer for his or her department in the Legislative Assembly the sole source of approval, and I made it.

My other recommendation was even more obvious. It concerned the situation where an application for waste disposal had been refused by the ministry but the applicant, by a simple application for appeal, could continue to operate in violation of the order of refusal. Such a situation was illogical and indeed intolerable to almost all members of the public not engaged in that activity. I recommended that violators be prosecuted forthwith.

My reasons for finding that the evidence disclosed no wrong-doing or impropriety, or the exertion of improper influence upon any politician or civil servant in connection with the $35,000 donation, I set forth at length in the "Findings" chapter of the report, and I was pleased that they were generally found acceptable.

In the autumn of 1978 I became sixty-five years old, and even though this was the normal retirement age for most people, I had never thought much about it, secure in the knowledge that as a judge I need not contemplate retirement for another ten years. Then early in 1979, when Helen and I were in Florida, Bill Davis called and offered me the chairmanship of the Ontario Securities Commission. I had been tipped off about this by Eddie Goodman, now so deep in the councils of the ruling party at Queen's Park that Davis once said at a dinner for Eddie, "I did not really know who was running the province, Goodman or me." The offer was tempting to an incorrigible experimenter, but in the provincial service I could only be sure of some five more years of work before retiring instead of the ten secured to me on the bench with the inviting prospect of becoming a supernumerary judge with undiminished pay and increased leisure. The incomparable Suzie Goodman said to her husband, "Why don't you leave him alone? He's happy where he is." And indeed I was, and after a few hours I told the premier that, having once forsaken the bench, doing it a second time was giving too many hostages to fortune. I wanted to stay where I was.

Our family had been augmented in the seventies by two Clappison granddaughters, Sarah, born in 1973, and Susie, in 1976, both in Toronto; in 1977 a Hughes grandson was born in St John's, Newfoundland, where Sam and Jane had gone to live when Sam became associated with John Weston, an engineer and inventor and a friend from Queen's University days. Helen and I consequently journeyed to Newfoundland before and after this event, and apart from the domestic excitement and preoccupation we renewed our friendship with Bill and Gert Crosbie. In spite of his deep roots in Newfoundland, Bill was a Toronto Zete and an ex-Horse Guard whom I had not seen since my first visit to Newfoundland on Civil Service Commission business in 1960. Like Eddie Goodman, he had been a tank commander of note, winning the DSO in Italy in 1944. He was also chairman of the board of Pelcon Ltd, the company of which Sam was executive vice-president. On our last visit in the seventies he was in hospital following a heart attack and I visited him there. On leaving, I asked him if there was anything I could do for him, and Bill, a great pipe smoker, said, "Leave your tobacco pouch." He recovered then but not long after had another attack in Toronto which was fatal. His was a great loss to Newfoundland and to Canada.

At the beginning of the 1970s we became, somewhat late in life, habitual visitors to Florida. In every one of twenty-five years or more we stayed at Boca Grande on the Gulf coast in the agreeable and spacious hostelry known as the Gasparilla Inn, situated on its own very private golf course on the Charlotte Harbour side of Gasparilla Island. We always went in the first half of January, this being the only time in the winter I could rely on as free from work in the courts. It must be a common experience for periodic visitors to the south that not the least of its charm is seeing old friends who have a similar predilection for the same time every year; what with these friends and the people with permanent residences and inveterate hospitality, life can be very pleasant indeed.

When we first went down with the Beattys and the Cromartys, the island, with the exception of a few elegant houses and the inn itself, was sparsely settled along miles of wonderful shelling beaches flanked mainly by a sea-grape landscape, now only a memory and the subject of many nostalgic watercolours. In the last quarter of a century the development and populace have risen relentlessly, although a fairly high standard of opulence and comfort has been secured. The village of Boca Grande now bulges with boutiques but fortunately the serenity and singularity of the inn has not changed, clearly I think because of its ownership by a member of the Dupont family well able to resist indiscriminate change. There is to my mind no comparison to be drawn between this leisurely part of the state, with its velvety beaches and even-paced existence, and the coarse sands and often coarse environment of the Atlantic coast of southern Florida.

As I have said, I have no desire to make these recollections a parade of cases in court. However, where there is a case of considerable consequence, one where the Court of Appeal first and the Supreme Court of Canada second overturned my judgment on all the principal issues, it must not be overlooked. The trial occupied forty-five days in court, almost exclusively devoted to the reading and filing of documents, with no interruption for cross-examination by the many counsel involved for the defence, and my reasons filled almost two hundred pages of the law reports. It was in fact two cases tried together, *Wotherspoon* v. *Canadian Pacific Railway Ltd* and *Pope* v. *Canadian Pacific Railway Ltd* (to abbreviate the styles of cause in both [22 O.R. (2d)385]). They arose from transactions beginning in 1881 when the Canadian Pacific Railway was first given its charter by Parliament to operate a railway extending from Callender, a village close to North Bay in Ontario, across Canada to Vancouver, a coveted privilege but, without traffic generated in Ontario and Quebec, a privilege only. Moreover, the Grand Trunk Railway, long established and jealous of any competition, was fiercely determined to deny the newcomer any extensions into the rich farmlands and prosperous towns of southern Ontario. Nevertheless, to save its life, the CPR set out in search of acquisitions among the smaller lines in this area, existing and projected. The Ontario and Quebec (O&Q) Railway, after a decade of stagnation, was reincorporated by Parliament in the same year as the CPR had been to construct its line between Toronto and Montreal through Peterborough and Smith's Falls. Valuable and appurtenant lands were acquired in those two cities and along the route, and the line's construction continued rapidly in collaboration with the CPR itself.

I have kept this account as brief as possible in view of the complexity of my reasons for judgment, which – so David Guest of the Blake, Cassells and Graydon firm said – read like a detective story. I can only give the simplest outline here. In due course, the CPR system extended from the Detroit River to the Atlantic Ocean, but the main line between Toronto and Montreal was the O&Q line. In 1885 the O&Q had leased this line to the CPR in perpetuity, a legal absurdity nevertheless authorized by Parliament, which, as it used to be said, could do anything except make a man a woman, an aphorism probably now out of date. To put the matter as simply as possible, the lease said that if the CPR failed to operate and maintain the O&Q line, the leased property had to be returned to O&Q, the latter retaining its corporate entity with bondholders and shareholders. And so it remained, although the CPR for years – indeed until after the Second World War – confined the affairs of the lessor (the O&Q) to a back room in Windsor Station in Montreal and the care of a couple of clerks pushing paper back and forth while the lessee (the CPR) sold off the railway lands from time to time, ignoring and perhaps forgetting that the real owner was still in existence.

When the CPR ceased to run trains over the leased line from Peterborough to Smith's Falls and tracks were torn up from Havelock eastward, rails and ties being sold, some shareholders wanted the provisions of the lease enforced and their railway back. One action was brought by the trustees of the Eaton Retirement Annuity Plan. This was led by their chairman, Brigadier-General Gordon Wotherspoon, on behalf of the trustees and other shareholders of the Ontario and Quebec Railway Company against Canadian Pacific Ltd (since 1971 the name of the Canadian Pacific Railway Company), Marathon Realty Company Ltd (as the former property department of the CPR was now constituted), and the Ontario and

Quebec Railway Company itself. A second was brought by Joseph Pope, a Toronto stockbroker. When Marathon Realty had called meetings of ratepayers in the western confines of Rosedale about developing the lands on which the North Toronto station stood, Pope had kept turning up and pointing out that neither Marathon Realty nor Canadian Pacific had title to the property in question. His action was also on behalf of himself and all the shareholders of o&q and against the same defendants. I ordered that both these actions should be tried together, and the trial opened on September 19, 1977, concluding on December 15.

No judge in such a situation was better served than I by counsel. Jake Howard, who had represented Disposal Services before the Waste Management Commission, appeared with Jim Garrow and R.S. Bruser, all of Blake's firm, for the Eaton trustees. John Sopinka, later a judge of the Supreme Court of Canada, and A.C. Millward appeared for Joseph Pope. Allan Findlay, who had been to Cyril Carson what Carson had been to W.N. Tilley, led D.S. Maxwell, F.J.C. Newbould, and Maureen Sabia for Canadian Pacific; and Pierre Genest, Eric Murray, and W.G. Scott appeared for Marathon Realty. Finally, John Robinette, at the height of his powers and reputation, represented the Ontario and Quebec Railway Company and its impeccable directors recruited by the CPR to breathe new life, and at least an appearance of vitality, into the company which had been comatose for nearly a hundred years. After I had disclosed the fact that my father had been a senior employee of the former Canadian Northern Railway, a notable rival of the CPR, and had been courteously advised by counsel for the defence that I had their confidence, the trial began.

No doubt it was the exacting work of counsel that earned me compliments from the Court of Appeal and the Supreme Court of Canada about the statement of facts in my very long reasons for judgment, compliments I may say in some contrast to their observations on my conclusions of law. As to the work of counsel, I need only say that the Eaton trustees team abandoned their own offices in the Blake firm and engaged a whole floor in a neighbouring hotel so that they could concentrate on the assembly of the evidence in all its mass and complexity without interruption from the routine of their practice. As to the law that for centuries has applied the doctrine of *stare decisis*, or the rule of precedent, with the courts

proclaiming the sanctity of contracts as vital to human relationships, the case provided a fascinating look into the future; over
more recent years courts have endeavoured to show that there are
several ways – "reasonable," mind you – of circumventing the plain
meaning of words. I found that, however difficult it might be to
accept a perpetual lease, it was a lease nonetheless and not a deed,
that the CPR had no right to convey away lands which they did not
own and to abandon a railway which they had agreed to maintain
and operate. The Court of Appeal, admirably constituted, although
the chief justice had apologized to me for not having a five-judge
court, found that the covenant to operate and maintain did not
really refer to the line itself but to operations generally within the
CPR system, a concept I suggest even more difficult to envisage than
that of the perpetual lease. Mr Justice Zuber at least could not
swallow the selling of O&Q property in the name of the CPR, and
the court as a whole (Arnup, Zuber, and Goodman) preserved the
reversionary interest in the proceeds of these sales to be valued and
paid to the shareholders of the O&Q Railway. Although Chief Justice
Laskin gave the plaintiffs leave to appeal at large, not to be confined
to specific issues, the Supreme Court of Canada unanimously concurred in the judgment of Mr Justice Estey, dismissing the appeal
in toto. Indeed, there is no doubt that in our system the highest
court can consider the public interest in a way not open to the
lower courts; if necessary, it may decide that it can reconsider a
precedent and, if not exactly ignore it, at least explain it away.
There is no doubt that if my judgment had been upheld, the task
of unravelling all the impugned transactions and assessing the damages of the O&Q shareholders would have cost a great deal of time
and money. What that would have amounted to was indicated by
the remarkable rise in the market price of O&Q shares, which for
years had remained virtually unchanged at $60, but in the course
of the litigation were sold for as much as $20,000 each.

I had one other very long case involving a railway, under the
style of *Oakville Storage* v. *Canadian National Railways.* It was about
a spark thrown by one of the railway's locomotives which started a
grass fire, in the end consuming nine buildings and their contents,
for which the owners sought compensation. The railway, after
settling with the owners of the stored goods, counter-claimed,
citing an agreement whereby Oakville Storage, in consideration of

obtaining a siding from the CNR, covenanted to reimburse the railway if any such accident happened. Other than to say that the plain meaning of the covenant was applied by me, but not by the Court of Appeal, and that I dealt lovingly with the details of the operation of diesel electric engines, I shall not dwell further upon either the facts or the law. But the case itself established an important if frivolous point. As counsel for the plaintiff was delivering hammer blows against the tyrannical railway, describing how the fire raced across the accumulation of dried grass and upon reaching the space between the wall of the first building and its cladding spread into the interior, I said, "Of course this was the *coup de grâce*." That produced the only really spontaneous explosion of laughter that I can remember ever greeting one of my sallies, so often productive of polite amusement only.

This case, the last of the long ones I ever tried (it began in May 1985 and ended in March 1986 after ninety-five days in court), represented the consolidation of nineteen actions. My reasons, which were not reported, occupied 250 pages of typescript, and since the results were overturned by the Court of Appeal, readers of the law reports were justifiably spared. And since everything from nuts and bolts to novation was dealt with, I kept a copy so that I could take it out from time to time and marvel at all this expenditure of energy only a year away from my retirement. I do not know the final result, although I was told that leave to appeal to the Supreme Court of Canada would be applied for. As is so often the case, it was a battle of insurance companies, the railway being big enough to insure itself; but it was also another example of an appellate court substituting its own opinion for words which plainly mean something else.

Let no one think from the coincidence of these respectful observations on deviations from plain meanings that my respect, indeed admiration, for the Court of Appeal of Ontario, on which I have leaned so often in the course of my years as a trial judge, is in any way diminished. Were the court not always there for those who felt they had a proper case to bring before it, the life of the judge of first instance would be a torment of anxiety. As for the Supreme Court of Canada, just to have one's case brought before it is a triumph in itself. I count myself fortunate that I was a member of the Supreme Court of Ontario. Containing, as it did, judges from the

Court of Appeal and the High Court of Justice, working and eating in the same environment at Osgoode Hall every working day when in town, it provided a much-sought-after collegial environment.

At the end of 1978 I took advantage of the passage of time to apply for supernumerary status. This offered very substantial advantages: a lighter case load, in Ontario no more than forty-four weeks of sittings; and no reduction in pay, but by the same token no possibility of promotion to a higher court. Many of us were not looking for this last, but only the very exceptional would have refused to take the upward step, if only for the sake of novelty. Yet in the Supreme Court of Ontario all the judges were equal in status if not in learning. The judges of the High Court were ex-officio members of the Court of Appeal and those of the Court of Appeal ex-officio members of the High Court. There was no difference in pay except of course for the chief justices and latterly for the associate chiefs. The Council of Judges consisted of the judges of both courts, and seniority was measured and observed in the combined court. Nevertheless, I had mixed feelings when, on a holiday in England the following summer, we heard in a thatched cottage in Dorset from a pocket radio and a broken and fading wavelength the words "a new government in Canada." But the prospect of new faces and new measures would be snatched away and Joe Clark's leadership fatally compromised by his failure to bring George Hees into his short-lived cabinet, driving a large section of the party into the arms of Brian Mulroney at the next leadership convention.

Jane and our grandson Geoffrey were with us that summer. The cottage was on the land of her parents' friend Lord Wynford, ninth of the line started by Chief Justice Best of the Court of Common Pleas in Regency days. Wynford had lost an arm in the Italian campaign and was proprietor not only of broad acres but of large herds of cattle which made their retention possible. At dinner in the manor house, prepared by him and his wife without any discernible staff, he told us how only the election of Margaret Thatcher had persuaded him and others not to give up and leave England. From Wynford Eagle we drove across the south of England to Sissinghurst to stay with Jane's parents at Sissinghurst

Place, with its magnificent garden (not to be confused with the gardens of Sissinghurst Castle) and ancient oak tree of splendid proportions, which local opinion held to be eight hundred years old. Jane's father knew a man in the Forestry Commission and once asked him down to examine it and give his opinion. His guest said, "Eight hundred years old? That's nonsense." When the general asked him to suggest a more appropriate age, he said, "Well, hardly more than seven hundred."

CHAPTER EIGHTEEN

Out of Court

I must be careful not to allow this work to become a travelogue; nothing could be more tedious. But I must not leave the impression that normal and sometimes exceptional recreation was not available, and ignore, for instance, such experiences as the great gustatory journey beginning in Venice in 1978 at the Palazzo Gritti and thence to Paris by way of Lyons with John and Evelyn Connelly, whom we also visited regularly in Westport, New York. Nor should I forget to recall the return to England in 1983 under the high-sounding auspices of the Canadian Institute for Advanced Legal Studies at Cambridge, where we stayed in considerable comfort at Queen's College, then motoring to Buckinghamshire to stay with Bill and Lorna Doughty, companions of our winter visits to Gasparilla Island and much else. Bill Doughty, a Trinity College Dublin oarsman, had been managing director of a company with asbestos mines in South Africa. When asbestos became unacceptable because of its alleged cause of cancer of the lung, he made a new career for himself in hospital administration for which he was knighted on the recommendation of the prime minister herself. After our visit with the Doughtys, Helen and I travelled to Devon, where Geoffrey met us, escorted by his mother (then separated from Sam and later divorced), for an idyllic visit to Branscombe and the sea.

And two Swan Hellenic cruises cannot be overlooked. The first occurred in 1986, a critical year for us. Helen, after a long confrontation with the fragility of her heart, which had for years limited her activities, finally had to choose between surgery or an early, if not an immediate, death. I will never forget the agonizing days in the Wellesley Hospital when one occlusion after another would bring doctors and nurses to her room on the run to keep her from slipping away from life. Finally, as I have said before, she was moved to the Toronto General Hospital, where Hugh Scully and his assistants replaced all five arteries of the heart with veins extracted from a leg and restored her to an existence not enjoyed for twenty years. That was ten years ago and we are now both reasonably active octogenarians. Only months after her surgery, when we had cruised the Aegean with the Crookendens, a measure of her transformation was provided when she climbed the one thousand–foot hill of the Acropolis at Pergamum in Asia Minor, a rash but triumphant demonstration of her return to health.

The distinctive feature of the Swan cruises was the presence of savants as lecturers: historians, classicists, archaeologists, and the like whose lectures gave a heady sense of purpose as well as pleasure to the patrons of the cruises. Napier Crookenden was one of these as an expert in the history as well as the conduct of warfare. He conducted, for example, tours of the El Alamein battlefield, though not on this occasion; but as we approached Constantinople through the Dardanelles, he addressed the ship's company from the bridge in a brilliant reconstruction of the British attack on the beaches at Gallipoli in the first German war, with its appalling slaughter and high heroism, in terms which held his audience still and silent. It was a very moving experience, not unexpected by those familiar with Crookenden's writings on the history of the second German war.

The second Swan cruise, in the spring of 1989 after my retirement, took us through the Suez Canal to the Red Sea, Jordan, and back to the treasures of the Nile Valley from Luxor to the pyramids. This time we went with Tim and Pete Beatty. Fortunately, the onset of arthritis in my left hip, although troublesome, had not advanced to the point where I could not manage the exertions required in visiting tombs in the Valley of the Kings. In those days one could not combine a visit to Jordan with one to Israel; one had to choose because of the state of war between the two countries and the tour offered Jordan. Outside our bedroom window in the comfortable hotel we stayed at in Amman, an anti-aircraft gun and its crew were

stationed day and night, if only as an emblem of this melancholy
state. But Petra, the great crusader castle of Kerak, and the Roman
ruins of Philadelphia were ample compensation.

The eighties also provided divergences from the courtroom, in
particular two electoral boundary commissions, one, in 1983, to
redistribute electoral districts in Ontario for the provincial government and the other, beginning in 1984 shortly after the conclusion
of the first, to do the same thing for Ontario as part of a nationwide
redistribution. I was offered the chairmanship for the provincial
commission by Premier Davis; in the case of the government of
Canada's appointment, the matter was a little more complicated
because of the provisions of the Canada Elections Act giving the
Speaker of the House of Commons the right to appoint two members of the three-person commission but reserving to the chief
justice of each province the appointment of a chairman. Although
Chief Justice Howland was gracious enough to say that my work on
the provincial commission more than qualified me for his selection
for the federal commission, I believe that he would have appointed
my old friend David Cromarty if he had not suffered the effects of
a crippling stroke. As it was, I had acquired considerable experience doing the work for the province of Ontario, in many ways
more difficult than was required under the highly organized
arrangements made by the Office of the Chief Electoral Officer
for Canada.

In both cases I was entitled to two colleagues and in both cases
I was fortunate. Neville Thompson, professor of history at the
University of Western Ontario, I had known for some years. Eddie
and Suzie Goodman's daughter, Joanne, had been a pupil of
Neville's, and he had awakened in her a strong interest in history,
an interest which brought him and her father together. The two
men became particularly close when Joanne's studies at Western
were cut short by the motor accident which took her life in 1975.
In her memory Eddie, with Neville's collaboration, set up the
Joanne Goodman Foundation at the university to provide annual
lectures over three days by distinguished scholars and men and
women in the forefront of public affairs; the foundation was

enriched by the combined hospitality of the founder and the famous university, Joanne's alma mater. I was privileged to enjoy these lectures and the attendant hospitality and generosity of the Goodmans and the friendship of Neville and Gail Thompson. The first lectures, incidentally, were given by Charles Stacey and were derived from his fascinating study of the private life of Mackenzie King aptly entitled *A Very Double Life*, a characterization made by King himself.

My other colleague was Warren Baillie, chief election officer of Ontario, holding the title of vice-chairman of the commission. Warren and his staff were indispensable on the technical side of the redistribution, and Warren, who was then in the early stages of his long career in this important office (which he still holds at the time of writing), has since visited several countries around the world where the electoral process required skilled observation to ensure its credibility. As secretary I was able to recruit Alan Stewart, a young lawyer who in this capacity served both of the commissions of which I write and who did invaluable work in the preparation of our reports.

Fortunately, Neville Thompson was appointed a member of the federal commission also, and we were joined by Daniel Soberman, professor of law at Queen's University and a member of a predecessor commission, no doubt to add a touch of experience to our deliberations. Soberman's was an excellent appointment, and in addition to experience he contributed good sense and good humour, making the deliberations most enjoyable. On this occasion I was able to renew collaboration with Jean-Marc Hamel, the chief electoral officer for Canada, who had been secretary to the Civil Service Commission of Canada when I was chairman nearly twenty years before. Jean-Marc, an accomplished administrator, had ten provinces and the territories to look after, so that a very tight schedule was in place and a meeting of deadlines mandatory. As one might expect, this far-flung responsibility had produced excellence in the mapping and statistical aspects of the work, more elaborate indeed than the provinces were capable of maintaining for a provincial redistribution. I paid only one visit to Ottawa; Alan Stewart paid several as secretary and everything went smoothly.

Thus, in the traditional and authorized manner 130 electoral districts were provided for the Legislative Assembly in Ontario in

1984 and 99 in 1987 for Ontario in the Parliament of Canada. At
the time and, for all I know, during the currency of both redistri-
butions, there were only two specific complaints, and the chief
justice who appointed me, always the soul of courtesy, wrote me a
warm note at the end of the federal exercise. For the rest, the
experience of travelling the province twice in agreeable company,
with only a two-year interval in the middle of the ninth decade,
provided an ample, if unremunerative, reward.

One judgment given in 1987, a year before my retirement, I like
to remember because it dealt with the Charter of Rights and
Freedoms still in the early days of being applied rather gingerly by
the courts. This was *Re Jamorsky and the Attorney General of Ontario,*
an application under the new rules of practice, similar to the older
motion by way of originating notice, standing on its own feet and
not part of or incidental to a trial of an action. Evidence was given
by affidavit, always the rule in the old Chancery courts asking for
a declaration of law and findings of facts where necessary and
appropriate. Jamorsky, a Polish doctor, originally had some sixteen
fellow applicants in a like plight (which I shall describe), but these
had dwindled to four at the time the matter came before me. Most
of the applicants had practised medicine in Poland for many years
and were fully qualified to practise there; furthermore, they had
all passed the valuating examinations of the Medical Council of
Canada and were either Canadian citizens or landed immigrants
in this country. They had been uniformly unsuccessful in their
quest for licences to practise in Ontario and were working in
various jobs related to the medical profession, for example, as
hospital orderlies. As I said in my reasons for judgment (59 O.R.
[2d] at pp. 424–5), "they are, to an extent, the victims of a
change of policy by the government of Ontario in admitting to
post-graduate medical training the graduates of what are now
known as 'unaccredited medical schools.'" Because of numerous
adjournments of the application, the curse of latter-day courts, and
the prolonged uncertainty confronting these doctors, I gave an oral
judgment at rather greater length than I normally would have done
in writing, occupying virtually a whole day in court.

As is well known, a medical education leading to the issue of a licence to practise medicine requires not only the successful completion of examinations set by university medical schools but also service in teaching hospitals as an intern and subsequently as a resident, generally attached to a senior physician or surgeon on the hospital staff. So great had been the development and growth of technical apparatus in medical training, and so increasingly high the cost, that the provincial government had committed itself to funding 603 internships and residencies a year. The result was that for practical purposes these were the only places available to aspirants for a licence to practise. So much was this the case that my inquiries as to how many internships and residencies were available to those in a position to finance their own training produced expressions ranging from knowing smiles to blank disbelief, convincing me that there was really no alternative to qualifying for the taxpayer's bounty. But there was a further and challenging limitation.

Government funding of hospitals affecting internships and residencies had gone through three stages. First, and up until the seventies, the Ministry of Health simply gave the hospitals a lump sum that they could apply to the cost of operation as they saw fit. Following this arrangement, funding was directed to specific needs and internships and residencies were the objects of specific grants. Finally, there was the policy that was under attack in Jamorsky's case, which provided that funded internships and residencies must be held by graduates of certain accredited medical schools in Canada and the United States, accreditation being awarded by committees in both countries working in close collaboration. As I said in my reasons, "It may seem strange to those who have been accustomed to consider great medical schools abroad, Edinburgh, Vienna, London and Paris to name only a few, to find that they are in the category of unaccredited medical schools, just as it may seem strange, but undoubtedly fair, that Canadian students who go overseas to qualify in Commonwealth and foreign medical schools are in exactly the same situation as the applicants in this case." The policy of the Ontario Ministry of Health, although apparently reasonably restricting these professional posts paid for by the Ontario taxpayer to use by graduates of accredited medical schools, in fact barred the door to applicants whose undergraduate medical training had been taken elsewhere than in one of the accredited North American medical schools.

The regulations that produced this result had taken effect in 1985 after a period of study and discussion, and had attracted protests from people situated like the Polish doctors. These representations had reached the ear of the then leader of the Opposition in the Legislative Assembly, David Peterson, who had promised some relief if his party were victorious at the general election of 1984. The result of this promise and its redemption was the creation of twenty-four funded internships exclusively available to graduates of unaccredited medical schools, but by regulations made in 1987 these were accessible only to those graduates of "acceptable unaccredited medical schools" who had successfully completed a "pre-internship" program taken at an accredited medical school in Ontario. There were other provisions and requirements which I will not impose upon the reader who has followed me this far. Those who are dissatisfied with what I confess is a simplified description of the effect of the regulations may pursue their researches in the reasons for judgment which I have identified and in the elaborate regulations to which they refer. In fact, they will be reassured to know that the facts recited were agreed to by the various counsel, not only representing the Polish applicants, but the attorney general and the medical schools and hospitals involved as well, and that my disposal of the matter was endorsed by the Court of Appeal. The applicants' attack was based upon certain provisions of the Canadian Charter of Rights and Freedoms, which, as I have observed elsewhere, has placed overwhelming power in the hands of Canadian judges. Enactments of Parliament and provincial legislatures can now be struck down in a situation where they are contrary to the Charter's provisions, thus placing the judges of courts of competent jurisdiction in a situation where they never were, nor wanted to be, in relation to the Crown and Parliament and to legislatures hitherto supreme.

Counsel for the Polish doctors were asking for wide-ranging relief based upon every section of the Charter that they felt gave the slightest opportunity for exploitation. In the main they wanted a declaration based upon sections 1 and 15, which are as follows:

1.   The Canadian Charter of Rights and Freedoms guarantees the rights and freedoms set out in it subject only to such reasonable

limits prescribed by law as can be demonstrably justified in a free
and democratic society.

* * *

15(1) Every individual is equal before and under the law and has the
right to the equal protection and equal benefit of the law without
discrimination and, in particular, without discrimination based
upon race, national or ethnic origin, colour, religion, sex, age
or mental or physical disability.

As Walter Tarnopolsky, who spent the last years of his sadly curtailed life on the Ontario Court of Appeal, prophesied in his book
Discrimination in the Law, "discrimination" is now firmly established
in the negative sense. It seems idle to point out that discrimination
in taste, reading, and so forth is more authoritative, established in
an earlier and more forthright age and accepted by those who have
an interest in the meanings of words and precision in the use of
language. Walter's colleague, George Finlayson, has pointed out in
one of his judgments that discrimination by legislators occurs every
day in favour of women who take maternity leave, receive the baby
bonus, and enjoy provision for child care, paid for in large part by
taxpayers who themselves do not qualify for these benefits.

Having negotiated the labyrinths of the law developed by inter-
pretations of the Charter as they then existed, I expressed the
opinion that the object of the legislation in Ontario was to bolster
efficiency and avoid waste of public funds, and not to discriminate
against the applicants or those similarly situated as prescribed by
section 15. It was unnecessary to resort to section 1 of the Charter
to find the reasonable limits on the rights of the applicants which
undoubtedly existed in this case. A well-known legal maxim says
that hard cases make bad law. This was a hard case, but I hope it
did not make bad law. At least the Court of Appeal did not think so.

Fortunately for me, the destruction of the Supreme Court of
Ontario to which I have referred was in the future, though not
long delayed, and on the 24th day of October, 1988, my seventy-
fifth birthday, I was dismissed by operation of law. Like all judges
in my situation, originally appointed for life but who had reached
this milestone, I could not say I was a retired judge with any degree

of accuracy because I had, in the brutal words of the Diefenbaker amendment to the British North America Act, ceased to be one. I was indeed vouchsafed ninety days in which to complete my outstanding written judgments; since I had none I spent this period, with the approval of my chief justice, Bill Parker, to retain my chambers, disposing of books, memorabilia, and the detritus of twenty-eight years' preoccupation with the law and the courts in the civilized security of Osgoode Hall. This period of disentanglement made departure easier and allowed for farewells, relaxed and unhurried. Indeed, I owed so much to so many who had made life easy and agreeable: Marilyn Archibald, my secretary since my return from Ottawa, whose energy and ability elevated her to be secretary to the chief justice of the High Court (and its replacement), and her successor, Polly Diamonte; Warren Dunlop, then I think personal assistant to the chief justice of Ontario, who went personally to Ottawa to track down a computer which, having deprived me of my health insurance coverage, was sending me huge bills without any explanation, much less remorse; and Mary Dayton, who among her numerous responsibilities expertly directed traffic for judges' cases and courts. I mention only a few of those many to whom I am indebted for peace of mind and enjoyment of judicial life.

I was not one to accumulate reserved judgments, and except in the longest and most laborious cases, I dispatched my business promptly. I had before me the example of Wilfred Judson, who on being advised by the prime minister that he was appointed to the Supreme Court of Canada was asked how soon he could begin his duties. "Tomorrow," he said.

CHAPTER NINETEEN

The Evil That Men Do

In the early aftermath of my becoming euphemistically a "retired judge" I had a talk with Ian Scott, attorney general for Ontario, and told him that I felt bereft of purpose and anxious for some work. On our return from a trip to Jamaica to stay with John and Betty Osler at the end of March 1989, he was good enough to call me and say that the attorney general of Newfoundland was looking for someone to conduct a royal commission to investigate some aspects of the grim revelations of child abuse at the Mount Cashel orphanage in St John's. These revelations had recently caused a sensation in the province and bid fair to cause one on a national and perhaps international scale. Ian had been kind enough to recommend me to the minister, and if I were willing to act, she would call me to discuss the necessary details. Call me she did on the following day. In that conversation with the Honourable Lynn Verge, minister of justice in Newfoundland, everything was settled between us in principle, including the appointment of counsel David C. Day, QC, of St John's and Clay M. Powell, QC, of Toronto, suggested by her and agreed to with enthusiasm by me. Although I did not know David Day, I knew his reputation, and Clay Powell I knew well because of the work we had done together at the time of the Atlantic Acceptance case (he was then a senior officer of the attorney general's ministry in Toronto) and later because of his eminence as counsel and expert in the criminal law of Canada. As it turned out, my third royal commission was to be, like its

predecessors, blessed by the excellence of counsel. Henceforth I
was not to deal or meet with the attractive and able politician who
had offered me a commission of critical importance, a commission
issued by authority over an order in council dated April 14, 1989.

Newfoundland was in the throes of a general election and the
minister was opposed by no less than the leader of the Liberal
opposition, Clyde Wells. The deputy minister and his colleagues
pondered the terms of reference until Mr Powell and I arrived in
St John's to confer with Mr Day and take the first steps to set the
royal commission in motion. As a complement to counsel I was
fortunate indeed to secure the services of Herbert A. Vivian, an
officer of the Department of Justice, to act as executive secretary
and take into his hands all those administrative affairs for which
his experience as an officer of the Royal Canadian Mounted Police
was an additional and important qualification. Although much
travelled in that famous service, he was a native Newfoundlander
of wide experience and comprehension of the local scene.

With all arrangements apparently in train, and the commission
document issued to me and in my pocket, Clay Powell and I flew
back to Toronto on April 20 over Newfoundland's magnificent,
forbidding coastline. On this deceptively sunny day the voters of
the province were busy dismissing the Progressive Conservative
government from office and giving Clyde Wells's Liberal party a
substantial majority. Wells, indeed, was defeated in his own west
coast riding by Lynn Verge and had to seek the resignation of one
of his own followers in a safe seat. This may have had something
to do with the uncertainty which followed. Would the new government consider itself committed to the investigation? It seemed
fairly certain that it would, but the deputy minister I had been
dealing with, Ronald Richards, was replaced by James Thistle, and
it was apparent that, whatever happened, the terms of reference
in my commission (if it was still to be my commission) would be
changed and the existing document replaced. The first hearing,
already advertised, had to be postponed.

At this point it might be useful to indicate what I then knew
about the situation at Mount Cashel. First of all, it was no longer
an orphanage and had not been one during the period some
fifteen years before when the transactions requiring investigation
had taken place. That is not to say there were no orphans among

its inmates, but strictly speaking it was a foster home operated on a large scale by the Christian Brothers of Ireland, a papal institute of the Roman Catholic Church. The members of the order were not clergy in the strict sense, but they wore a distinguishing habit and had all taken vows, including one of chastity. Founded in 1800 by Edmund Rice, a prosperous merchant of Waterford in Ireland, the movement, with episcopal blessing, spread rapidly in Ireland and received papal recognition twenty years later, Rice being appointed superior general of the order. The circumstances which moved Brother Rice in Waterford were repeated in St John's, Newfoundland. Many Waterford people had settled in the province as recruits of the annual fishing fleet expeditions from Bristol and other west-of-England ports for which the fabulous fisheries of the coasts of Newfoundland were an abundant lifeblood. Without becoming involved in describing a period of the maritime history of Britain and of Newfoundland well known to every studious reader, I want only to say that the Royal Navy discouraged organized settlement of the island lest it interfere with the use of the coasts for drying fish and generally with the operations of a trade known as the "nursery of British seamen." Such settlement as did take place was therefore haphazard and clandestine, and the education of children, except among a few families of prosperous merchants, practically unknown. By the middle of the last century the state of affairs in St John's had reached a point where boys were neglected and running wild in a town where only rum was plentiful. In response to many appeals the Christian Brothers of Ireland, after much hesitation, agreed to go to the rescue of the Catholic boys of Newfoundland. An important part of their teaching method was instilling a strict discipline in their charges, sustained by swift and often painful punishment of those who failed to observe it.

Although Newfoundland saw the first overseas venture of the Christian Brothers of Ireland, in 1976 when they celebrated one hundred years of teaching in the colony, dominion, and province, the congregation was established around the world, with a sophisticated and thriving organization in North America. Teaching was still its prime concern, not by any means confined in Newfoundland to the capacious Mount Cashel buildings on the farm on the outskirts of St John's given to the archbishopric by an earlier incumbent, Archbishop Howley. Only a small proportion of the order lived there to look after a community of boys ranging in age from infancy to near man's estate. This community had long ceased to be significantly one of orphans as such, being mainly composed of wards of the director of child welfare in the provincial Department of Social Services, the sons of broken homes or of parents who could not afford to raise them. A few were at Mount Cashel because their fathers had been there and remembered boarding school life and education with satisfaction and pride. A mere handful of the boys were found to be delinquent. Only the younger boys were taught at Mount Cashel, the brothers generally teaching at various Catholic schools in and around St John's by day and, where not otherwise accommodated in monasteries, returning to Mount Cashel by night to assist in the operation of the institution.

At the time of the centennial celebrations referred to, Mount Cashel was highly valued by the provincial government and in particular by the director of child welfare of that era, F.J. Simms. But if up to this point the relations between the government and the administration of Mount Cashel had become closer and outwardly cordial, they had also reached a point where the Department of Social Services was anxious to put at least one social worker on the premises. The Christian Brothers and in particular the superintendent regarded such a move as an intrusion and were determined to resist. This controversy led to a compromise whereby the designated social worker would be a visitor only, without authority to make other than formal contact with the wards of the state, a result reached mainly because of the high reputation of Mount Cashel in particular and the Christian Brothers generally and a public awareness of their indispensability to the Catholics of Newfoundland.

Yet while the Christian Brothers of Ireland had made giant strides around the world in the century since their arrival in Newfoundland and had endeavoured for many years to nurture young boys deprived of any effective parental guidance, the order had unwittingly provided in St John's a haven for the loathsome practitioners of child abuse, destroyers of the innocence of boys in their infancy and adolescence. If child abuse is correctly categorized by the terms emotional, physical, and sexual, it may be said that those who prey on young boys are in varying measure guilty of all three but are mainly involved in abuse that is sexual, ranging from brutal buggery to the more insidious but milder type of corruption known as paedophilia.

All boarding schools, whether for boys or for girls, or perhaps, as is nowadays the fashion, for both, have special problems with nascent sexuality in their charges, but rarely must they contend with corruption induced by members of the staff. In Newfoundland there had been a handful of suspicious occurrences sufficient to warn the Christian Brothers of the ever-present danger, particularly among those brothers who were in charge of boys' dormitories and summer camps. At the critical time, indeed, it was known by some members, although certainly not by the majority, that the superintendent of Mount Cashel himself was a homosexual abuser of children.

Half buried and seldom expressed for at least thirty years had been the belief in St John's that things were not quite right in Mount Cashel. The growing reluctance of its administration to allow the Department of Social Services access to their wards in the orphanage enhanced the mystery and the uneasiness it caused. But the departmental official most closely connected with the orphanage, the director of child welfare, was timid in his dealings with the superintendent. In the rare cases where complaints were made by parents or friends of boys who were either wards or their companions, the director referred each one to the superintendent and accepted his assurance that they were groundless. In 1974 this delicacy frustrated the courageous efforts of a seventeen-year-old girl who took her badly beaten cousin out of the orphanage and brought him to the Harvey Road office of the department, to display his bruises and file a complaint. This local office, in spite of containing the office of the liaison officer for Mount Cashel, had no authority to deal with any complaints or matters of policy affecting the orphanage. All such issues had to be referred to the director of child welfare in the Confederation Building, and it was here that the girl's complaint was quietly dropped into limbo.

In the following year a better opportunity of shedding light on the malpractices of the Christian Brothers at Mount Cashel presented itself through the tribulations and activities of the Earle family. Because of the parents' marital estrangement, three Earle boys were supplied to the orphanage, two of whom were beaten and sexually abused. An initial complaint brought by their father on behalf of Billy, the elder of the two abused boys, suffered the same fate as the young girl's complaint in 1974; the local St John's office made a report to the director of child welfare, who evidently took no action beyond discussing the matter with the superintendent at Mount Cashel. But the case of Shane Earle, who had been an inmate of Mount Cashel since the age of six, was epic. His beating was discovered by a friend of the family who was doing repair work at Mount Cashel. The friend confronted the director of child welfare in his office in a menacing manner and had the boy sent to hospital. The hospital then issued a report to the police.

Furnished with the report and with a statement from Carol Earle, mother of Billy and Shane, twelve and nine years old respectively, the Royal Newfoundland Constabulary, headed by Chief of Police John Lawlor, detailed detective Robert Hillier to investigate. Over the previous two or three years some isolated complaints had convinced Hillier that there were irregularities at Mount Cashel, and he went at once to Brother Kenny, the superintendent, to arrange interviews of his staff and young charges. Twenty-one boys out of the ninety-one at that time resident in the orphanage were interviewed at police headquarters, delivered there and taken back by the superintendent himself. Two of the Christian Brothers were interviewed on church premises; one made what amounted to a confession of sexual approaches to younger boys, his companion remaining silent. To his astonishment Hillier was then told by the assistant chief that his superior had instructed him to tell Hillier to file his report forthwith and that negotiations were proceeding at the Department of Justice. This was indeed the case, the provincial superior of the congregation of Christian Brothers having arrived from Ontario to offer the removal from the province of the brothers interviewed by Hillier in exchange for immunity from prosecution. This was agreed to by Deputy Minister of Justice Mr (later judge) Vincent McCarthy. Hillier was then asked to write a second report removing all references to sexual misbehaviour; he complied but managed to insert some such references which were accepted. At that point the investigation by Hillier and his colleague was shut down.

This brief outline I consider necessary for making sense of what I have to say further about my task in Newfoundland, but it is in no way a substitute for what is written at length in my report. The report, with the approval of counsel, I entitled "The Report of the Commissioner of the Royal Commission of Inquiry into the Response of the Newfoundland Criminal Justice System to Complaints," and with good reason. On June 1, 1989, the new government had decided to confirm the actions of its predecessor in respect to the commission, its commissioner, and counsel, and, generally speaking, its terms of reference, but to amend the latter by extending the commission's mandate to a degree which completely reduced the dominance of the Mount Cashel story in favour of other concerns of the Department of Justice, the constabulary, and the Department of Social Services. On the whole, I thought that the terms of reference had been improved, but their enlargement would certainly require more time and more money than hitherto contemplated.

The reputation of the Mount Cashel Boys' Home and Training School, as it was now called, and the Christian Brothers of Ireland residing there had come perilously close to destruction in December 1975. Various improvements in administration were introduced and care was taken in the appointment of superintendents for the remaining fifteen years of the institution's useful existence. From time to time over the next thirteen and a half years the concealment of the transactions of that dark period was threatened. In particular, this was the case when a certain Sergeant Pike, Hillier's immediate superior in the "assault" section of the constabulary, gave evidence *in camera* in April 1979 to a judicial inquiry, presided over by Judge (later Mr Justice) Soper, investigating a fire in a St John's apartment house. Pike gave explicit evidence at length on the nature of the Hillier investigation, its termination, and the absence of any charges in connection with it. In the same proceeding the director of public prosecutions expressed the view that it would not be unusual for immunity to be granted provided the offenders in the circumstances in question were removed from the jurisdiction, although he later stated that this should not be considered his official view. A transcript of this evidence was released at the time that the judge presented his report, thus indicating in the unusual circumstances of its release his concern for its content. Two of St John's newspapers, the *Telegram* and the *Daily News*, referred guardedly to these important revelations, and only the latter mentioned the Christian Brothers and Mount Cashel.

But if public indifference testified to the apparently unassailable reputation of the Christian Brothers within their community, consternation reigned. A new provincial superior wrote to his predecessor who had negotiated the settlement of 1975, now the superior general of the order in Rome, saying: "You can imagine the shock and embarrassment of the Monks in Newfoundland at this unexpected revelation – since so many of them had absolutely no inkling whatsoever of the episode." He expressed fear that in the provincial election called for June 1979 the Liberal party might, as he said, "play it dirty" in their efforts to unseat the Progressive Conservative government. If Sergeant Pike had not been embroiled in a controversy of political significance, his allegations might have been taken more seriously.

In 1982 there occurred a classic case of paedophilia at Mount Cashel in which a delinquent child was involved with one of the brothers in fellatio over a period of a year, costing the abuser only four months imprisonment. Yet the situation at Mount Cashel was stable and apparently secure. What other conclusions could the Mount Cashel authorities have drawn when in the case mentioned the Court of Appeal not only reduced the four-month sentence to time served (twelve days) but substituted for the probationary terms imposed by the trial judge an order that the convicted brother should submit to such treatment as might be decided by the provincial superior?

When in the winter of 1990–91 I came to write my report to the Lieutenant-Governor-in-Council of Newfoundland, I headed the chapter dealing with the period from 1974 to 1989 with the words *De Profundis*, and the chapter dealing with the reopening of the investigation of the events of 1975 *Dies Irae*. By February 1989, after a long period during which a combination of public indifference and careful contrivance had succeeded in covering up the depths of depravity to which foster care had been reduced at Mount Cashel, the day of wrath was about to dawn. Although the Department of Social Services had long had information about sexual misbehaviour at Mount Cashel which its senior officers maintained they knew little or nothing about, the repulsive activities of Father Hickey in Portugal Cove and Father Corrigan in Pouch Cove, and their conviction of sexual offences under the Criminal Code, aroused widespread anger in the Catholic community in 1988 and led to the appointment of an investigative committee by Archbishop Penney in the following year. The committee was headed by the Honourable Gordon Winter, a distinguished former lieutenant-governor of the province and notably not a coreligionist of the archbishop's. This body did important work in examining the causes and consequences of sexual aberration in the priesthood and did not flinch from identifying the many occasions on which the archiepiscopal see had sought to suppress the complaints of victims of child abuse; its investigation resulted in Archbishop Penney's resignation being tendered to and accepted by the pope. Thus, in the early winter of 1989 the flanks of the seemingly invulnerable order of Irish Christian Brothers were dangerously exposed. In February two chance telephone calls to the associate deputy attorney general indicating concern about Mount Cashel led him to unearth Detective Hillier's thirteen-year-old report. Its surrounding circumstances induced him to recommend to his minister the reopening of the 1975 investigation.

News of the resumption brought Shane Earle back into the limelight. He had returned to Mount Cashel in 1976 and had never formally complained to the police. When the emphasis appeared to change in favour of aiding the victims of child abuse, he enlisted the help of two people, first Superintendent Power of the constabulary, who was in charge of the renewed investigation of Mount Cashel, and second Michael Harris, editor of the *Sunday Express*, a lively journal which had obtained a wide readership in St John's under his management. Harris had already written a book entitled *Justice Denied*, about the case of Donald Marshall, a young Micmac Indian imprisoned for many years after conviction for a murder he did not commit. In the result Marshall was released and compensated by the government of Nova Scotia. Then and now a fearless and fertile writer, Harris is better known as a television panellist with a national audience and an important position in the world of journalism. After hearing Shane Earle's story, he wrote at least two masterly newspaper articles that effectively convinced the government of the province that a resumption of the investigation of 1975 was not enough to appease the public sense of outrage. It was thus that the issue of my revised commission to conduct proceedings under the Public Enquiries Act ensued. I should say parenthetically that this statute had not, as I recall, been amended for many years.

The new terms of reference for my commission must now be briefly examined. Issued in the queen's name (indispensable after being described as "royal"), the commission's recitals, as they must, dictated the focus of the inquiry.

> Whereas it appears desirable and expedient in the public interest and in the interest of the administration of justice that an Inquiry be held relating to the investigation conducted by the Royal Newfoundland Constabulary into allegations of child abuse at Mount Cashel Orphanage in the year of our Lord 1975 and in relation to the police reports dated December 18, 1975 and March 9, 1976 respectively, and into the handling of the said investigation by the Royal Newfoundland Constabulary and by the Department of Justice,
>
> And whereas there have been suggestions made that there existed within the Department of Justice a policy that criminal charges would not be laid in some cases of physical or sexual abuse of children, where the alleged assailants agreed to leave the Province of Newfoundland,
>
> And whereas recent investigations have resulted in a substantial number of charges being laid, particularly against members of the clergy, relating to incidents dating back in some cases to the year 1970 ...

I was then instructed to determine issues in the form of questions dealing with the police investigation, whether charges should have been laid and who had concluded the investigation before this had been done. In view of what was alleged after the production of my report, the following should be noticed as a specific direction to determine "whether any bargain was made by any person acting on behalf of the Crown or the police with any member or members of the Irish Christian Brothers or any other person not to proceed with criminal charges and, if so, the terms of such bargain."

The spotlight then turned upon the Department of Social Services, the questions being what reports had been made to the director of child welfare under the Child Welfare Act, and if they had been made, were they acted upon; did the department share with the Department of Justice a policy (apart from the Mount Cashel incident) of suppressing allegations of physical or sexual child abuse if the alleged perpetrators left the province; did such a policy or practice extend to areas of the administration of justice other than the problem of child abuse; and if such a policy did exist, was it justifiable. The commission was then to decide whether existing police and government departmental policies were sufficient to prevent avoidance of "the due process of law in instances of allegations of physical or sexual abuse of children" and what should be done to prevent a recurrence of the events giving rise to the inquiry. Finally, I was to "bring forward conclusions and any recommendations which you consider desirable to further the administration of justice."

At the conclusion of these terms of reference and after words giving the commission authority to hold hearings *in camera* where considered necessary, there was a flourish dear to the hearts of the executive powers plus an inadvertent slip: "and further, we require you to report your findings within ninety days of the commencement of Hearings." Since ninety days would have to pass before a syllable of testimony could be uttered, given the time it would take to locate suitable premises for the conduct of our business, recruit and organize staff, draft and serve subpoenas, and make the multitude of arrangements necessary in every inquiry of this type and magnitude, such a direction was clearly absurd. In any event, this was recognized, bringing me into contact with Premier Wells, whose hand lay heavily but expertly on the levers of power after his party had been in opposition for seventeen years.

Michael Harris wrote *Unholy Orders* against a publication deadline for the fall of 1990. When one considers that the last witness testified in July of that year, the fact that he could write and his publishers produce a readable and, for the most part, accurate account of what transpired before the royal commission reflects credit on them both. Of course, Harris was more familiar than most with the facts and particularly the flavour of the happenings at Mount Cashel, and he pays tribute to the help and cooperation of all the staff from the commissioner down. It was an impressive achievement. The book, one of those breathless accounts which only gifted journalists seem able to produce at short notice, is, though sadly maimed by the lack of an index, a good and reliable read.

Unholy Orders was of course published before my report was completed in the following spring (and not, be it said, released by the provincial government until 1992), and consequently did not record the dramatic prosecutions responsible for that delay. But in the midst of paying many graceful compliments, he said in the epilogue that the commission could be justifiably criticized for being ill-organized, unfocused, and soft on witnesses. I do not take seriously the reflection on organization. Our able investigators, Buck Orser and Fred Horne, both ex-RCMP officers, had travelled far and wide in Newfoundland and the rest of Canada to interview and where necessary secure the attendance of somewhat over 250 witnesses. All were in turn interviewed by counsel, who spent long and exhausting hours in the process. Then the evidence flowed almost without pause for the 156 days of hearings on Strawberry Marsh Road. But as for lack of focus and being soft on witnesses, Michael Harris accurately reflected what the public felt deprived of: in a word, blood. To say that the public did not understand the difference between a commission of inquiry and a court of law is to make the unfounded assumption that it understands either one. Bullying cross-examination, measured for effect in decibels, and voluble condemnation of the perpetrators of sexual abuse of boys in Mount Cashel – in effect, assuaging a hunger for vengeance, felt even by an experienced observer like Harris – would have stood in the way of calm deliberation, particularly the requirements of relevance, without which much expensive and prejudicial delay would be created. I invite the reader to look again at my summary of the terms of reference and to see that the focus of the inquiry was not on the pathetic plight of the victims of sexual abuse but on the reaction of the authorities – police and social services – to the complaints of the victims such as they were. I was asked, as counsel was well aware, to examine the mechanism of the system operated by these authorities in the mid-seventies and after, and to suggest, to put it briefly, how it could be improved. I was not asked to examine the mechanism of homosexual perversion or how it can affect and destroy the innocence of childhood, or to look over my shoulder at the not-so-distant past when retribution was measured by the lash.

Nevertheless, and in spite of the professional restraint of the lawyers appearing before the commission, parts of the evidence were highly charged with emotion. Herb Vivian had negotiated an agreement with a television company whereby we, in exchange for granting the company exclusive rights to televise our proceedings, were supplied with videocassettes that reproduced all that transpired on each of the 156 days of sittings. At the same time, from first to last the hearings were televised live during the daytime and reproduced again at night. Newfoundland, particularly the Avalon Peninsula, was saturated with this record, and so too were other parts of Canada as the producers saw fit.

Two cameras were employed, so that instead of the rather wearisome pictures of witnesses waiting to field questions, both the counsel's questions and the witnesses' answers were visually portrayed as well as heard. With this service it was unnecessary to engage stenographers to make a written record, and when it came time for me to make my report, I took copies of all the cassettes to my office in Toronto. I confess that a lot of time was spent listening, but with the aid of a computer the time spent sorting things out was greatly abbreviated. There were two advantages in this form of record: first, if I died, another commissioner could replace me and be furnished with a record that showed the demeanour of the witnesses, enabling him or her to assess their credibility. Second, since in the winter of 1991 I was developing macular degeneration of the retina, poring over typed transcripts of evidence was spared me. And all of this was free, saving a province with financial problems many tens of thousands of dollars.

To return to the issue of the commission's organization, it seems to me that to have produced all the evidence, in terms of documents yielded by government departments by the truckload, and heard all the witnesses, all sworn or affirming, from October to

July constituted a memorable feat, one that militates strongly against any suggestion of lack of organization. It will be appreciated that all the participants in the events under investigation were almost fifteen years older than when the events took place. The victims of abuse had grown to manhood and were widely dispersed in Canada; some had even left the country. The minister of justice of the day had become Chief Justice Hickman of the Trial Division of the Supreme Court of Newfoundland; Hickman's deputy minister had become Judge McCarthy but he had had died before the investigation of 1975 was reopened; and the Department of Justice's legal adviser to the Department of Social Services had become Madam Justice Noonan of the same court. All of these still living testified under oath, a handful perhaps by affirmation, as did the superior general of the congregation of Christian Brothers, Gabriel McHugh, who came from Rome for the purpose, and the provincial superior of the province of Canada and the West Indies, Brother Burrows, who travelled from Toronto. David Day went to Antigua to take a deposition from Brother Nash, who had conferred with Brother McHugh and Vincent McCarthy when the bargain had been made to substitute banishment for due process of law. James Lawlor, who had, as I found, collaborated with McCarthy in the suppression of Hillier's investigation at the orphanage, gave the testimony of a sick and haunted man taking refuge in denial and evasion. Almost equally pathetic was the evidence given by the director of child welfare, F.J. Simms, newly retired and seeing his career reduced to insignificance and worse with every question put to him by counsel. Most affecting of all was the spectacle of strong young men given over to convulsive sobbing by the mere recollection of the appalling indignities inflicted on them by those to whom they should have been able to look for guidance and comfort in their childhood.

Putting paedophilia on one side if possible, it was evident that the Christian Brothers in Mount Cashel continued their order's tradition of inflicting excessive, if not savage, punishment. Disobedience, often inadvertent, would like as not provoke a blow to the face of the offending child by the bare fist of a grown man, difficult to explain and impossible to condone. While the evidence of offences against the boys who had made complaints to Detective Hillier in the winter of 1975–76 and of others was being heard day after day, the constabulary were conducting their own investigations and, based upon what was revealed before the commission and what they had learned and tested independently, laying charges of buggery, sexual assault, beating, and other infamies for subsequent presentation in court.

But in many respects what happened at Mount Cashel was overshadowed by the accumulation of evidence that complaints of neglect and cruelty had been ignored or mislaid by the authorities, who were hampered by inadequate liaison between government departments like Justice and Social Services, exaggerated respect for established institutions, and plain disbelief. We were told of a little girl dead at the age of three who had never walked because of the repeated fractures of nearly every important bone in her body, fractures inflicted by her parents and particularly and incredibly by her mother. This woman solemnly took her daughter to hospital where the doctors, on seeing the child, were deeply concerned but also, at a time when the battered-child syndrome was not defined or understood, bewildered. Again, evidence was given of an infant boy recovering miraculously from the torture of twisted arms and legs, broken and torn by parental brutality and sadism.

Since an abundance of the province's children – the victims of broken homes, simple abandonment, poverty, or parental dissipation – were made wards of the director of child welfare, the department was always faced with the difficulty of finding foster parents suitably housed and responsible. There was frightening evidence of irregularity in the treatment of foster children, culminating in the instance where a woman had filled her house with foster children, keeping some in the basement and feeding them like animals, driving them out of the house in the middle of winter to defecate as best they could, while her own progeny and husband were regaled with the best that government money could provide. On the occasion of regular inspections by social workers, the little waifs were paraded by this virago freshly scrubbed and neatly dressed, too terrified to make any complaint. This foster home was regarded for years by authorities as a model environment.

When subpoenas came to be issued to the Christian Brothers already charged by the police, counsel for the commission were surprised by the alacrity with which counsel for these persons responded favourably to the prospect of their clients giving evidence before the commission. Just in time and in the middle of a sleepless night I saw the dimensions of the gulf yawning before our feet. The law governing the use of evidence in the proposed situation in its most modern form was contained in section 13 of the Charter of Rights and Freedoms:

> 13. A witness who testifies in any proceedings has the right not to have any incriminating evidence so given used to incriminate that witness in any other proceedings, except in a prosecution for perjury or for the giving of contradictory evidence.

As I saw it, this meant that little of the evidence to be given by the alleged perpetrators could then be used against them in subsequent criminal proceedings. I quickly gave instructions that they must not be called before the royal commission as witnesses, and by doing so we – Day, Powell, and myself – incurred the censure of many observers. We were "soft" on witnesses, particularly the Christian Brothers. As noted above, even Michael Harris leaned towards that view, although he does acknowledge that my scruples might have been attributed to some such consideration.

What happened at Mount Cashel was horrific and deeply damaged the work and reputation of those who operated the institution, but the bulk of the evidence and the main emphasis of my report dealt with the relevant statutes of Newfoundland, the Departments of Justice and Social Services, and perhaps most of all the police. This was not because the Royal Newfoundland Constabulary needed reform in a comprehensive way. What the force needed, I believed, was to be disentangled from the Department of Justice and given a policy-making shelter of its own in the form of a police commission. It also needed, in my opinion – controversial as it was – observance of the right to lay charges upon reasonable grounds and not to have this vital function left in the hands of government lawyers as had formerly been the case. How gladly I would have written "reasonable and probable grounds" but for the decision of the Supreme Court of Canada to follow American authorities in finding that "reasonable and probable" meant "reasonable" alone. I have already expressed my difficulties with the word "reasonable" as is now enthroned in this particular context in all the statutes of Canada without the rivetting word "probable," which has for so long protected innocent bystanders on the criminal scene. In the public hearings of the commission we heard a good deal about "prosecutorial discretion," a doctrine for which no less an authority than the present chief justice of Ontario, the Honourable Roy McMurtry, was an advocate when he was attorney general of the province. This would reserve to Crown officers the right to decide whether a charge should be laid, a right which I have always maintained should be exclusively in the hands of the police officer investigating the commission of an offence. This does not preclude the police officer from asking for advice from superior officers or Crown lawyers as to what an appropriate charge should be in any given circumstance. Nor does it preclude counsel for the Crown from deciding on grounds of insufficient evidence or technicalities of the law that a prosecution should not proceed. No doubt there is a fine line to be drawn here between the functions of a police investigation and Crown prosecution, but in my report I advised the government of Newfoundland and Labrador that it should be firmly drawn. It need only be imagined what the result of Detective Hillier's investigation of the Mount Cashel situation in 1975 would have been had he enjoyed the right to lay charges – without interference from the Department of Justice – when he was satisfied that he had reasonable (and in those days probable) grounds for doing so.

Yet, whatever the true focus of our commission's mandate was felt to be by Mr Powell, Mr Day, and myself, for whom every word of the terms of reference had special significance, public opinion was mainly and understandably concerned with what I described as a "national crisis" at page 458 of my report. I had been referring to the evidence given by panels of experts, all under oath (a creative and valuable approach to the giving of evidence before a commission of inquiry instigated by commission counsel), and had referred to the Badgley Report of 1984 on sexual offences against children and the magisterial report of Mr Rix G. Rogers entitled *Reaching for Solutions* and published in 1990. Rogers, special adviser to the minister of health and welfare, the Honourable Perrin Beatty, was one of the experts who testified before my commission. Indeed, his evidence and the discussion surrounding it represented the first airing of this issue since his report had reached the hands of his minister. Both these seminal documents were initiatives of the government of Canada and cast a strong light upon a subject which had long been a hidden part of human existence, an almost normal part if one can use that term about such a monstrous perversion. After listening to the statistical evidence, I expressed my feelings at page 459 of my report as follows:

> My immediate and overwhelming impression was one of a national crisis not by any means confined to one or two provinces, a crisis involving some two million families across Canada in which child sexual abuse has occurred and is occurring during the span of Mr. Rogers' investigation, in and outside the family where one in every two boys and one in every three girls have been to a varying extent demoralized by an abuser. As an additional horror we have begun to realize that across the country there is a welling-up of complaints which only partly indicates the dimension of the duration of child sexual abuse hitherto hidden away and unrevealed. All the resources of Canada and its provinces capable of being brought to bear on corruption so massive and so damaging to society must be mobilized, trained and deployed.

But among these resources I did not include counselling for paedophiles. This ancient and evil fraternity, preying mostly upon prepubescent boys, is irreclaimable and the weight of expert evidence is against squandering public money on trying to persuade its members to relinquish the obsession which holds them in its grip. The state has no sanctions for them except the prison house. One can only hope, in the words of the death sentence, that the Lord will have mercy on their souls.

CHAPTER TWENTY

A Very Distinct Society

It may only be an historian's pleasing fancy that when Jacques Cartier was returning home from his first voyage to the Gulf of St Lawrence in 1534 he found St John's harbour full of ships. If this cannot be supported by existing authority, it is nevertheless probable, for the ships of England, France, Spain, and Portugal had even then been long familiar with the snug but wonderful inlet which provides the only refuge from the winds and weather of the North Atlantic along the unyielding coast of the Avalon Peninsula from Cape St Francis to Cape Race. There are several points of similarity between the societies of Quebec and Newfoundland, however much the Labrador decision of the Judicial Committee of the Privy Council and the Churchill Falls hydro-electric power agreement may have envenomed their relations. Both were harnessed by their colonizing powers of France and Britain and thus isolated from immigration. Both have large family connections, more like tribes than families, sharing the same names from the highest to the lowest. Both have language peculiarities reflecting an inheritance from the seventeenth century, distinguishing them from their modern counterparts in France and the British Isles. Both have high birth rates and high rates of emigration to the rest of Canada and the United States reflecting the relative poverty of their own environments. Both can legitimately be called "distinct societies."

Throughout the ten-month period of our life in Newfoundland, Helen and I were able to renew and expand our knowledge of the awesome landscape, albeit never going west of the east side of Trinity Bay and only rarely able to sally further than the confines of the Avalon Peninsula. "Confines" is certainly not the right word for even that comparatively small part of the great sparsely settled island affectionately known as "the Rock."

Only once during the months of my last sojourn in Newfoundland was I treated with hostility, this being by a distressed woman who would not look me in the eye while she denounced the royal commission. Considering the painful revelations which accompanied our work, this was almost miraculous. It was the more remarkable because our proceedings in the commission had been, as I have described, displayed on television day and night and I had certainly been overexposed. I was often accosted on weekends in stores and on the streets by well-wishers, and for all I know ill-wishers too, with perfect courtesy. Starting with our oldest friends in Newfoundland, including those of Sam and Jane, we made many more, Helen especially. Setting on one side the stimulating transactions of the commission, we never had a dull moment while we lived in St John's. Bill Crosbie's widow, formerly Gertrude Murray, known to all her friends as Gert; the chief justice of Newfoundland, Noel Goodridge, and his wife Isabelle; Ian and Margot Reid; Gordon and Bump Winter; Olga Ayre; Burf and Patsy Ploughman; Cam and Betty Eaton; Herb and Gladys Vivian; and Randy and Ginny Bell – all offered friendship that has endured and that enriched our lives in those memorable months of 1989 and 1990. As I write, Cam Eaton and Noel Goodridge have departed this life. One of Newfoundland's favourite soldiers, Cam won the Military Cross while serving with the 166th Newfoundland Field Regiment, Royal Artillery, in Italy; his service to Newfoundland and to Canada after the war was prodigious and earned him the Order of Canada. On his seventieth birthday on June 1, 1990, we were invited to a great party in his honour, and hearing that a number of rhymes and epigrams were in season, I wrote the following:

To C.E., 1 June 1990

Welcome, warrior, to the ranks
Of them whose guns and trucks and tanks
Have long since rusted in Elysian fields.
A new recruit? No, re-engaged

> For service with the middle-aged
> Without the panoply of swords and shields.
>
> Come to away and sing the praise
> Of dusty nights and torrid days
> And forward observation skills,
> Or how the thud of hidden guns
> Under remote Italian suns
> Starts echoes in the Southside hills.

Needless to say, in the crush and enthusiasm of the party, plans to read verses were delayed if not cancelled, and since I was beginning to suffer from arthritis in my left hip during this period, I departed early but managed to get my offering passed to him and enjoyed his telephone call the following day.

By this time I myself was seventy-six and had enjoyed a fine celebration of my birthday with my colleagues and friends at the Woodstock Inn on the road to Portugal Cove. Helen's seventy-fifth birthday was celebrated at a dinner party in the Hotel Newfoundland, where Sam appeared for a surprise visit and tribute to his mother. Lynn also flew out from "away" and enjoyed the hospitality of our friends in St John's.

When the hearings of the royal commission ended in July of 1990 and Helen and I flew back to Toronto, I moved into an office at 180 Dundas Street West, the Ontario government building where commissions of inquiry of one kind or another were housed. Here I was joined by Pat Devereaux from our staff in St John's, bringing all the video and audio recordings of our sessions and the equipment necessary to transcribe my dictation and print the report; its composition with her expert management and help went quickly enough. We were housed next to my friend and fellow-townsman Bill Colter, former chief judge of the county and district courts and then a member of the Ontario Court (General Division) engaged on his five-year-long commission of inquiry into the Niagara Regional Police Force. Here we were visited by Herb Vivian. Herb was maintaining our office in St John's, where the report would be published and all the exhibits and cassettes retained until final disposal in the archives of Newfoundland. In Toronto Clay Powell read the chapters as they appeared in the early stages, as did Herb Vivian in St John's, but Pat and I did most of the proofreading and this simple yet laborious process, vital to the production of a book of any quality, was remarkably accurate. Writing took about half the time between starting the project and final preparation for presentation to the government. The other half was easily taken up in the preparation of the two volumes, the second being appendices, among others the valuable series of profiles of abused children prepared by David Day and reports of my oral reasons for deciding some of the important points at issue. Finally, the vital task of preparing an index was done and done well in St John's, making the report ready for publication.

It was in the course of writing that I found myself in difficulty when I tried to read the smaller print of various documents. One day not long afterwards I stepped out of the club onto University Avenue and in the bright sunlight was distressed to find that I could not see in any detail the faces of the passers-by. My ophthalmologist, Robert Wagman, told me that this was the onset of macular degeneration of the retina in both eyes, progressive and irreversible. Perhaps it was a premonition that forced me to have the report printed in unusually large type; more likely it was my inability to see clearly anything smaller than was adopted. I was sorry about this but not distraught. I was not destined for total darkness as my friend Edward Dunlop had been since the day during the war he had snatched up a live grenade dropped by one of his men. In the act of throwing it away from the rest of his platoon, he had lost both eyes and his right hand in the inevitable explosion. The George Medal for this act of heroism, sparingly awarded as it was, could not compensate for the terrible disability visited on a young man in the bright morning of life. Edward bore his disability cheerfully in the course of a career which included being a minister of the Crown in Ontario, receiving the Order of Canada, and adopting the role of a much sought-after adviser and counsellor to his generation. For me at seventy-seven the race was over, and although the inability to read was a serious inconvenience, it was alleviated by instruments of one kind or another and of course by Helen's constant willingness to read to me as often as possible. As I write six years later, I can still see much that makes life enjoyable and am resigned to whatever may befall.

When the two-volume report was ready, Helen and I again journeyed to Newfoundland, arriving on May 31, 1991. The famous harbour, sanctuary of ships, was shrouded in snow but all was warmth and hospitality when Herb Vivian and I went to the Confederation Building to present the report to the government of Newfoundland and Labrador represented by the acting premier, Winston Baker, and the minister of justice, Paul Dicks. This was done in form, the press was represented, pictures were taken, and the ceremonies concluded with an excellent luncheon and much agreeable conversation. Here Helen and I received the parting gifts representative of the literary and sculptural genius of the province. We left with many expressions of mutual regard and a determination to return as yet unfulfilled although still contemplated.

Nevertheless, the report was not then released to the public, the government's stated reason being that the release of the report would seriously impair the prospect of a fair trial for the accused. I had many calls about this, particularly from newspaper, radio, and television people who sensed a "cover-up," as they called it, and who on the whole refused to take seriously the stated reason for the government's decision. I believed, as I hope any conscientious lawyer would, bearing in mind that there were almost a dozen prosecutions in train and that there had been extraordinary province-wide publicity given the hearings of the commission, that the government had decided wisely. The rationale also applied to the screening of a television production entitled *The Boys of St. Vincent*, based, it was alleged, on the Mount Cashel affair and typically designed to stimulate public prurience. A book by Derek O'Brien, a former inmate of the orphanage, was also banned in the province for the same reason. Whenever I was asked, and I was asked often, why this should be the case, I always adopted without question the government opinion, believing then as now that it was entirely correct, but to many it seemed to be excessive interference with free expression. There is no question that there is room for debate in the matter. Even such a statesman as Gordon Winter, notably free of any legal preoccupations and always taking a long view, felt that the government's action was heavy-handed. My own view about the screening of *The Boys of St. Vincent* was that had the royal commission – and the subject of the telecast – been about the control of highway traffic or some other issue devoid of sexuality, the media would not have cared as much.

When the report was finally released in April of 1992, the following year, some twenty pages were missing from the text because
of an ongoing prosecution in the case of a foster home at Mount
Pearl. These were subsequently replaced, but the incident testified
to the concern of the provincial government to find a balance
between public impatience and the securing of fair trials. In case
it should be felt that the government was overly sensitive about the
rights of the accused in criminal prosecutions, it should be remembered that a trial repeated for technical reasons that should have
been foreseen is expensive and an injury to the taxpayer, so here
there are two faces of justice to be confronted.

At the time of the release of my report, Paul Dicks had resigned
his portfolio (he has since returned to the front bench) and had
been succeeded by Edward Roberts, a long-time pillar of the Liberal party in Newfoundland and once the designated successor of
Joseph Smallwood. From him I received a charming letter acknowl-
edging the importance of my work in generous terms for which I
was and am grateful. I received many other letters generally
expressing approval, although there were some that indicated abiding mystification as to what had really happened in the corridors
of the Department of Justice in December 1975. I for one am not
troubled about my findings in that respect. I heard the witnesses
and I watched them while they made the most solemn statements
under oath, and I did my best as an experienced judge to reach
the right conclusions. There I think it must rest.

CHAPTER TWENTY-ONE

As for Myself

When we were in Ottawa in the sixties, John MacNeill, clerk of the Senate, sent me a piece of white silk ribbon which his secretary, a Lindsay girl, had found being used as a bookmark in her family Bible. One side of it was printed with a legend which identified it as an election favour distributed to the loyal Tories who were supporting Sir John A. Macdonald in his last election campaign. At the top of the legend appeared the Canadian Ensign much as it appeared before the adoption of Mr Pearson's version of the Canadian flag. Under it was the image of Sir John and below that the words: "The Old Flag, the Old Leader, the Old Policy" and "Sam Hughes." Obviously each candidate across the country had his name attached in bold type as was that of my grandfather. This is one of my cherished possessions and I had photostatic copies made of it, one of which I sent to John Diefenbaker, provoking an enthusiastic response from a notable collector of Macdonald memorabilia.

Three observations now occur to me. The first is that the use of the Union Jack as Canada's national flag had not begun by 1891, and indeed did not begin until Sir Wilfrid Laurier, returning from the euphoria of the Imperial Conference of 1896, ordered the Jack to replace the Ensign, consigning the latter to no doubt its technical use, on ships of the Canadian merchant marine. The second is that the Old Policy was of course the one eventually abandoned by Sir John's party under the leadership of Brian Mulroney in favour of free trade with the United States, an act which many people thought might better have been introduced by the Liberal party, which was as strongly in favour of it until it became a convenient weapon for belabouring that prime minister. And the third concerns the abiding personal faith of Macdonald which was expressed in the last paragraph of his election address to the people of Canada in 1891. The first sentence of that last paragraph was as follows: "As for myself my course is clear, a British subject I was born and a British subject I will die." This was an important part of his testament to the people of Canada and animated his successors in various degrees to the present day, certainly vital to the preservation of Canadian independence from the United States in the last century, and if less so today by no means a negligible support. Every oath of allegiance I have taken on entering upon various public employments has been one to the sovereigns, George VI and Elizabeth II, their "heirs and successors according to law." This is the universal experience of men and women situated as I have been. Let no one think that it is inconsistent with Canadian citizenship in either law or logic. The Crown is tightly woven into our constitution. It is a symbol of impartiality and the fair play which we all celebrate and extol even when we have doubts about some transactions of the state. An example of this is the familiar phrase dear to the hearts of prosecutors in court, "the Crown never wins, the Crown never loses." Corruption on the part of the Crown is not to be thought of; if its servants are found to be corrupt, they are dismissed. If this observation is received with a knowing smile, then I invite whoever is amused by it to live in a country where it is assumed that the governing bureaucracy is corrupt and has to be paid off. The prefix "Royal," used for instance by the Royal Victoria Hospital or the Royal Canadian Golf Association, is fiercely sought after and carefully bestowed.

In October 1970 I spoke for the second time to the Empire Club of Canada in Toronto. In an address entitled "Imperial Legacy," I examined what was left of the towering structure of the British Empire upon which the sun never set in the days of my childhood, and what indeed it had left to us in Canada. Victorious in two world wars it had effectively ceased to exist, and the Commonwealth, however intellectually satisfying, was not a tangible bequest. But for law and language I had much to say. The law of England, which has never countenanced torture or the presumption of guilt, and the English tongue are thriving around the world, not only in lands where the writ of the modern empire once ran but in the United States of America as well. Then again we owe to England the tradition of our civil service, a professional, impartial, and honourable career. On this I found it easy to speak with feeling. Finally, I spoke of the Crown and the sovereign who wore it who had seen so much of the material assets of imperial rule almost cheerfully dispersed since the last ministry of Winston Churchill. It will be remembered that Churchill said he had not become the king's first minister in order to preside over the liquidation of the British Empire. But the Crown endures as a symbol of stability and a focus of loyalty and its wearer as the incarnation of duty and propriety.

Helen and I are now both octogenarians. I never thought that either one of us would see the momentous twentieth century out, but 2000 is approaching fast. "Seeing" is a doubtful word for me and hearing is a problem for her. We are very dependent on each other but we have complementary disabilities. Otherwise we are in good health by octogenarian standards.

In 1992 to our great joy Sam, after twelve years of bachelorhood, married Martha Blackburn of London and became at once a husband and a stepfather. Once again we had a charming and affectionate daughter-in-law. Yet after a rapturous life of almost two years the marriage was dissolved by Martha's sudden death after some energetic waterskiing in Georgian Bay, and misery descended on our son. Our own grief was sharpened by anxiety for his willingness to survive. With the help of his family and friends and the promise of his son in England, he was able to reach resignation at last, with undivulged reservations which one can only guess at. I vividly recall the great funeral in St Paul's Cathedral at London, Ontario. Against much prudent advice, Sam insisted on speaking about Martha from the pulpit, doing so with simple eloquence. I remember how Marjorie Blackburn left her wheelchair to take his arm to lead the congregation with head held high behind the casket, out into the sunshine. And then the long two hundred miles to Lindsay for Martha's burial beside Sam's forebears.

I contemplate with more tranquillity the end of this attempt to record the personal past. Its composition has been an agreeable exercise, helped at every turn by the Joanne Goodman Foundation of the University of Western Ontario. For many years I have enjoyed the privilege, replete with hospitality, of attending the annual three-day lectures given by scholars and men and women of affairs from many lands. The climax is a dinner given by the founder, Eddie Goodman, whose influence on my career since the war has already been celebrated in these pages. In the fullness of time he has become Lieutenant Colonel the Honourable E.A. Goodman, PC, OC, QC, DU, LLD, but the weight of these honours and awards has been shouldered with elegance and ease and has not in any sense quenched the fire of his spirit and questioning mind. The local habitation of the foundation is the Department of History of the university, personified by another old friend, Professor Neville Thompson. In 1994 the decision to write this book sprang from a reminiscent conversation with Eddie and Neville (umpired by his charming wife, Gail) at the University Club in Toronto. As I said earlier, in 1994 I was commissioned as a special lecturer for the Joanne Goodman Foundation. I entitled the address "Canadian Historians I Have Known" and delivered it at Western on October 20 of that year. By that time I was no longer able to read a paper and I had the stimulating experience of recalling extemporaneously my recollections of W.L. Grant, Chester Martin, Donald McDougall, Donald Creighton, Frank Underhill, Harold Innis, Charles Stacey, Gerald Graham, Eric Harrison, and others to a generously appreciative audience of friends, faculty, and students. I was four days short of my eighty-first birthday and my enjoyment of the occasion and gratitude for the opportunity were profound.

The mandatory retirement of superior court judges has in Ontario, at least for those who reach the age of seventy-five in good health, been, as the saying goes, a licence to print money. Arbitrations and mediations which now flourish because of the insupportable delays of proceeding in the regular courts have convinced many people to pay retired judges more handsomely than they were ever paid when in office and get a swift decision; the trend is so strong that the idea of an informal extra-curial appellate court is beginning to be canvassed. My retirement in 1988 was a little ahead of the surge in popularity of this medium, and then my absence in Newfoundland plus the onset of blindness effectively excluded me from participation, although, with John Robinette, I was briefly a member of the Private Court. Recently I have had limited activity, together with John's daughter Wendy Collier, my old friend Harold Adamson, and young friend John Tentardini, sitting on a conciliation committee to weigh claims against the operations of the St John's Training School at Uxbridge in respect of child abuse – all at the instance of Peter Shoniker, busy lawyer and son of another old friend, E.J. Shoniker, much mentioned above.

These activities make retirement less formidable and the domestic round offers scope for seasoning the incapacities of old age with curiosity about the doings of one's heirs and successors according to love: the wonderful wife with whom I go hand in hand down the gentle slope; the wonderful daughter who, while sustaining a busy life with a leader of the accounting profession, with my two granddaughters at universities only eight hundred miles apart, can find time to oversee rather than overlook the fortunes of her parents; the wonderful son, sharing the last of these tasks with humour and confidence; and my English grandson, freshly returned from a seven-month backpacking expedition to half a dozen South American states, preparing now to explore the academic life in the University of Edinburgh, Athens of the North.

Index